Tough Plants
for
SOUTHERN GARDENS

Low Care, No Care, Tried and True Winners

Published by Cool Springs Press, a Division of Thomas Nelson, Inc., P.O. Box 141000, Nashville, Tennessee 37214.

Rushing, Felder, 1952-
     Tough plants for southern gardens : low care, no care, tried and true
          winners / Felder Rushing.
          p. cm.
     Includes bibliographical references and index.
     ISBN 1-59186-002-4 (pbk. : alk. paper)
     1. Landscape plants—Southern States. 2. Low maintenance
     gardening—Southern States. I. Title.
SB407.R88 2003
635.9'0975—dc21

                              2003007392

First Printing 2003
Printed in the United States of America
10 9 8 7 6 5 4 3

Managing Editor: Jenny Andrews
Copyeditor: D. Michelle Adkerson
Designer: Starletta Polster

On the Cover: "Grandma's Irises" by Robin Conover

Author's Note: According to several members of the American Iris Society, the plant on the book cover is *Iris germanica*, collected in 1753 by Linnaeus—the same one painted by Van Gogh in his *Iris*. So, it's been a tough plant for a long, long time.

Visit the Thomas Nelson website at www.ThomasNelson.com

Tough Plants

for

SOUTHERN GARDENS

Low Care, No Care, Tried and True Winners

Felder Rushing

COOL
SPRINGS
PRESS

A Division of Thomas Nelson, Inc.
www.ThomasNelson.com

Dedication:

This book is dedicated to the gardening women in my family: great-grandmother Pearl, who taught me about wildflowers and daffodils; grandmother Louise, whose daylilies were garden club blue-ribbon winners; Wilma, who just grew zinnias by her concrete chicken; Wilma Gene, my mother, whose zest has inspired everyone around her; Terryl, my longtime best friend and wife whose dracaena won a state fair ribbon; and daughter Zoe, the gal who grows the sweetest turnips on Earth—in a purple tire planter.

Great-Grandmother,
Pearl Townsend Boyer

Acknowledgements:

Thanks to all of y'all who helped inspire and tweak this book—Master Gardeners from every Southern state, garden club and plant society members, and my gardening friends. Special credit for "who my garden is" goes to Rita Hall, a transplanted English gardener who taught me to see our own native plants as worthy of the garden, and Leon "Dr. Dirt" Goldsberry of Edwards, Mississippi, whose enthusiasm for growing everything he can get his hands on taught me to ignore the "rules" and just enjoy growing stuff.

And I'd also like to credit all the horticulturists, especially university kinds, who have overcome their scientific training enough to learn to relax and be better "garden variety" gardeners.

Special acknowledgment also goes to Jenny Andrews and Hank McBride at Cool Springs Press, who had to pull down deep for patience as we turned this lifelong love of tough plants into something I can share with others. There are special crowns in Heaven for them both.

Table of Contents

Foreword

In my part of the South, the mountains, there's a humorous folk tale with a repeating refrain: "Everybody knows Ol' Dry Frye." Well, everybody knows Felder Rushing, leastways everybody in the South who gardens, does. He was a Mississippi horticultural extension agent for twenty-two years. His garden writing appears about everywhere, from his regular newspaper columns to magazines, even the Internet. He hasn't missed a Saturday of his garden radio talk show in over twenty years. And he speaks somewhere just about every weekend.

Felder isn't a stuffed-shirt, Latin-only horticulturist. He's a good old, hands-in-the-dirt gardener. He knows his bottle plants (made by hanging bottles on a bush), and has a special love for that refined accouterment, the tire planter. He goes out of his way to photograph outlandishly tacky gardens. He has a true sense of the real South and a true love for people.

One night, after Felder and I had both spoken in Memphis, he led me on a two-and-a-half hour drive down some flapjack-flat road so he could show me some "real Mississippi Delta Blues." We finally reached an almost empty hole-in-the-wall nightclub in some scruffy little town, just in time to see an old, suited black man step up and take the microphone from the local white band. He played guitar and he sang . . . and . . . and . . . he was *awful*. Around two in the morning, as we were driving all the way back to Memphis, I finally said, "Felder, that old guy, I didn't really think he was too good."

"Oh, he was poor as gully dirt," Felder quickly agreed. "Most of them were so bad they couldn't buy hay to feed a nightmare. That's the authentic Delta Blues, though."

The point of all this is that Felder is "real people." He knows gardeners. He knows gardens. *And he knows plants.* If Felder tells you something is so easy to grow it'll thrive anywhere, believe him. And if you follow the suggestions in this wonderful distillation of decades of experience, well, my friend, your gardening will become a whole lot more successful.

And a whole lot easier as well.

Pat Stone, the Garrison Keillor of gardening, publishes Green Prints: "The Weeder's Digest," *the only magazine that shares the personal side of gardening; the former editor of* Mother Earth News *also wrote* Real Gardeners' True Confessions *and co-authored* Chicken Soup for the Gardener's Soul.

Green
SIDE UP

This book is about unkillable plants. Its aim is to increase the number of people who garden—without a lot of "bells and whistles" science—by highlighting what decades of experience have shown to be the toughest survivors of the South.

Some of the plants are common as dirt, but can be used very successfully—indeed they are often found growing in the finest botanical gardens on Earth. Think of the old fable of Rumpelstiltskin, who wove golden garments from common straw.

Americans are constantly told by pollsters that we are a nation of gardeners, yet an observant drive around any neighborhood usually shows that few of us actually garden with gusto. The late garden author Henry Mitchell wrote that "there are only two kinds of people—those who garden, and those who do not." Truth is, we're mostly lawn mowers and shrub pruners, with maybe a potted plant or two by the television to keep us in touch with Nature.

Yet most of us remember grandmothers and aunts, even dads and uncles, who grew all sorts of interesting flowering shrubs, trees, bulbs, perennials, and lots of other weird plants. Most of us today have a pot or two of something tropical in our home or office. Truth is, we **need** to grow something—anything—that depends on us at least a little bit, or as my friend Russell Studebaker, world famous horticulturist from Tulsa, Oklahoma, says, "We'd just as well be sittin' around polishin' silverware."

I have spent a lifetime scratching and sniffing around landscapes and gardens all over the world, coast-to-coast and top-to-bottom in our great country, and especially in every nook and cranny of the beloved region we call the South. And I have written and lectured for many years on how we treat the outdoor rooms we develop as our "guarded areas."

My opinions on plants and gardening come from being raised by real gardeners, including a horticulturist great-grandmother who showed me her over three hundred fifty different kinds of daffodils and shared her love of wildflowers, a grandmother whose daylilies and African violets won many blue ribbons, a country grandmother who just loved zinnias and her concrete

chicken, and parents who struggled with vegetables and a lawn while raising a bunch of rowdy kids and pets.

Throw in years of experience working in garden centers, a couple of university degrees, over two decades as an urban "consumer horticulturist" with a university Extension Service (and over twenty years as host of a call-in radio program), and you can imagine how much I have learned from the experiences of hard-working but fun-loving gardeners.

I have also taken copious notes while on many intimate "behind the scenes" plant safaris to Africa, from steamy jungles on both sides of South America and sojourns into Mexico to the snowy peat bogs of northern Canada, from wind-swept cemeteries on tiny Caribbean islands to the temperate rain forests of Alaska. I have evaluated plants and their combinations on several trips to Europe—one on which I took an educational television film crew to show how the English and French use our native wildflowers, including at Louis XIV's ultra-formal Versailles and Monet's overstuffed Giverney. Not to mention the countless flower shows I have "done" in every corner of our country and Europe as well.

Sadly, many people seem to have gotten away from gardening. Blame it on TV or fast food or El Niño, or preening dilettantes who make us feel bad if we don't garden exactly the way they recommend. Better yet, forget the excuses—there are at least **eight very simple and understandable reasons** good people, even flower lovers, have miserable gardens:

- Too tied up mentally, physically, and emotionally with other parts of our lives—family, church, meetings, sports, housework, the Internet, and myriad other distractions that preoccupy us. There isn't enough time to dedicate to all the gardening we love and need to do, so that much of it becomes a chore. Might as well just have a big lawn to cut mindlessly every other weekend.
- The weather won't cooperate when the mood for gardening strikes us right; it's either too hot or cold, too wet or dry, too dark after work, or

just plain too much humidity to overcome. One week the dirt is hard as concrete, the next it's gummy and sticks to the shovel. And the Weather Channel says more is on the way.

- Our bodies ache just thinking about the physical challenges of gardening. After even half a day of digging or planting, our backs, knees, and hands aren't always up to the task, and the easy chair by the TV beckons.
- Spiders, snakes, and bees unnerve us, and we are worried about whatever mosquitoes might be carrying this year. It's less scary to just stay inside and stare through the plate glass window as birds flock to their feeders stocked with store-bought sunflower seed.
- Too many rules to remember for how to garden, what to do, and when. We feel daunted, as if we will mess up or waste time and money no matter what we do. And the experts just pile up stuff we are supposed to do or know.
- The neighbors will talk about us if we garden publicly, as if our efforts will make their plain landscapes look bad. We don't want to look like fanatics, so we just hide in the backyard and mow the front.
- Bugs and blights ruin our best efforts. They kill our attempts at gardening—or worse, make our gardens look bad and perform poorly. And though there seem to be way too many pests in the South, we are beginning to realize that pesticides are bad for the environment and our health. Even "natural" kinds of bug-and-blight-and-weed controls are expensive and a lot of fuss.
- Plants die anyway, no matter what we do or how hard we try. So we give up.

There is a simple solution to all the above: Find and plant things that grow themselves whether we tend to them or not! And arrange them in combinations that make neighbors at least think we know what we are doing.

This book is filled with the kinds of plants that have proven themselves over many decades, even centuries, to be useful, beautiful, adaptable, and downright easy to grow. In fact, some are all but unkillable, having performed for generations of Southern gardeners with little or no care. They just keep on going, even when planted in miserable soils, and survive back-to-back floods, droughts, freezes, torrid summer heat, and benign neglect.

That's the premise of this book—to highlight perennials, bulbs, annuals, vines, shrubs, trees, and even roses that have been planted by a wide range of gardeners—of all styles and abilities—for many years and that have proven themselves to grow well without "artificial life support."

These many dozens of easy-care plants have been gleaned from country homesteads, cottage gardens, less affluent parts of town, abandoned gardens, and even cemeteries. They're popular, rewarding, and tough, plus they can be displayed and enjoyed in any landscape style, even in the front yards of suburban homes. And most are easy to root, seed, divide, or otherwise propagate for sharing with family, friends, and neighbors.

Criteria Used for Selecting the Plants for This Book

Of the thousands of plants we can possibly grow, including old favorites and exciting new cultivars, only a few pass muster to survive "garden variety" gardens across the South; many disappear because they simply aren't tough enough. I have personally seen the plants in this book being grown across the entire South, in botanical and collectors' gardens, and in rural cottage gardens alike, all enjoyed because they have these benefits:

- Possess strong values, such as beauty, better flavor or fragrance, multiple-season effects, and are heirlooms.
- Grow in ordinary soil with little or no watering or fertilizer.
- Tolerate local climate and weather extremes, including heat, drought, rain, and sudden freezes.
- Resist insect pests and diseases.
- Don't require the gardener to have a horticulture degree—these plants all but grow themselves.
- Are "no fuss" and easy to groom in the off season.
- Can be found at local garden centers or through mail-order sources.

I deliberately avoided scientific horticulture in this book, for two reasons: It is covered thoroughly in nearly every other garden book, which you probably already have, and most of these plants simply don't need a lot of fuss. Most require only two acts on your part: Dig a little dirt, and plant them "green side up."

MASTER GARDENERS are men and women who have been given forty, fifty, or more hours of intense training in all aspects of home horticulture by university Extension Service professionals. In return, they have given an equal number (sometimes many, many more) of hours teaching others about gardening. They are the "take it to the streets" part of university horticulture departments. Find out more, or how you can become involved, by calling your county or parish Agricultural Extension Service office, or click on The American Horticulture Society Master Gardener link at AHS.org for your state's Master Gardener program. The entries in the book have passed muster with Master Gardeners, who gave excellent insight on which plants are truly hardy—and which ones some thought I should omit because they are too easy!

In this book you will find chapters on annuals, which have to be planted from seed every year; perennials and bulbs, which generally stay around for many years but "die down" or go dormant part of the year; and shrubs, trees, and vines, which have "woody" trunks and stems and remain a visible part of the landscape year-round. There are also short chapters on low-maintenance lawn care, ornamental grasses (which fall sort of between perennials and shrubs in how they are used in gardens), and the toughest tropical plants, which are easily kept for years in pots and other containers in our home or office.

Also throughout the book you will find fast-reference lists of plants for unique growing conditions and uses, based on what many gardeners, especially Master Gardeners, have discovered in average gardens. Also included are quick tips for planting and caring for tough plants, plus landscaping ideas and simple how-to garden shortcuts, all aimed at saving you time, money, effort, and worry.

This book is for both beginners and "old hands" who just want pretty plants, without all the fuss. **Have fun, then share with others.**

Where in the World Are We As Southern Gardeners?

The region covered in this book is shaped more or less like a **sweet potato**, extending west to east from somewhere in Texas to somewhere in Maryland, and north to south anywhere there is rain in the winter and hot, muggy nights in the summer. Allow for uneven edges on the "sweet potato" to include those people along the fringes who want to think they're in the South. Hardiness-wise, it roughly includes Zones 6 to 9, give or take.

Why can't we grow peonies and blue spruce or bananas and orchids? The truth is that some of us can grow those things—depending on our climate. Trouble is, our climate ranges from the upper South's below-zero winter temperatures and the mild summer nights of our mountains to the coastal South's torrid humidity and balmy, usually freeze-free subtropical "winters." And everything in between.

In the upper South, blue spruce, peonies, lilacs, rhubarb, and raspberries are commonly grown, yet we pine for figs and camellias, and have to dig our cannas and gladiolus in the winter. Our lawns are ryegrasses, fescues, and bluegrass—making our gardens look more like they are in the "bottom of the North" instead of the top of the South.

The middle South gets very cold, and even has snow, for short periods in the winter, but with long stretches of mild temperatures that cause our plants to soften up; we have plants that can tolerate minus 40 degrees Fahrenheit, but that will freeze in the mid-20s, if it follows three weeks of 60s and 70s. Still, we enjoy tea roses, azaleas, sweet potatoes, cannas, and rabbit-eye blueberries; even if our bananas freeze to the ground, they come back up as foliage-only plants every summer. Cherry trees and most peonies and lilacs simply won't flower well this far south, for lack of cold in the winter.

The lower South, which is all the way down to, but not quite on, the Gulf Coast and the Atlantic Ocean, is blessed for the most part with mild winters, fewer freezes, and rarely any snow. It's hot and sticky more of the year, with mosquitoes and spring peeper frogs active in February. It stays hot and humid all night long, which is fine with figs, elephant's ears, windmill palms, and pansies all winter. We have paper-white narcissus in bloom in December and January, and camellias from October to March.

The coastal South rarely frosts but has very rainy winters and stays warm and humid even at night. The huge Southern Indian azaleas grow in full sun or under majestic live oaks; lantana can flower year-round; and gingers, philodendrons, bananas, even citrus fruits are common outdoor plants.

For a more detailed description of your state's climate, check out the *Month-by-Month* books published by Cool Springs Press, written by well-known garden experts from your state.

Note on Hardiness Maps

The USDA Hardiness Zones are based on "average low temperatures," which are often way off base; the American Horticulture Society's Heat Zone Map is based on average high temperatures and is another good indicator, but not entirely useful by itself. What we need is to overlay both maps, plus a humidity map, and a wet winter map, a hot humid dry summer map, a clay/sandy/alkaline/acidic soil map, and a "too tired and hot to garden" map. **Then** we'll have some useful information! Given the vast array of factors that determine what plants will do well and where, and the vagaries of Nature, Hardiness Zone and Heat Zone maps have not been included in this book.

Plant Names

Elvis sang about how his "Mama loved roses" and getting "all shook up" because you're his buttercup. You know what a rose is; so what's a buttercup? You don't have to know a plant's scientific or Latin name to grow and enjoy growing it. But proper names are important when you want more information about any plant, especially its myriad varieties. Just remember that generally similar plants are lumped into **families**, with really close relatives clustered

into the same **genus**, and individual kinds sorted into **species**. Plants with minor variations are named as **cultivars** (which are simply "cultivated varieties"). Got that?

Common names are the designations most gardeners relate to, but they can be misleading for serious identification purposes. For example, there are quite a few plants called "buttercups," including nearly anything with pollen that rubs onto your nose when you smell it too closely. Most common buttercups include yellow daffodils, wild ranunculus, and the roadside "Mexican primrose" with big, floppy, pale pink and white flowers, sometimes called "showy evening primrose" even though it blooms in the day.

The plant names used in this book, both the generally accepted common names and the official Latin names, are important as reference, but not important to the enjoyment of the plants themselves (though some of them are fun to say, and some have very interesting histories). What is important is that you give the plants a try and, if you like them, make an effort to get to know their names in case you want to tell other folks about them.

"Best for Beginners" and "Kinda Tricky" Lists

One man's weed is another's wildflower. No two gardeners will ever agree on a list of "best" and "worst" plants, based on personal experiences as well as social acceptance; goldenrod, one of our most common roadside beauties, is generally considered "weedy" in America, yet is one of the most popular summer and fall cut-flower perennials in European gardens. One gardener can grow tomatoes with no trouble at all, while neighbors struggle with the challenge. My grandmother grew blue-ribbon African violets, but they quickly melt under my hit-or-miss care.

Yet some plants are so easy to grow that they are considered common, or a weed. Instead of holding our noses in the air, they should be celebrated as great "intro" plants for new or beginner gardeners, especially children who have no expectations, and new home gardeners who are too busy or horticulturally "green" to give them much care. These "Best for Beginners" plant lists scattered throughout the book are good for starters, and often remain popular long after their success has started to wear thin with more advanced gardeners.

On the other hand, after a quarter-century of watching all sorts of gardeners, and helping them with problems, I have seen too many popular plants succumb to insect or mite pests, foliage and root diseases, poor adaptation to our climate, or they require regular maintenance such as pruning or deadheading. These plants—again, very popular, and widely sold in garden centers—tend to cause headaches for beginning gardeners, or gardeners who don't get around to preventive mainte-nance. They generate a lot of calls to garden experts; I put them in my "Kinda Tricky" lists. Again, they are all great plants, but may take a little extra planning or thought into their planting, or a little extra care in their growing.

I got much help on these lists, including from Leon "Dr. Dirt" Goldsberry, whose overstuffed Deep South cottage garden in Edwards, Mississippi, has seen it all. The gardener in him helped the horticulturist in me narrow our list to a defensible few.

You can grow them all, from both lists, but don't say we didn't warn you about some of them!

Myth of the Five-Dollar Hole

Even though plants have been grown well in "just plain dirt" for centuries, many modern gardeners have been taught to overprepare soil. While adding a little organic material can help soils drain better and roots penetrate farther and more quickly, too much can cause soils to hold water during wet seasons, dry out quickly in hot summers, and keep roots in a small area. A moderate approach usually works best.

Think "crackers in chili"—a bowl of chili usually doesn't need any crackers at all, but a handful of crumbled crackers can fluff it up and cool it down; more than that turns it into mush. Dig your soil a solid shovel's depth, turning it upside down and chopping up the clumps. Spread over the area a thin layer of organic material (compost, manure, potting soil, finely ground bark, whatever), and stir it into the native soil.

A rule of thumb for how much organic matter to add: trees, tough shrubs, and bulbs, none; roses and perennials, add a one- to two-inch layer of new material over the native soil, and stir it in; annuals, add a two- to three-inch layer. I **never** add more than three to four inches of organic matter to a shovel depth of soil!

SPECIAL NOTE: Many tough plants die from being pulled out of pots and plugged right into the ground "as is"—their potting soil keeps roots in a wet-dry cycle that leads to rot. **Always** loosen potting soil from around store-bought plant roots—trees, shrubs, perennials, even annuals—and mix it into your soil.

Mulches Make a Difference

Covering the soil with a blanket of porous material has several strong benefits: It keeps the soil surface from packing and crusting in heavy rains, cools the soil in the summer (like a hat on a bare head), reduces rapid temperature changes during sunny winter days and cold nights, prevents many weed seeds from getting the sun they need to sprout, and keeps things looking neat. Landscape fabrics do a fair job, but natural mulches of leaves, pine straw, or shredded bark "feed" the soil as they compost or are eaten and taken deep around roots by earthworms.

It is best to use the mulch evenly over the root area under shrubs and around flowers—don't pile it up around trunks and stems like a fire ant mound.

A rule of thumb for how much mulch to use: Spread your preferred material over the area just deep enough to barely but completely cover the soil, then add that much more to compensate for settling and natural composting. Refresh once a year or as needed.

Two Rules for Composting

Too much has been written and said about composting. It makes me tired just thinking about all I'm supposed to do: small particle sizes, correct carbon-nitrogen ratio, thermophilic bacteria, bins an exact size, turning and aerating, and all the rest of that **stuff**!

As anyone with a leaf pile will attest, there are only two rules for composting: Stop throwing that stuff away, and pile it up somewhere. The rest is finesse. If you want to get in a race with someone, call your county Extension Service office for a handout on how to speed things up. Below are a few tips for composting:

- Mix a little green stuff, including grass clippings and vegetable scraps, even weeds, with brown stuff (decaying manure, shredded autumn leaves, etc.), or add a little nitrogen fertilizer.
- Keep the pile moist, but not wet (moisture is needed by good bacteria).
- Turn the pile occasionally to mix and fluff it up (air is also needed for good bacterial action).
- Chop big stuff into smaller particles.

Really, you can forget the rules—just do it!

Water Wisely

There is no good advice for watering tough plants—after all, most have survived the neglect of many, many gardeners with no watering at all! Most can be found around abandoned homes and even cemeteries.

Well-established trees and shrubs rarely need any water at all. But of course, potted plants, summer annuals, and a nicely maintained lawn need help from time to time. Still, a general rule of thumb is that when you have to water, do it deeply, then leave plants alone so their roots can grow deep and strong, and you won't have to water as often. Watering frequently and a little at a time keeps roots shallow, susceptible to damage during dry spells, and needy.

HINT: When you do water, do it twice, an hour or so apart, to give the first watering time to soak in; the second watering really pushes it down deep. Sometimes I even water my plants after a light rain, to maximize the effect. And remember that for the plants in this book, too much water (like too much fertilizer) is worse than none at all.

Feed Plants for Quality, Not Quantity

Most of these tough plants can go for years without fertilizers—just look around and see for yourself. But giving them an occasional feeding can boost their performance, and invigorate them with healthier leaves, stems, roots, and flowers.

Keep in mind that most of the people telling you to feed, feed, feed your plants either sell fertilizer or are in a race with someone in a plant-nut club or society. All the plants want is a little pick-me-up from time to time, particularly with nitrogen, phosphorous, and potassium (the "big three," N, P, and K, whose numbers are on the fertilizer bag).

In a nutshell, here are what those three ingredients do for plants:

Nitrogen (first number, letter N) makes plants grow, especially with green leaves and stems. Foliage plants (the lawn and ferns) like nitrogen, but too much at a time can cause the plants to grow too quickly, making them weak and tender, and even burn them. Too much nitrogen often forces green growth at the expense of flowers or fruit (all vine, no tomatoes); once or twice a year, lightly, is the most I'd ever use nitrogen.

Phosphorous (second number, letter P) doesn't "make" flowers and fruit, it **helps** them; too much too often can interfere with other nutrients, especially nitrogen. Once every year or two is usually plenty.

Potassium (potash, the third number, letter K) helps make strong stems and roots, and lowers a plant's freezing point (it's the so-called "winterizer" ingredient); like phosphorous, it lasts two or three years or more.

BOTTOM LINE: Use an all-purpose, numbers-all-the-same plant food (like 10-10-10) every year or two, with maybe a little pick-me-up shot in between. For foliage plants, it's okay to use a fertilizer with a higher first number; for flowering or fruiting plants, use one with a higher middle number. Just don't ever overdo it—lean and mean is the best way to keep plants growing but still tough.

WHAT YOU CAN'T SEE usually won't hurt you or your plants; if your shrubs or flowers have little bugs or blots or spots or raggedy edges, try looking at them from ten feet away. Take off your glasses, and a lot of garden headaches disappear. If a plant continues to suffer, dump it for another plant—it ain't like y'all are married!

Share the Wealth

Multiply and share your own plants by saving seed, digging and dividing in-ground parts of multiple-stemmed perennials and shrubs, or rooting pieces of stems. Dare to share by holding informal plant swaps. Keep it simple by having participants offer only one plant, which should be given a number, and a corresponding number put in a pot to pass around; pull a number, and that's the plant you get—whether you want it, like it, already have it, or even brought it yourself! The real swapping begins afterwards.

THREE HINTS: Save seed indoors in a cool, dry place, and they'll last much longer; divide perennials in the season opposite of when they are in full bloom or leaf-growth; and root mature stems of evergreen shrubs in the summer and deciduous shrubs and trees in the late fall and winter.

Seven Seasons of the South

Southeastern gardeners can savor at least seven subtly overlapping but distinct gardening seasons. A good starting point in this segue of seasons would be January and February, the mid-winter, architectural "bare branches and bark" **first season** that keeps us on our toes as we expect sudden deep freezes to waste our magnificent *Camellia japonica*, fragrant paper-whites, and sweet olive. The only sure-fire dependable color in our winter comes from wild birds at our feeders.

Second season is when flowering shrubs pique our interest and give us hope. Most notable are flowering quince, forsythia, and mahonia, with flushes of daffodils naturalized around old home sites and cemeteries, complemented by white baby's breath spirea and white "flags" iris. Color quickly moves up into mid-story Oriental and star magnolias, flowering buckeye, ornamental pears, and redbuds to really get our gardening juices flowing.

The **third season**, riskiest of them all, usually brings a "blackberry winter" (the late frost that seems to always catch us and our too-early tomatoes by surprise); it's a reminder that summer is still a long ways off. Iris, wildflowers, and the new furled foliage of cannas and ferns get our hopes up more. Worst of all, we get intoxicated by wisteria, dogwood, and azaleas—breathlessly exotic but fickle beauties that remind me of the "fun girls from Mount Pilot" on the old Andy Griffith show—gaudy to behold, but usually nothing but trouble. Could it be said that these plants **cause** a late freeze?

By the **fourth season**, the lawn is up and running, and choked with late winter weeds (henbit, wild garlic, oxalis, dandelion); pansies begin to burn out in the heat, but it's a transition to summer with amaryllis, daylilies, Southern magnolia, and verbena. **Fifth season** lasts the rest of the summer, with crape myrtles, vitex, lots of perennials (salvias, liatris, cannas, lantana, rudbeckia), and taller summer annuals such as pentas and zinnias. This is when okra, squash, and tomatoes start coming in. **Sixth season** is when our summer starts to test our mettle and wear us out. The lawn becomes a chore and needs water, yet it's time to plant a second fall crop of flowers, tomatoes, and peppers. Bugs begin to get the upper hand, but it's too hot to spray.

The **seventh season** brings a hint of cool—and fall color in the trees. Lots of summer stuff still hangs on, but it's time to plant pansies and daffodils as native goldenrod and narrow-leaf sunflowers get frosted. *Camellia sasanqua* comes into flower, and a merciful hard freeze wastes the cannas and tomatoes. Time to plant pansies and daffodils, to egg-on the full-circle coming of the winter architectural season.

Regardless of your current season, it's just a transition. Relax, look around, see what you have—or don't have—and start planning and planting for this time next year.

Annuals
THAT ENDURE

It's a given, in the gardening world, that a lot of popular plants live for only a short time and then die no matter what you do. But they are so fun or productive that gardeners continue to replant them, year after year, in spite of the trouble and expenses of time, effort, money, and maintenance.

These **annuals**—so-called because they have to be replanted every year—are often **perennial** in some parts of the world, but they are killed here in the South by either cold winters or hot summers. Some, in fact, are borderline and may survive for a couple of years or more, but they are so "iffy" that they are considered annuals for most gardeners.

Still, a surprising selection of annuals are tougher than others, tolerant of bad weather and pest-resistant to boot, making them worth planting in an "unkillable plants" garden. Some reseed themselves to "come back" many years on their own; others have seeds that are easily saved from year to year or are readily available at garden centers or through mail order. A few are hard to grow from seed, but cuttings are easily rooted or they can be purchased as rooted plants.

What makes most annuals high maintenance is the soil preparation often required at planting time, plus fertilization, mulching, weed control, and watering during extremely sunny, windy, or hot spells (even in the winter).

Every seed catalog and garden book has lots of information on growing annuals, but the best knowledge comes from experience. The annuals in this book have been grown for many years with little or no effort throughout the South and are presented here in a "best of the best" list to help you get started with as little effort as possible.

Soil preparation involves digging your soil at least a shovel's depth, chopping up the larger chunks, and smoothing the surface. This can usually be done by hand or with a small power cultivator. The expense and storage problems of large power tillers are usually not justifiable except for large areas where lots of annuals are replanted year after year, such as in a large vegetable garden; even then, a large, powerful tiller can often be rented for a few dollars.

Organic matter such as compost, soil conditioner, peat moss, composted manure, or potting soil can be added to the soil to encourage annuals to grow roots quickly and deeply, improve drainage in heavy clay soils, and help hold moisture in sandy soils. Generally, a layer of organic matter two or three inches deep, no more than four inches deep, laid over the previously dug area and then tilled in, will work wonders throughout an entire season. It is better to use a little each of two or three different kinds of organic matter, for a total of two to four inches, than a lot of just one kind.

Fertilization means adding a small amount of a balanced or all-purpose fertilizer to your soil during soil preparation or at planting time. Most gardeners overdo this, causing plants to get "leggy" or grow too fast, resulting in poor flowering, or making plants more susceptible to weather, moisture problems, and pest pressures. A general rule of thumb, regardless of what kind of fertilizer you use, is to apply no more than one pound (about a pint jar full) of all-purpose fertilizer for every hundred square feet (ten by ten feet, four by twenty-five, five by twenty, etc.) of planting area. Adding more fertilizer later in the growing season is often helpful, but never overdo it.

Mulching simply means covering the newly worked soil with a layer of pine straw, or shredded or chipped bark, to keep the sun from overheating the soil, to keep the soil from crusting over after hard rains or watering, and to slow the germination of weed seeds. Synthetic fabric mulches do a fair job of weed control, but do not decay and "feed" the soil or its worms. A rule of thumb for how much mulch to use is to see how much it takes of your favorite kind to completely but barely cover the soil, then add that much more to compensate for packing and natural composting.

Weed control is usually done by hand pulling, chopping with a sharp hoe, mulching to keep seeds from sprouting, or, in last-case scenarios, using chemical weed killers—which are not always dependable or safe for other plants. For information on weed control, consult your county agriculture extension agent or ask a dependable, trained garden center employee to show you products that have your kinds of weeds and your kinds of plants listed on the labels. When in doubt, just put on gloves and pull!

Watering is necessary for most short-lived annuals, especially when it is hot and dry in the summer or during long spells of sunny, windy weather in the winter. Some annuals simply do not need it, but most will, at least every few weeks; container-grown annuals need regular watering, sometimes even in rainy seasons. How often to water and how much to use is so variable that no one can tell you an honest answer; the rule of thumb is to water only when needed, but do it deeply. I almost always water twice when I water, so the first time "sets up" the soil and the second one, done a few minutes after the first, really soaks in and lasts longer.

Note on Pest Control

Most of these plants have few pests, practically none that are major. Occasional leaf spots and minor insect infestations can make some plants look bad, but it is still a good idea to avoid pesticides whenever possible in order to protect bees, butterflies, and other beneficial creatures. When possible, choose a "natural" product such as insecticidal soap, neem oil, or diatomaceous earth to control minor insect pests and be prepared to simply pull up annuals that are suffering intolerable problems—something else is always waiting to go in that hole! Also be aware that overwatering or overfeeding can cause tough plants to be more susceptible to problems.

Note on Seed or Plant Sources

Always shop locally first! While the quality of seeds and annual transplants that arrive at garden centers is usually similar, in many cases—though not always—independent or family-owned garden centers have better-trained staffs who care for plants longer than some mass-merchandisers and who have

more knowledge about the plants and their challenges. Shop at a variety of sources for the best buys and the best service. Mail-order firms often have a larger selection of unusual or old-fashioned plants and seeds. And never overlook the value and fun (and heritage) of swapping seeds and plants with friends and neighbors!

ANNUALS are used for fast color or screening, as container plants and hanging baskets, for vegetables or herbs, and in long-blooming masses or specimen plants. They provide all-season "color bridges" as perennials flush in and out of show, can give solid color in the winter or summer (even in the shade), and add interest to shrubbery when it is out of season.

 Best for Beginners:

- Celosia
- Dusty Miller
- Coleus
- Gomphrena
- Moss Rose
- Okra
- Pansy
- Pentas
- Pepper
- Periwinkle
- Sweet Potato
- Zinnia

Kinda Tricky: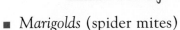

- Marigolds (spider mites)
- Impatiens (root rot)
- Tomatoes (pests, training)
- Annual Verbena (mites)
- Sweet Peas (weird weather)

Felder's Top Annual Picks

The following annuals, which by no means include all of the toughest, have proven themselves in millions of Southern gardens as beautiful and low maintenance.

Black-Eyed Susan

Rudbeckia hirta

Sun or very light shade

This very familiar native wildflower is one of the best butterfly and cut flowers ever for growing on a sunny hillside or in a meadow.

FLOWER: Thin, sunflower-like rays of mostly golden yellow on long, stiff stems in the spring and early summer, usually with dark cones or "noses" that become covered with butterflies.

PLANT: Low-growing, linear leaves over the winter; flowering stems sent up in spring and summer. Prefers fall seeding in poor but well-drained soils.

INTERESTING KINDS: Gloriosa daisy and 'Green Eyes' ('Irish Eyes') are outstanding summer cut flowers.

Castor Bean or Mole Bean

Ricinus communis

Full sun to light shade

The word for castor bean is **bold**—big summer plant, large leaves, perfect for backs of borders or in the center of a bed or large container. Roots are said to repel moles, but no evidence backs that up.

FLOWER: Stalks up to a foot tall with not very showy flowers but large marble-sized spiny burrs of seed, the same color as the stems, sometimes bright red (seeds are very poisonous, so remove them where children might garden or play).

PLANT: Tall, branching, woody-stemmed summer annual up to six feet or more tall and half as wide, with large, lobed leaves up to two or more feet across in burgundy or green.

INTERESTING KINDS: 'Sanguineus' has leaves tinged blood red, and 'Zanzibarensis' has green leaves with white veins.

Celosia
Celosia argentea var. *cristata*
Sun

These plants will grow in sidewalk cracks and reseed themselves for years to come.

FLOWER: Cockscomb (Cristata group) has rounded, fissured heads up to a foot across of blood red and other colors; plume cockscomb (Plumosa group) has smaller plumes of red, pink, golden, or white; another type (Spicata group) has long, slender flower heads in pink or yellow.

PLANT: Summer annual with pointed oval leaves of medium green or purplish, up to two feet or more tall and half as wide. Use as a specimen, in combinations, or in masses.

INTERESTING KINDS: In the Spicata group, 'Flamingo Feather' is four feet tall with long, narrow spikes of pink and white; 'Flamingo Purple' has dark purplish green leaves and pinkish purple spikes; 'Pink Castle' has rose pink spikes.

Cleome or Spider Flower
Cleome hassleriana
Sun or light shade

Tall fluffy plants with marijuana-like, palmate leaves. Good cut flower that wilts when first cut but perks up in water. Excellent butterfly and hummingbird plant, great in masses behind other flowers or combined with bold textured plants in large containers.

FLOWER: Airy heads six inches wide and loosely arranged, with open flowers that have spidery "cat whisker" stamens and long narrow seedpods, in white, pink, or dusty purple.

PLANT: Four- to six-foot branching summer annuals (there are dwarf forms also) with palm-like foliage that is sticky and has a not-so-nice aroma when cut, and small prickly thorns.

INTERESTING KINDS: 'Helen Campbell' is snow white, and there are a number of Queen varieties (cherry, pink, rose, purple, mauve, ruby) that indicate color.

Coleus
Solenostemon scutellarioides
Light shade or sun, depending on the type

Coleus is an old-fashioned tropical foliage plant grown mostly in light shade as a summer annual, either in beds or containers. Large masses are spectacular all summer and fall, and when in flower are fair butterfly plants. Very easy to root in water or moist potting soil and kept indoors over the winter.

FLOWER: Tall flower spikes are not very showy, but are studded with small, salvia-like blue trumpets. Most gardeners pinch the stalks off to promote new leaf production.

PLANT: Shrubby, many-branched member of the mint family with large leaves, up to six or more inches long and nearly as wide, in many colors, including red, green, yellow, chartreuse, orange, salmon, pink, and purple, most variegated, splotched, or with contrasting edges. Grows best in moist conditions, with light but regular feeding. Leaves can be steeped to make a tea-like tonic.

INTERESTING KINDS: Seed-grown coleus come in a wide array of leaf shapes and colors. The "hottest" kinds are so-called "sun" coleus, many with burgundy or red foliage, which can tolerate hot sun, even in a pot on a sunny patio; common varieties include 'Plum Parfait' and 'Burgundy Sun'.

Copper Plant or Copperleaf
Acalypha wilkesiana
Sun

Bulky mainstay foliage plant for hot summer beds, often overlooked because it is sold as rooted cuttings in larger pots, which are relatively expensive compared with typical "six pack" flowers. Lots of bang for the buck, though.

FLOWER: Not very showy tassels of reddish brown hanging from leaf axils.

PLANT: Three-foot or taller mass of mottled bronze, red, copper, orange, and green foliage, held densely around the plant. Grows all right in the shade, but has outstanding heat and sun tolerance; a great "anchor" for companions in a large container, in groups, or as a short summer hedge behind other flowers. Must be pruned and brought in during the winter if you want to hold it over for next year.

INTERESTING KINDS: 'Macafeeana' has large reddish leaves tinged with crimson and bronze; 'Hoffmannia' has narrow, twisted leaves; 'Obovata' has leaves ruffled and serrated, in pink, bronze, and red.

Coreopsis or Tickseed
Coreopsis species
Sun

Common prairie wildflowers that "tame" very well in urban flower borders, containers, and butterfly or cut-flower gardens. State wildflower of Mississippi. Many species are perennial, though some are short-lived.

FLOWER: Cheerful yellow disks two or more inches across from mid-spring through midsummer.

PLANT: Short, stocky clump of linear foliage appears in early winter. Some species have wide, strap-like leaves; others have very delicate, needle-like foliage.

INTERESTING KINDS: *Coreopsis tinctoria* is an airy, openly branched plant, which has a reddish aura around the flower center and finely divided, almost ferny leaves. Interesting relatives include black-eyed Susan, other coneflowers, and sunflowers. A similar plant is *C. basalis* or calliopsis.

Cosmos
Cosmos sulphureus
Sun

This summer and fall flowering showstopper is one of the most impressive flowers of the season and reseeds itself to the point of being a nuisance. But it's easy to thin out seedlings in the spring and summer.

FLOWER: Showy, single, flat, daisy-like flowers in deep orange-yellow.

PLANT: Large branching plant to eight feet with deep-green, divided, marigold-like leaves.

INTERESTING KINDS: Common cosmos (*Cosmos bipinnatus*) has pink, white, rose, or crimson flowers with yellow centers that bloom in the spring, summer, and fall; very easy from seed sown in spring.

Dusty Miller
Senecio cineraria
Sun or shade

This is the first "white" companion plant I reach for when looking for contrast in container plantings or especially when working on a patriotic planting. Good, solid white all year.

FLOWER: Fairly showy, loose clusters of creamy yellow held above the foliage in summer.

PLANT: Upright, spreading, many-branched shrub-like mound to two feet or taller of soft, dusty white foliage; sometimes needs shearing to thicken up the foliage near its base. Perennial in the lower and middle South.

INTERESTING KINDS: 'Cirrus' is a dwarf form; 'Silverdust' is very compact and finely textured. Other silvery or white garden plants in the aster family include *Artemisia* and several *Centaurea* species that are also called dusty miller.

Globe Amaranth or Bachelor's Button
Gomphrena globosa
Full sun

Historic summer annual, the perfect companion for other flowers because of its tall, airy growth. Super easy to dry for long lasting flower arrangements. Fair as a butterfly plant.

FLOWER: Bristly, round, button-like clover heads of red, purplish red, pink, or white on long stems up to three feet tall.

PLANT: Often-reseeding summer annual with narrow foliage that is not much to look at. Very pest resistant and incredibly drought- and heat-tolerant.

INTERESTING KINDS: Compact purplish red 'Buddy', tall red 'Strawberry Fields', and pink 'Lavender Lady'.

Johnny Jump-Up
Viola tricolor
Sun or light shade

Favorite "old garden" winter annual, planted in the fall and flowering through the worst winter. Perfect for containers, mass planting over taller daffodils, or borders.

FLOWER: Sweetly fragrant, purple and yellow pansies about the size of a quarter. Blooms spring into summer; seedlings pop up in the fall.

PLANT: Floppy many-branched mounds of small roundish leaves, to a foot or more tall and wide, set out in the fall or late winter as transplants. Reseeds.

INTERESTING KINDS: Various cultivars exist, with flowers ranging from soft lavender to nearly black.

Joseph's Coat
Alternanthera ficoidea
Sun or light shade

Grown entirely for its generally compact growth and solid green, golden, or variegated foliage, this is the most popular annual for creating living floral emblems or to spell out words in flower beds. Tolerates close shearing and roots readily (fallen clippings often root in the mulch).

FLOWER: Insignificant white stars throughout the foliage.

PLANT: Solid little "mini-shrub" from six inches to three feet tall with small leaves.

INTERESTING KINDS: There are many varieties in green, gold, burgundy, rosy red, scarlet, and chartreuse forms. 'Rosea Nana' has rose-colored leaves; 'Golden Threads' has narrow leaves in green, yellow, and white.

Larkspur
Consolida ambigua
Winter sun, summer light shade

Larkspur is our main "delphinium" plant, producing prolific racemes of pastel colors, perfect for a cut-flower garden or as a companion to irises and other late spring or early summer perennials.

FLOWER: Narrow, dense spikes of interesting violet-like flowers, a half-inch or longer, of deep or pale blue, pink, or white, produced in late winter through midsummer; some are double flowered.

PLANT: Airy, branching, three- to five-foot-tall plant grows best over the winter. The old-timey single form reseeds prolifically.

INTERESTING KINDS: Giant Imperial and Regal strains are many-branched.

Melampodium
Melampodium paludosum
Full sun

Its unfortunate lack of a "common" name scares new gardeners off, but this is one of the top ten summer flowering annuals for massing in hot, dry, parking-lot type garden spots.

FLOWER: Buttery yellow daisies produced in nearly solid sheets, from spring to frost.

PLANT: Mounding plants from two to three feet, deep green foliage. Requires heat to grow.

INTERESTING KINDS: 'Showstar' is compact, under two feet tall; 'Medallion' can get over three feet tall and half that wide.

Mexican Sunflower
Tithonia rotundifolia
Full sun

Fast-growing tall screen or accent that flowers nonstop in heat, drought, and humidity, all the while covered with butterflies and hummingbirds.

FLOWER: Marigold-like flowers up to four inches across with orange petals and yellow centers. Blooms spring to frost, good as cut flowers and outstanding for butterflies.

PLANT: Large (to six feet or more) multi-branched summer shrub with hand-sized leaves. Reseeds well.

INTERESTING KINDS: 'Sundance' and 'Goldfinger' are more compact, to three or four feet.

Moss Rose
Portulaca grandiflora
Full sun

This solid mass of bright flowers opens only for people who are outdoors in the middle of the day. Perfect for rock gardens, edging, and spilling out of containers in hot, dry locations.

FLOWER: Compact, inch-wide, rose-like clusters of brilliant red, magenta, pink, yellow, and white that open only when summer sun shines directly on them, right up until frost.

PLANT: Low mounds, six inches tall by a foot wide, thick with fleshy, cylindrical leaves to an inch long. Reseeds prolifically in hot, dry areas.

INTERESTING KINDS: There are double- and single-flowered strains of cylindrical-leaf moss rose; the popular flowering purslane (*Portulaca umbraticola*) has flat leaves and flat, single flowers.

Okra

Abelmoschus esculentus

Full sun

Vegetables as ornamentals? You bet! Tall, leafy okra has gorgeous foliage, flowers, and fruit, and makes a statement in large containers or behind other summer flowers. Stems with seedpods make super additions to dried arrangements.

FLOWER: Three-inch, pale yellow hibiscus-like cups produced near ends of stems.

PLANT: Tall (to six feet), slightly branching stems covered with almost foot-long, deeply divided leaves. Requires hot weather for best growth. Long narrow seedpods are edible when small.

INTERESTING KINDS: 'Burgundy' has reddish green foliage and maroon fruits; 'Blondie' has creamy white fruits.

Pansy and Viola

Viola X *wittrockiana* and *Viola cornuta*

Full winter sun or part shade

Pansies and violas have become some of the most popular annuals, and probably the only truly reliable ones for providing color and interest in the cool weather months, connecting fall to the following spring.

FLOWER: Flat and up to four inches across, in white, blue, purple, red, yellow, orange, sometimes with large blotches or contrasting "eyes," produced from fall to late spring. Remove spent flowers for the most optimum continued production.

PLANT: Compact six- to eight-inch-tall mounds of slightly lobed, roundish leaves. Requires cool weather for best growth; generally dies from heat by early summer in the South. Best grown from transplants.

INTERESTING KINDS: There are many hybrid strains and colors of pansies, from big floppy kinds to compact freer-flowering ones. New hybrids, called bedding pansies or violas, between the smaller *Viola cornuta* and the larger pansies have mid-sized flowers and more compact growth, and come in many hues of white, yellow, apricot, blue, purple, and others.

Pentas or Egyptian Star-Cluster

Pentas lanceolata

Sun or light shade

This medium-tall shrubby plant was grown for many years as a Victorian "pot plant" and has made a tremendous comeback as one of the best butterfly plants for the summer garden.

FLOWER: Six-inch-wide clusters of small, starry florets of deep red, white, or pink bloom atop the foliage.

PLANT: Upright, branching shrub to two or more feet tall. Grows best in hot weather.

INTERESTING KINDS: Several strains on the market, all about the same.

Pepper

Capsicum annuum

Full sun or light shade

Ornamental peppers, with a huge array of sizes and fruit colors, are seriously overlooked additions to flower beds, herb gardens, and containers. Most ornamental peppers are edible, but very hot!

FLOWER: Small, starry, white flowers from late spring to frost; fruits are tiny birds-eye pods to long and thin, from green to yellow, orange, red, purple, and almost black.

PLANT: Shrubby summer annuals from six inches to four feet or taller, many branched with oval leaves of green, purple, or variegated with white or yellow.

INTERESTING KINDS: There are many, many forms of *Capsicum annuum*, including sweet, jalapeno, and chilli peppers. *Capsicum frutescens*, the tabasco pepper, is a large shrub with hundreds of narrow fruits in green, yellow, and red held upright; *C. chinense* includes the habanero pepper which is fiery hot and has beautiful, gnarly orange fruits.

Perilla
Perilla frutescens
Full sun or light shade

This reseeding annual in the mint family has coarse, attractive toothed leaves and a shrubby form, making it a good background or filler plant. The purple-leaved form is a nice foil for pink flowered plants or plants with silver foliage.

FLOWER: Spikes of lavender mint-like flowers, with the spikes remaining after a frost has killed all the leaves.

PLANT: Shrubby stems of burgundy or green, toothed leaves, very similar to basil but with a different scent. Reseeds prolifically all over, including into mulched areas and nearby walkways, but it's easy to pull the ones you don't want.

INTERESTING KINDS: 'Atropurpurea' has purple leaves; the form *rosea* has variegated foliage and looks something like coleus, to which *Perilla* is related. Another mint family member, sweet basil, which has many cultivars, is more fragrant but not as drought tolerant.

Periwinkle
Catharanthus roseus
Full sun

One of the most drought-tolerant plants on Earth, periwinkle flowers continually with no care at all.

FLOWER: Flat, five-petaled disks of pure white, pink, or red, sometimes with a darker "eye," produced in masses atop foliage from spring to frost, more in hot weather.

PLANT: Compact mound of glossy green foliage up to two feet tall, usually a foot or less. Reseeds prolifically into nearby hot, dry areas. Resents water and heavy wet soils.

INTERESTING KINDS: Many strains on the market, with more or less creeping or compact habits and larger flowers.

Petunia

Petunia × hybrida

Sun

Old "grandmother's garden" varieties are not as showy as modern hybrids, but give a wonderful cottage-garden element to mixed borders and containers.

FLOWER: Flat or ruffled trumpets of white, pink, red, purple, blue, or rose, with or without stripes; some strains have flowers four inches or more across. Blooms best in cool weather.

PLANT: Sprawling vine-like summer annual that tolerates a little cool better than extreme heat. May need "pinching" to thicken scraggly growth. Often reseeds.

INTERESTING KINDS: Too many to mention, but cascading 'Purple Wave' takes the most summer heat, needs no pruning to thicken it up, and smells of heavenly spices, all day and night.

Salvia

Salvia coccinea and *Salvia splendens*

Sun or light shade

Salvias are summer mainstays with spikes of red or blue, sometimes pink, purple, white, or peach.

FLOWER: Spikes of small exotic trumpets, mostly red, from spring to frost, great for butterflies and hummingbirds.

PLANT: Upright, branching, small shrubby plants to two feet tall or more; solid green leaves give great contrast to the spikes of flowers. Reseeds prolifically everywhere, including into hard clay.

INTERESTING KINDS: *Salvia coccinea* is the most heat- and drought-tolerant plant of all, will be covered with butterflies, and reseeds everywhere. It's the last annual besides periwinkle to die from drought. The most common other summer annual salvia (*S. splendens*) is a mistake to plant in full sun—it does much better in light to moderate shade and needs watering.

Sunflower

Helianthus annuus

Sun

Classic tall annual for the back of the border or even the vegetable garden. Easy to grow from seed directly sown in the ground. Newer cultivars make this "country cousin" look at home even in more "sophisticated" gardens. Plant something in front to hide its bare legs.

FLOWER: Wide, usually flattened heads of golden flower disks surrounded by rays of yellow, gold, cream, rust, and red. Edible seeds mature by midsummer or fall.

PLANT: Tall, to eight feet or more, sometimes branching, with large, pointed, oval leaves up to a foot wide. Sometimes needs staking, or grow it with annual vines to help as a support.

INTERESTING KINDS: Too many to single out, varying in plant height, flower size and color, and quality of seeds (for birds or people); pollen-free kinds are best for cut flowers.

Sweet Potato

Ipomoea batatas

Full sun to moderate shade

Ornamental sweet potatoes are fast growing, trailing (not climbing) vines with beautiful foliage color for large containers, hanging baskets, or ground covers. Astounding in masses or entwined with other summer plants.

FLOWER: Not very showy, small "morning glories."

PLANT: Heart-shaped or lobed foliage on long, trailing vines that root as they "run" from spring to frost. Does best in poor soils with low fertility. Forms edible tuberous roots.

INTERESTING KINDS: 'Blackie' has deep burgundy, almost black foliage that is deeply divided; 'Margarita' has shocking chartreuse foliage; 'Pink Frost' ('Tricolor') has variegated white, green, and pink leaves, and is not as vigorous as the other two.

Zinnia

Zinnia elegans and *Zinnia angustifolia*
Sun or very light shade

One of the very best "starter" flowers for kids and adults alike, outstanding for butterflies and cut flowers, best used in masses or behind other plants to hide its ugly lower foliage.

FLOWER: Flat or double daisy-like flower heads, up to three or more inches across, in all possible colors, even white (no black), usually with yellow stamens; produced freely all summer and fall on long stems. Deadheading can increase the number of flowers produced.

PLANT: Many-branching, compact mounds or tall specimens to four feet or more, with pleasing oval leaves. Sometimes prone to powdery mildew but plants keep on flowering. Usually reseeds.

INTERESTING KINDS: Narrow leaf zinnia (*Zinnia angustifolia* or *Z. linearis*) is a loose mound of smaller, non-stop, orange or white flowers, with outstanding heat and drought tolerance in containers, edging, or rock gardens.

Other Annuals Worth a Try:

Ageratum (*Ageratum houstonianum*) is a blue-flowered edging plant that can offer good cut flowers.

Bluebonnet (*Lupinus subcarnosus*) or **Texas bluebonnet**, seedlings have interesting winter foliage and blue spring flowers. Soak or knick seed before sowing in fall. Avoid wet, fertile soils.

Burgundy Mustard (*Brassica oleracea*, Acephala group) has winter foliage of deep red or maroon, sometimes with white midribs, and tall airy spikes of clear yellow spring flowers. Edible, but hot.

Calendula (*Calendula officinalis*) is like a cross between marigold and zinnia, for winter and early spring color. Flowers are edible.

Candlestick Plant (*Senna alata* or *Cassia alata*) has dramatic, big, fall blooms with a tropical touch.

Cornflower (*Centaurea cyanus*) is a fall-sown plant that makes knee-high masses of white, purple, blue, or pink flowers suitable for drying before the plants die from summer heat.

Cushion Mum (*Dendranthema* × *grandiflorum*) is best used as one-shot masses of autumn glory; expensive but showy. Compost them when they freeze, and replant with bulbs and pansies.

French Hollyhock (*Alcea rosea* 'Zebrina' or *Malva sylvestris* 'Zebrina'), a prolifically reseeding, overwintering shrub with lavender flowers streaked in purple, is much better adapted to the South than "regular" hollyhocks.

Hollyhock (*Alcea rosea*) has overwintering mounds of large round leaves that erupt into tall spires of single or double flowers in white, pink, red, or burgundy. Suffers in summer heat and can be riddled with insect damage.

Impatiens (*Impatiens walleriana*) must have shade and lots of water. Great with caladiums.

Kales (*Brassica oleracea*) (pictured) include curly, burgundy, and other interesting varieties (including bold-textured collards) for winter and spring color in containers, raised beds, and kitchen gardens.

Lettuces (*Lactuca sativa*) offer incredible variations of leaf shape and color (mostly greens, golds, and burgundies) for winter foliage in containers or empty summer beds. Edible and easy from seed.

Marigold (*Tagetes* species) has showy yellow or gold flowers and fragrant foliage. Often peters out in midsummer from spider mites and heat but can be replanted for a fall show.

Nicotiana (*Nicotiana alata* or *N.* × *sanderae*) or **flowering tobacco** blooms with panicles of white, red, pink, yellow, or mauve in cool weather; the tall, white flowering tobacco (*N. sylvestris*) is a knockout in the summer shade garden. Some types are highly fragrant.

Poppies (*Papaver* species) produce exotic spring flowers from fall-sown seed. Round pods are also attractive; the pods of opium poppy (*P. somniferum*) are the source of opium, which is why this plant is illegal to grow.

Queen Anne's Lace (*Daucus carota*) is the reseeding parent of the carrot, with ferny foliage and large, flat, white heads of flowers. Great for butterflies, in meadows, and in poor soil.

Snapdragons (*Antirrhinum majus*) (pictured) have tall dense spikes of white, yellow, red, or pink flowers from fall to spring. Tolerates winter in the lower South, better for spring and fall in upper South.

Sweet Alyssum (*Lobularia maritima*) creates a mass of white or pale purple for spring edging.

Touch-Me-Not (*Impatiens balsamina*) or **garden balsam** is an impatiens relative with larger leaves; more tolerance of sun and drought; and pale white, pink, or red flowers close to the stems. Reseeds vigorously.

Fast-Reference Lists for Annuals

In Shade or Semi-Shade
- Ageratum
- Alyssum
- Begonia
- Caladium
- Coleus
- Impatiens
- Pansy
- Pentas
- Salvia
- Snapdragon

For Hot, Dry Spots
- Castor Bean
- Celosia
- Copper Plant
- Cornflower
- Cosmos
- Dusty Miller
- Globe Amaranth
- Joseph's Coat
- Melampodium
- Mexican Sunflower
- Moss Rose
- Okra
- Perilla
- Periwinkle
- Queen Anne's Lace
- Sunflower
- Sweet Potato
- Zinnia

For Poor, Unimproved Soils
- Bluebonnet
- Castor Bean
- Celosia
- Cleome
- Coreopsis
- Cosmos
- Globe Amaranth
- Moss Rose
- Okra
- Perilla
- Periwinkle
- Queen Anne's Lace
- Sweet Potato

Plant in the Fall or Mid-Winter
- Alyssum
- Black-Eyed Susan
- Bluebonnet
- Calendula
- Cornflower
- Cosmos
- French Hollyhock
- Hollyhock
- Johnny Jump-Up
- Larkspur
- Lettuce
- Mustard
- Pansy
- Poppy
- Queen Anne's Lace
- Snapdragon

Usually Reseed Themselves for Years
- Castor Bean
- Cleome
- Coreopsis
- Cornflower
- Cosmos
- Globe Amaranth
- Impatiens
- Johnny Jump-Up
- Larkspur
- Moss Rose
- Periwinkle
- Perilla
- Petunia
- Queen Anne's Lace
- Zinnia

Good Annual Cut Flowers
- Ageratum
- Celosia
- Cleome
- Cornflower
- Cosmos
- Globe Amaranth
- Larkspur
- Pentas
- Poppy
- Queen Anne's Lace
- Salvia
- Snapdragon
- Sunflower (pollen-free varieties)
- Zinnia

Colorful Foliage
- Basil
- Caladium (in Bulbs)
- Castor Bean
- Coleus
- Copper Plant
- Dusty Miller
- Joseph's Coat
- Kale
- Lettuce
- Mustard
- Perilla
- Okra
- Sweet Potato

Easy Edging
- Ageratum
- Alyssum
- Begonia
- Dusty Miller
- Joseph's Coat
- Marigold (dwarf)
- Pansy
- Petunia
- Sweet Potato
- Zinnia (dwarf or narrow-leaf)

Fast Backgrounds or Screens
- Candlestick Plant
- Castor Bean
- Cleome
- Copper Plant
- Cosmos
- Hollyhock
- Mexican Sunflower
- Okra
- Sunflower
- Zinnia

Butterfly Plants
- Coreopsis
- Cosmos
- Globe Amaranth
- Mexican Sunflower
- Okra
- Pentas
- Periwinkle
- Queen Anne's Lace
- Zinnia

Wedding of the Flowers

My great-great-aunt Bernice, a retired New Orleans school principal who visited her old home place in north central Mississippi quite often, was a heck of a gal. It was she who first told me that flying saucers were coming out of the center of the earth, through a hole in Antarctica (and had a magazine with pictures to prove it). She studied teaching in New York City, and took flying lessons from Charles Lindbergh himself (for that, we have REAL photos).

After she passed away, I found some of her old notes and stuff, including a crumbly, printed Victorian parlor word game in which a story was told with blanks left in the narrative, to be filled in with plant names. This particular one was called "The Wedding of the Flowers" and its faded penciled-in answers were hard to read. With help from friends and family, I took on the project of filling in the blanks. Here is the complete story, with the answers underlined:

Black-Eyed Susan married Sweet William after he Aster. His rival had been Ragged Robin, but the groom's Tulips sealed the engagement under towering Sunflowers. Their Four O'Clock wedding in Virgin Bowers was announced by Bells of Ireland and Bluebells. The bride was given away by Poppy, as the groom's mother whispered to him "Forget-Me-Not." Jack-in-the-Pulpit officiated.

Though the groom was giving up Bachelor Buttons, he brought to his bride Peppermint and Candytuft. The rings were made of Goldenrod and the bride's Paper-White gown was trimmed with Queen Anne's Lace (with Cowslips underneath). Bridesmaids were Quaker Ladies, including Lily, Iris, Daisy, and Rose. Their dresses were Lilac and Pinks, and they received Foxgloves and Cockscombs. The groomsmen were Jon-quil, Dan-delion, and Chrys-anthemum.

There was a crowd at the wedding—Phlox—but Seven Sisters and Old Maids were left behind. Singers included Larkspur and the great Bird of Paradise. A brief scene was created when Johnny Jump-Up objected to the wedding, but Bleeding Heart, Bittersweet, and Weeping Willow, all rejected lovers of the American Beauty, kept their Peace.

They ate their wedding cake from Buttercups, and had Lady Slippers tied behind their carriage. Their new home will be on Cape Jasmine, where they will spend the rest of their Everlasting lives in Sweet Peas (peace), hopefully with Baby's Breath.

Here's hoping their Passionflower love affair, made under the Star of Bethlehem, doesn't turn into Touch-Me-Not!

UNBEATABLE
Bulbs

My great-grandmother Pearl, who lived right across the street from my childhood home, had over three hundred fifty varieties of daffodils—and knew all their names. I was raised thinking bulbs are about the toughest garden plants there are, and to this day, I can't imagine my garden without a single one of its dozens of nearly zero-maintenance beauties.

Flowering bulbs and bulb-like perennials are overlooked mainstays of Southern gardens. They have traditionally been planted as afterthoughts or all by themselves, partly because so many of them have temporary shows and we forget about them the rest of the year. But they can easily be worked into overall landscapes to add or prolong color and provide foliage even in "off" seasons.

Not all the plants in this section are true bulbs. Many are rhizomes, corms, tubers, and other forms of underground structures. In addition to traditional spring bulbs such as daffodils, there are summer-blooming rain lilies, gorgeous cannas, native blazing star, and winter-foliaged painted arum.

Flowering bulbs need plenty of sunlight, at least when their foliage is out; spring bulbs get all the sun they need even when planted under summer-shady oaks and tall deciduous shrubs since the trees still haven't leafed out by late winter and early spring. Be careful, however, to avoid planting them in the shadow of the north side of a building or evergreen shrubs, because the winter and early spring sun is so low in the southern sky, combined with the low-light setting, that the bulbs won't get enough light.

Bulbs also usually require well-drained soil and certainly shouldn't be planted where water stands for hours after a rain. Avoid water-related bulb rot by working plenty of organic matter or coarse sand into heavy soils, or plant in raised beds or containers.

Garden centers, mail-order catalogues, and specialty nurseries have many dozens of different kinds of bulbs, each with several distinct species and sometimes hundreds of unique cultivars. It's always a great idea to try new kinds—you never know when one will turn out to be an all-time favorite in your garden. But for long-term success, see if there aren't enough different kinds of bulbs described here to keep you entertained for many years with little care.

The planting rule of thumb for true bulbs, unless otherwise indicated, is "twice as deep as they are tall." Big bulbs go deeper than smaller ones. You can even plant smaller ones above larger ones!

Interplanting with Bulbs

Daffodils are dormant in the summer; lantana is completely bare in the winter. Why waste precious garden space for "one shot" plants, when you can plant one in between the other to prolong the season? Bonus: The emerging foliage of one can hide the fading leaves of the other. Large shrubs, bare winter lawns, and overstuffed patio pots can all be gussied up with bulbs.

The biggest considerations for interplanting flowers include making sure that all of them get the amount of sun or shade they need and that watering or fertilizing one type doesn't harm the others.

Good companions include: daffodils with daylilies and chrysanthemums, liatris with goldenrod, hosta with liriope, iris with larkspur and artemisia, and canna with nandina.

Bulbs for the Shade

Ever see bulbs growing in old home places that are all grown up with trees? These "naturalized" beauties have spread by seed, because their fruiting pods were left intact instead of being mowed or clipped before their seed ripened.

The trick to getting them to grow and multiply in the shade is planting them under trees which lose their leaves in the **winter**, giving them winter sunshine, and leaving them alone after flowering so they have time to form flower buds underground inside the bulbs for the next season. This is especially important for daffodils, which form their next year's flower buds in the six weeks or so after they flower.

The bottom line is, plant bulbs, especially early-flowering kinds, where they get winter sunshine, and then **leave them alone** after they flower—and don't cut or braid their foliage!

Protect Bulbs from Critters:

Voles are small, mouse-like rodents that burrow and eat roots and especially tender bulbs. I have actually seen them in action, watching plants start to wobble and then disappear into tunnels! Not much will control these destructive pests—they are even hard for cats to catch! Here are some "tricks of the trade" used by hard-core gardeners, and in botanical gardens:

- When planting bulbs, surround them with gravel or other coarse material, which voles hate to dig through.
- Place "live" traps near burrows, baited with something smeared with peanut butter.
- When digging beds, place hardware cloth (mesh wire with half-inch openings) in the bottom and up the sides, like an upside-down fence, at least six or eight inches tall, partly sticking out of the ground (mulch will cover the exposed part). Make sure the bottom edge is curved outward, away from the bed, to guide voles and moles away, not under.
- Plant individual bulbs or plants in wire baskets buried partially in the ground.
- Surround bulbs with other plants like daffodils, which voles will not eat.
- Protect from digging squirrels, chipmunks, and cats by laying "chicken wire" over the planted area, which bulbs will grow up through.

How to "Steal" Bulbs

Got an old abandoned homeplace in mind, where you are sure no one will miss a few daffodils, iris, daylilies, or hyacinths? Take your time—don't rush out when plants are in full bloom, for two reasons: Digging when in flower often causes them to skip a year blooming (which means it will be two years until the next flowering cycle), and someone you know will invariably come down the road just as you get back to your car with an armload.

Assuming you have permission to dig on private property, here's the way to do it: Cut the flowers from the ones you want, both for "instant gratification" in a vase, and to keep someone else from seeing them and "liberating" them first; then go back a couple of months later, when the plants have formed next year's flower buds and are nearly dormant, to dig. Be sure to put a plastic spoon or other discreet label by the ones you want, or you might not find them later.

Tulips Hate the South

Tulips are annuals in the South. Showy as they are, they're best used for one-shot foliage and spring flowers—just like equally beautiful (and intensely fragrant) hybrid hyacinths. Tulips are native to mountainous areas of the Middle East, where it stays cold all winter, and gets very dry in the summer. Because of our mild, wet winters and hot, humid climate, they usually don't get the "chilling hours" they need to rebloom in the Southeast or they sim-

ply rot from our wet springs and muggy summers. Plus, the new bulbs they produce take energy from the "mother" bulbs while requiring a couple or more years to get to blooming size, and everything just peters out. Sure, you could dig and clean and store them, and refrigerate them before planting again, but c'mon—what's the point? Buy a cheap sackful every fall.

Perhaps the best shot at a perennial tulip for the South is the lady or candy tulip (*Tulipa clusiana*), with small flowers that are rosy on the outside and either white or golden ('*Cynthia*', pictured) on the inside that opens and shuts for several days. It requires super well-drained soil and almost complete summer drought. Lower-South gardeners should dig and store them in a dry place, then refrigerate for six or eight weeks before replanting. Also try early-flowering *T. kaufmanniana*, *T. tarda*, and *T. turkestanica*. Good luck!

 ## Best for Beginners:

- Canna
- Chives
- Daffodils
- Iris
- Elephant's Ear
- Grape Hyacinth
- Gladiolus
- Hosta
- Lycoris
- Anemone

Kinda Tricky:

- Tulip
- Dahlia
- Amaryllis Hybrids
- Freesia
- Garden Lilies

Caladium
Caladium bicolor
Shade or part sun

Shade lovers, take note: This is one of your best friends! There's no better way to bring pizzazz to a shaded border, brighten a dark patio, or skirt a row of gloomy shrubs with color. Though caladiums will tolerate a lot of sun (with extra soil prep and watering, which is against the principles of this book), these summer annuals perform best by far in the shade.

Caladiums are so striking individually, they really don't need to be planted in large groups in long rows or circles around trees. Better to use them in clusters of three or more, repeated here and there for effect. They are also superb in pots on a shady porch or patio, especially when combined with impatiens.

FLOWER: Not striking at all, a calla-like whorl of white surrounding a pencil-like pollen stem, mostly hidden in the more desirable foliage. Admire the first one or two, then clip the rest off to stimulate more foliage production.

PLANT: Leaves are variable, but mostly pointed heart- or shield-shaped, up to a foot long, of red, white, pink, and green, in countless combinations. Produced in two-foot-tall masses.

INTERESTING KINDS: 'Freida Hemple' has dark red leaves bordered with green; the short, compact 'Miss Muffet' is light green with white ribs and red speckles; 'June Bride' is white.

SOIL: Plant tubers knobby side up, very shallowly in rich soil amended with organic matter, and occasionally water when rainfall is scarce. If plants go dormant, they usually pick back up after rains return. Light, regular feedings promote continuous foliage production.

PROPAGATION: Plant new tubers every year, well after danger of frost is past, or get them started earlier in pots in a bright spot indoors to set out later. Or dig, divide, and save old tubers before frost in the fall; let them dry thoroughly; and keep them very dry indoors over the winter.

TIP: WHAT'S THE DIFFERENCE between bulbs, tubers, rhizomes, and corms anyway? We tend to refer to most of them as "bulbs" and the distinctions can be subtle. All of them are underground structures developed for storing energy, water, and food for new growth, and to sustain the plant during dry spells and dormancy. Many plants with such structures are native to regions with regular seasonal dry periods. A tuber is a swollen stem, branch, or root (caladium). A corm is a bulbous stem and is annual, forming new corms from buds on the old ones (crocus). A rhizome is a stem also, but can vary in thickness and branching, and can be near the soil surface (iris). A true bulb is a modified bud, with a thickened stem section and modified leaves (daffodil). Clear as mud, right?

Canna

Canna X generalis

Sun or very light shade

Almost nothing says "South" more than cannas, perhaps the most widely planted perennial around. Because they are so common around "poor folks" gardens and homes, some upscale gardeners refuse to grow them. Yet the exotic Victorian foliage favorites are showcased in every botanical garden on Earth. The biggest problem is what to do with the huge gap they leave after gardeners clean up their wilted, frozen remains once they go dormant at first frost. One solution is to interplant with evergreen shrubs or ornamental grasses, or place a "hard feature" such as a gazing globe or statue nearby.

FLOWER: Sometimes very showy, gnarly masses of irregularly shaped flowers in orange, red, yellow, apricot, salmon, and mixed. Hard, round, bristly seedpods can be interesting as well, especially on old Indian shot canna (*Canna indica*). Cut faded flowers to promote more leaves.

PLANT: Large, almost banana-like, slick tropical leaves are long and wide, sometimes pointed, in green, bronze, dark burgundy, and striped. Plants grow in masses of leafy stems that can get up to six feet tall, although compact and dwarf forms are common. Very good for container culture, near pools or water gardens, around patios, and in Victorian mixed plantings.

INTERESTING KINDS: Cultivars include Pfitzer's dwarf varieties, which get two to three feet tall; 'Bengal Tiger' has bright yellow stripes with maroon margins and orange flowers; 'Tropical Rose' grows well from seed; 'Red King Humbert' has bronze leaves and reddish orange flowers; 'Tropicana' has shocking stripes of red, pink, and orange. There are many others available in nurseries or by mail order.

SOIL: Rich and moist soil preferred. Loves water, but tolerates extreme neglect and drought once established. Some fertilizer beneficial, but too much causes tall foliage to flop.

PROPAGATION: Divide thick rhizomes in fall, winter, or spring. Can be moved in summer, if stems and massive foliage are cut off first. Transplants recover rapidly.

TIP: WHAT ABOUT THOSE WORMS? Canna leaf rollers are the larvae of night-flying moths, for which little can be done. Chemical controls often burn the plants by concentrating in the leaf whorls, and even natural materials such as biological worm sprays or diatomaceous earth kill the caterpillars, but still leave plants looking ratty. What I do is simply cut the plants down low, throw away the debris (and the worms), and let new growth quickly return.

Chives or Onion Chives

Allium schoenoprasum

Full sun or part shade

Chives are a must in any herb garden. Their thin, grasslike leaves have a mild but distinct onion flavor and bouquet, and are excellent when cut fresh and used as a garnish for soups, salads, cream cheeses, herb butters, and especially over egg dishes. The plants are outstanding year-round, in all weather, even as container plants, and can be used in groups with other perennials, in a rock garden, or as a border—the spring flowers are an exceptional bonus. Interplant chives with daffodils for winter companionship or as a complement to cascading oregano or thyme. Great foil to iris as well, and both prefer dry soils.

FLOWER: Round clusters of lavender-pink florets, up to two inches across, on stems up to a foot or more tall. Edible as garnishes, even in soups. Cutting flowers results in more foliage.

PLANT: Small clumps of grasslike foliage. Leaves are hollow like quills and may get over a foot long. May die back in severe winter weather, but never fails to return by mid-spring.

INTERESTING KINDS: 'Forescate' is a robust grower with rosy pink flowers; 'Shepherd's Crook' has interesting contorted leaves.

SOIL: Well drained, high in organic matter. Can live in an old container of potting soil for years.

PROPAGATION: Seedlings grow slowly; so it's best to get more plants by dividing clumps in fall or spring. Readily available at garden centers. Small plants can be kept indoors over winter on a sunny windowsill.

TIP: PLEASE DON'T EAT THE DAISIES! But go ahead and munch on the flowers of chives, nasturtiums, pansies, and daylily buds. Edible flowers can bring more than flavor to the table—they can add beauty and a little surprise to dishes, especially if you're having friends over for dinner. There are more things to eat than vegetables in the garden!

Crinum

Crinum bulbispermum

Sun

No Southern garden should be without this big, coarse bulb! It has outlived cemeteries—I even photographed one growing in broken glass between the sidewalk and curb beside a beer joint. Its tropical foliage and tall umbel of large flowers make it a favorite for cottage gardens and formal borders alike. It is a tough, long-lived plant—noted Texas horticulturist William Welch once remarked that as far as he knows, "No crinum has ever died."

FLOWER: Stalks up to four feet tall topped with nodding clusters of slender trumpets up to a foot long, either white, pink, wine-red, or white with reddish stripes. Blooms late spring through fall depending on variety.

PLANT: Floppy, knee-high eruptions of long, wide, strap-like leaves remain in large clumps for many years. Dies down in the winter. Tips of new growth sometimes get caught in the twisted dried remains of the previous year's foliage, but simple leaf tip trimming untangles it.

INTERESTING KINDS: Nearly red 'Ellen Bosanquet', pink ruffled 'Emma Jones', pink with white streaks 'Carnival'. Interesting relatives include *Crinum americanum* and *Hymenocallis* species, native to Southern wetlands, with white flowers of long petals webbed with papery connective tissue. Take shade and will grow readily in areas that are wet all winter and hard, cracked blue clay all summer. Milk-and-wine lily (*C. latifolium* var. *zeylanicum* or *C. zeylanicum*) has white flowers striped with red, hence the common name.

SOIL: Well-drained or heavy, but won't tolerate standing water. Bulbs seem to flower best when "rootbound" or at least settled in one spot for a couple of years.

PROPAGATION: Bulb division, which isn't easy, considering how large and deep they are. Always dig way away from the plant, and at least a foot deep, before angling inwards until you cut into a bulb. Then dig deeper to get the rest. The thick bulbs are easy to separate and should be planted as deep as they were found.

TIP: RESCUING HEIRLOOM BULBS is a new possibility, thanks to "test tube" laboratories. Of all the bulbs passed around between gardeners for centuries, even in this country, many varieties are thought to have been lost forever. But some are being "rescued" from old gardens, small towns, and even cemeteries by observant gardeners who share their finds with specialty bulb growers. The use of "tissue culture" (taking hundreds of microscopic bits from a bulb's basal plate and growing them in test tubes as identical clones) has made antique bulbs readily available and affordable in commerce. Now there is no excuse for letting a fantastic, hardy bulb disappear from gardens; remember, the more you share, the more everyone grows!

Daffodil

Narcissus species

Full sun, mostly in winter and early spring

It isn't "right" for a garden expert to have a favorite flower, so I won't admit to my passion for daffodils. But my earliest childhood memories are of row upon row of many different kinds, including the very fragrant paper-whites (with multiple flowers on each stem) and the skinny yellow jonquils with their heady bouquet. They herald spring for me and everyone else in the South.

Besides, it isn't just me—hands down, daffodils are the most popular true bulb in the South. Old home sites can be located deep in the woods by the naturalized daffodils left behind to spread on their own. Deer and chipmunks, even voles, leave them alone; many varieties (though not all) multiply rapidly year after year, and they come in a wide array of flower forms and fragrances. When I smell them, I'm transformed into a little boy in the garden of my ancestors.

FLOWER: Varies with the species. Stalks from six inches to over two feet tall produce single blooms or clusters of six-petaled flowers, usually with an elongated cup in the center. Double forms, large-cup, short-cup, split corona (cup looks like it has extra petals), in white, yellow, gold, pink, orange, and many combinations. The biggest flush of flowers is in March and April, but early, fragrant paper-whites may appear around Thanksgiving, with 'Twin Sisters' blooming into early May.

PLANT: Leaves are mostly strap-shaped, butter-knife-like in clumps, from a few inches to a foot or more long, depending on species. *Narcissus jonquilla* has distinct, reedy foliage similar to a porcupine quill. Leaves first appear in mid-fall, and begin to die down by early spring. **Very important:** Do not cut or braid old foliage, which reduces food transported to the bulbs and cuts down on next year's flowers; let leaves yellow and flop naturally. To help hide fading foliage, interplant daffodils with white or pink yarrow, silvery artemisia, or lantana, all of which are dormant in the winter but whose emerging foliage hides the flopping leaves of daffodils in the spring.

INTERESTING KINDS: Though there are many dozens, even hundreds, of great daffodils to try, these have proven themselves to be long-lived and prolific bloomers in the South: 'Mount Hood', 'Unsurpassable', 'Ice Follies', 'Carlton', 'Tête-à-Tête' (a great short variety for planting in front of others), 'Hawera', 'Thalia', 'Peeping Tom', 'February Gold', 'Jetfire', 'Baby Moon', 'Cheerfulness', 'Minnow', 'Geranium', 'Grand Primo', and 'Actaea'. 'Twin Sisters', with two yellow and white flowers per stem, is the latest bloomer in the South. Other good types are *Narcissus jonquilla* (the sweetest scented of all), *N.* × *odorus* (campernelle jonquil, a type dating back to Shakespeare), and *N. poeticus* (pheasant's eye daffodil).

SOIL: Any well-drained soil, even in the lawn or under trees with a sunny southern exposure in the winter. Will not tolerate standing water in winter or irrigation in summer (best to not plant daffodils with roses, hostas, or other flowers that may get a lot of summer water, or they'll rot).

PROPAGATION: Bulb division. Dig as soon as foliage is beginning to disappear in the spring by lifting entire clumps and pulling off bulbs that come apart easily. Best to replant immediately or store in a cool, dry place until early fall planting. Because daffodils make their next year's flower buds after they finish blooming, avoid digging when in flower or risk losing a couple of years of blooms. Mark the ones you want, cut their flowers for an arrangement, and come back to dig when the foliage has died down or at least six weeks after flowering.

Why Daffodils Don't Bloom:

- Too much shade in the spring.

- Poor drainage, and bulbs rot.

- Too much nitrogen fertilizer or no fertilizer at all.

- Crowded bulbs may need lifting and dividing.

- Leaves were cut off too early in the spring.

- Plants were moved when in flower.

- Varieties planted are not suited for the South.

For more information, varieties, and sources for this popular old Southern bulb, contact the American Daffodil Society, 4126 Winfield Road, Columbus, Ohio 43220-4606. Or on the Internet: www.daffodilusa.org. The site has lots of tips, but most important, it lists the e-mails and phone numbers of daffodil clubs in every part of the South.

TIP: WHAT'S IN A NAME? Daffodils are narcissus, and vice-versa. Common name, Latin name. Some folks call yellow ones by the common name (or even "buttercups") and fragrant white ones by the Latin, but no matter. Different species sometimes have distinct common names—paper-whites and jonquils, for example. But they're all daffodils. And narcissus. If anyone wants to argue about it, just smile and say "Yes 'm" and let it go.

THE EASIEST BULBS to force indoors are the inexpensive paper-white narcissus. They don't require as much cooling to flower. Simply put a few in a small pot, fill around them with gravel to keep them upright, and fill halfway up the bulbs with water. Keep in a cool place indoors until they start growing; then move them to a sunny window and keep them watered. **Note:** After being forced in water, these bulbs will not survive outdoors. Compost them.

Elephant's Ear
Alocasia macrorrhiza and Colocasia esculenta
Shade or sun

If any bulb typifies the tropics, it's elephant's ear. Big, bold, coarse foliage spreading along creek banks and low wet areas translates into a perfect complement for ferns and a backdrop for other moisture-loving plants, sun or shade. They grow well in large pots, adding lushness to pools and decks, even in full sun if they are kept watered. They're also perfect where large, quick screening is needed from spring to fall.

FLOWER: Unusual, calla-like spathe, rarely seen, hidden in the foliage canopy. Most gardeners ignore them, or cut them off to promote new foliage production.

PLANT: *Alocasias* are the "upright" elephant's ear, having huge, heart-shaped leaves with tips pointing upwards. Very slow to spread, but large bulbs are easily dug and divided in the fall. Several colorful cultivars are found in tropical nursery catalogs, including some with deep coppery leaves and white veins; most are ground-hardy only to about 10 degrees Fahrenheit, but can survive with mulch—or dig and keep them indoors over the winter. *Colocasia*, also called taro or dasheen, has giant, heart-shaped green leaves, tips pointing downward, on stalks up to four or more feet tall, forming a mass of tropical boldness. It has a tendency to "run" in wet or moist soils and can become a pest. Dies down in the winter, but returns from root-like tubers. Large leaves may need protection from strong winds, which can tear them.

INTERESTING KINDS: There are dark colored and white-variegated forms of both species. 'Hilo Beauty' is a smaller plant with cream mottling and 'Black Magic' is wine colored. *Alocasia* 'Variegata' has cream blotches and 'Violacea' is tinged purple. *Colocasia esculenta* 'Fontanesii' and 'Illustris' have dark markings. The related dragon plant or dragon arum (*Dracunculus vulgaris*) is a most unusual shade plant with huge leaves atop leopard-spotted stems. Each leaf looks like a giant green hand with fingers splayed outward like a fan. Sometimes called Voodoo lily, it is an awesome plant, to say the least, worth seeking out! Tolerates a good bit of sun if kept moist. Excellent container plant for a tropical collection.

SOIL: Performs well in areas that stay damp or wet, along creek banks or in low areas near houses. Also grows in raised beds and big containers, if the soil is enriched with moisture-holding peat. For extra performance, feed these fast-growing foliage plants lightly but regularly and keep moist during hot spells.

PROPAGATION: Division of bulbs or runners in fall, winter, or early spring.

TIP: PLANT ELEPHANT'S EAR, dragon plant, and other tropicals where they won't be missed as much in the winter, when they're either dormant or in storage in your basement. Most likely spots: between trees, in front of evergreens, or near an attractive feature that can carry the scene through the dormant months.

Garden Lilies
Lilium species
Light shade to full sun (if well mulched)

Garden lilies are among the proudest of garden plants. Generally tall spring and summer bloomers, they have three main requirements for long life: deep well-drained soil high in organic matter, moisture year-round (their roots never really stop growing), and lots of mulch or leaf litter to keep roots cool. In other words, edge-of-the-woods conditions or well-prepared garden soils. They are outstanding cut flowers and perfect for the backs of flower beds where their lower stems and any support stakes are hidden.

FLOWER: Mostly large trumpets produced from late spring into the summer atop straight, tall (three to six feet or more) stems. White, orange, red, yellow, pink, and often spotted.

PLANT: Dark green rosettes of leaves come up in mid-winter and begin throwing out flowering stems covered with narrow finger-like leaves in the spring. Some flowering stems turn yellow soon after blooming, but always wait before cutting back until all the leaves are totally yellow; never pull on faded stems or you risk pulling up the plant, bulb and all, or creating a situation conducive to bulb rot.

INTERESTING KINDS: Regal (*Lilium regale*, early summer, white and fragrant), Madonna (*L. candidum*, pure white, fragrant, may rebloom in the fall—Madonna needs shallow soil), Formosa (*L. formosanum*, late summer, white, very good for the lower South), tiger (*L. lancifolium* or *L. tigrinum*, pendulous orange flowers spotted with dark brown), turk's cap (*L. martagon*, pink, curved-back petals on downward-facing blossoms), Easter (*L. longiflorum*, white, early spring, very fragrant), 'Stargazer' (hybrid Oriental lily, raspberry red with creamy white edge).

SOIL: Must have deep soil (at least a foot), high in organic matter, that does not stay wet all winter or completely dry out in summer. Mulches and leaf litter help keep roots and bulbs cool and moist. Moderate fertility is good for steady growth.

PROPAGATION: Seeds sprout slowly but surely; better to dig and split apart bulbs, which have many smaller "bulb scales" encased in papery sheaths around a central stem (like garlic). Plant each bulb scale about three times as deep as it is tall, cover with mulch, and leave alone—don't go poking around to see what's coming up or you'll break the new stem.

TIP: PLANTING EASTER LILIES AFTER THE HOLIDAY IS A SNAP. Carefully loosen potting soil, stirring it into deeply dug garden soil, and plant where the foliage can get at least half a day of sunshine. Mulch well to keep roots cool and moist, and allow the plants to die down naturally. They will come back and bloom year after year, but usually won't flower until May or so (commercial growers "force" Easter lilies to bloom early by shining bright lights on them at night, fooling them with artificially long days).

Garlic Chives
Allium tuberosum
Sun

Though grown exactly like onion chives, garlic chives is an entirely different plant, with narrow leaves that are flat rather than quill-like. The moderately strong garlic aroma can be telling after a rain. Garlic chives are not really invasive, but they do spread readily and are best kept in borders or containers. Mine have gone entire summers in pots with no supplemental watering whatsoever!

FLOWER: Summer and fall flowers, larger than regular chives, are white and have a faint violet scent. Believe it or not, they make an excellent long-stemmed "filler" in summer and fall cut-flower arrangements.

PLANT: Clumps of blue-green, narrow, flat leaves can be a foot tall. Foliage is attractive even when the plant isn't flowering. Might die down in severe cold but will rebound when the weather warms in the spring.

INTERESTING KINDS: Ornamental onions are striking architectural gems for the sunny border. Most have onion-like leaves and spectacular flower heads ranging from the size of golf balls up to softballs or larger. Examples are *Allium aflatunense, A. atropurpureum, A. christophii* (star of Persia), *A. cernuum* (nodding onion, a North American native wildflower), *A. sphaerocephalum* (drumstick allium), and *A. roseum*. True garlic (*A. sativum*) is a winter-hardy bulb planted in the fall and harvested in the late spring or early summer. Its softball-sized white flowers are on stems up to four feet tall and can often be found around abandoned home sites.

SOIL: Not picky about soil. Can withstand dry spells without missing a beat.

PROPAGATION: Easy from seed (and will seed itself readily, though not annoyingly, throughout the garden); collect seed by clipping dry, papery seedheads into a paper bag and shaking. Clumps can also be dug and divided in spring or fall.

TIP: WHAT MAKES ONIONS SMELL? The distinctive scent of members of the genus *Allium* is due to sulfur compounds, and is released when plant parts are slightly bruised. For the most part ornamental onions do not spontaneously waft their aromas through the garden as do such intensely sweet-smelling plants as hyacinths. Not that onions smell bad to everyone, though chopping vegetable onions can bring us to tears. But the onion fragrance can also remind us of new-mown lawns in summer and favorite foods being prepared, and some alliums even have a faint violet-like scent. So dry your tears and embrace this sensory aspect of alliums in the garden.

Gladiolus

Gladiolus species and hybrids

Sun

Gladiolus, the ultimate summer cut flower, is as easy as any plant can be. Just stick a handful of corms into reasonably good dirt, and add a stake to keep the tall rocket from falling over under its heavy flower load. Most Southerners have to treat "glads" as annuals, but they are cheap, and you can plant a few every month for a continuous glorious show and cut-flower harvest.

FLOWER: Narrow, tall, three- to four-foot spike of showy flaring flowers that open a few at a time all on the same side of the stem, from the bottom up, as the flower stem grows. Usually requires staking to keep from falling over under its own weight. Outstanding cut flower in red, yellow, orange, apricot, white, purple, and many combinations.

PLANT: Each corm produces one upright fan of tall, sword-like leaves, from which the flower stem also grows. Most effective in groups, especially when planted behind another kind of plant to help hide the bareness down low.

INTERESTING KINDS: Hardy gladiolus (*Gladiolus communis* ssp. *byzantinus*) is a winter-hardy old-garden variety that usually has bright magenta flowers, sometimes white. Reliably hardy throughout all but the northernmost and mountainous areas of the South. Abyssinian sword lily (G. *callianthus* or *Acidanthera bicolor*) grows up to three feet or so tall and has large white flowers with a purplish brown blotch.

SOIL: Any well-drained soil. Tolerates moisture, but tough enough without. Corms should be planted two or three times as deep as they are big around.

PROPAGATION: Buy new corms every year, planting a few at a time beginning when the soil has warmed in early spring (late March) up until early August for a continuous show. Dig old corms, separate the new ones that form, and save them in a cool, dry place over winter to plant next year.

TIP: FLOPPY PLANTS SHOULD BE STAKED DISCREETLY. Gladiolus often flops under its own weight, as do dahlias, garden lilies, and other tall boys and girls of the summer. In the late winter and early spring, as their new foliage begins to emerge and the soil is still moist, push curly rods, teepees made of bamboo or other slender but sturdy sticks, or even specialty plant support stakes, deep beside each plant, up to about half as high as you expect the plants to get. As the plants grow, tie them loosely to the stakes with soft twine.

You may also use sections of low, prefabricated, picket-fence type border materials as part of your bulb garden, which will work well to prevent the worst flopping.

Grape Hyacinth
Muscari botryoides
Sun, especially in the winter

Old cemeteries are covered in a mid-winter haze of blue from this prolific little bulb; rock gardens burst into color with short stalks of juicy-looking flowers; lawns become "infested" with fragrant patches of the self-seeding native of the Mediterranean region. Great winter companions for the little bulb include the short violas or Johnny jump-ups, ferny-leafed anemones, and inexpensive Dutch iris. Or just plant it as a naturalistic "river of blue" across the lawn.

FLOWER: Many small, light- to dark-blue urn-shaped bells packed like grapes on short, six- to ten-inch stems formed in clusters, with a delightful faint scent of grapes. Many cultivars are available with various blues, all white, or combinations.

PLANT: Short clumps of thin, grasslike leaves from fall to spring. One of the earliest bulbs to send up foliage, it can get so thick it nearly chokes itself out.

INTERESTING KINDS: *Muscari latifolium* has much larger flowers than the old-timey grape hyacinth and is better suited for mixed-flower borders where it's less likely to get lost under the shade of other plants. *Muscari armeniacum* 'Blue Spike' has double flowers of pale blue; *M. comosum* has pinkish purple feathery flowers.

SOIL: Any well-drained soil, even in cemeteries, meadows, and under winter-deciduous trees.

PROPAGATION: Division of small bulbs, dug and replanted any time you can find them. Very inexpensive to buy lots and lots to naturalize in small groups, which multiply quickly if left alone after flowering so seed will form and self-sow into surrounding areas

TIP: PLANT SMALL GROUPS or rows of grape hyacinths in front of other bulbs, both as a "skirt" for tall specimens, and to use their early fall-appearing foliage to mark where other bulbs are planted (so you don't accidentally dig them when setting out pansies and other plants in the fall).

Hosta or Plantain Lily
Hosta species
Shade

Anyone who doesn't grow hostas, or has to buy one, must not have any gardening friends! Except for coastal areas, which are too warm and humid for hostas to live for long, these bold, easy-to-divide plants are the queens of the shade. They are grown in full sun up north, but they'll burn or look ratty in the hot Southern sun. Good companions for hostas include ferns, especially Southern shield and evergreen holly ferns, liriope for contrast and winter effect, mondo grass as a hosta ground cover, small daffodils such as 'Tête-à-Tête' where winter sun is possible, and painted arum for winter foliage. Also play hostas off a big rock or statue or other garden accessory.

FLOWER: A "plus" on some varieties. Long spikes with generally white or bluish, narrow trumpets up to three inches long, mostly on one side of the stem; blooms in the summer. Fairly good cut flowers. To prevent crown rot, don't pull—cut their old stalks from the plant.

PLANT: The reason for growing hostas is their leaves! Round, oval, heart-shaped, large, small, green, bluish, golden, variegated, with curly or smooth edges, there are so many kinds you really need to consult a catalog to choose your favorites. Some plants are miniature, growing less than five inches high, while others can easily get three or more feet tall and wide. All die completely to the ground at first frost, but come back readily in the late spring (don't get overeager and go poking around in March, or you'll pop off some buds).

INTERESTING KINDS: There are over two thousand registered varieties of hostas. A handful of common ones for the South include *Hosta sieboldiana* or 'Elegans' (green), 'August Moon' (chartreuse), 'Francis Williams' (green with gold edge), and 'Sum and Substance' (huge golden variety). Consult any garden catalog for more, or contact the American Hosta Society at www.hosta.org.

SOIL: Rich, woodsy, high organic matter content. Plant level with the soil around them, mulch to keep soil cool and moist, and water only when very dry. Moderate fertility will encourage steady leaf production.

PROPAGATION: Seedlings take years. Simply order new plants when you can, and divide what you have in the fall when the foliage begins to look like it's starting to "go down." Dividing in spring is all right, though the first summer the plants may go dormant a little early.

TIP: CONTROL SLUGS BY AVOIDING OVERWATERING and using slug baits, traps, and repellents. If voles eat your hostas, plant the hostas in metal or heavy plastic baskets buried with a little of their rim above ground.

Iris

Iris species

Sun or light shade

Iris, named after the rainbow goddess because of her range of colors, is one of the all-time great perennials of the world. I have seen the same, stubby-foliaged "sweet flags" iris (*Iris germanica florentina*, the one introduced to America as "orris root," an herbal fixative) growing both around hot metal storm sewer grates in blazing sun and nestled between the gnarly roots of an ancient oak. It is common in cemeteries, in both sun and shade, and was the original pattern for the French *fleur de lis*. Yet it is hardly available commercially. You have to get it from someone who got it from someone who got it . . . Luckily, it is easy to divide any day of the year, and about all you need to know to grow it is "green side up."

The range of different kinds of iris available for the gardener's palette (there are between two hundred and three hundred species alone, not counting thousands of cultivars) includes cut-flower bulbs, evergreen woodland ground covers, roaming masses of rhizomes, and erect swords for the water's edge. Because of several flower types and how, even when not in flower, the foliage texture is a fantastic complement to shrubs and other perennials, the choices are more than sufficient for several to suit every garden style.

The iris borer worm and rots are major problems. The borer is worst in the upper South, and fire ants take care of many. Rot is caused by planting too deep, overwatering, or covering rhizomes with mulch. The best way to deal with either case is by digging and cutting away infested parts, reworking the soil, and replanting. Avoid mulching or overwatering iris!

FLOWER: Variable in size, atop sturdy stems in the spring, in an astounding array of colors and combinations, including nearly black; some have a strong cinnamon scent, as well. The two main parts of the flower are the "standards" (three inner petals that generally stand upwards or are nearly horizontal) and the "falls" (three outer petal-like sepals that are held at various angles, mostly horizontal or drooping). "Bearded" iris have fuzzy caterpillar-like fur on the falls; "beardless" iris have smooth falls; and "crested" iris have comb-like crests on the falls. There are a few "remontant" (repeat bloomers) around, available mostly through specialty nurseries, but most iris flower in late March, April, or very early May.

PLANT: Narrow, pointed leaves ranging from only a few inches long on creeping rhizomes to thick stubby points to tall thin swords over four feet tall. Mostly evergreen in the South, perfect as a "skirt" for other flowers or to accent a water garden or focal point.

SOIL: Most iris require dry, well-drained soils, especially the thick-rhizome bearded kinds, which should be planted right on top of the soil with the tops of their rhizomes baking in the sun. Iris is also one of the few perennials that do not tolerate mulches, which can lead to rot, slugs, or other problems. Bulb types cannot tolerate standing water. However, Siberian, Louisiana, and yellow flag (*Iris pseudacorus*) can tolerate weeks of standing water and perform best along water features.

PROPAGATION: Dig and divide thick, root-like rhizomes in the fall or spring, or any time you can get them. If abundant foliage causes new plants to flop, cut it back and new growth will resume shortly.

TIP: TO GIVE IRIS DIRECTION, new rhizome growth of iris goes where the tips are pointing. When setting out iris for the first time, situate rhizomes so the new or leaf end is pointing in the direction you want the plant to grow. Planting three or more in a group, eight or ten inches apart and facing outward from the center, like spokes in a wheel, will produce a nice clump quickly that will continue to grow into a mass of foliage.

MOST COMMON IRIS TYPES:

BEARDED (sword-like leaves grow from stubby rhizomes planted nearly on top of the soil, various species and hybrids)

DUTCH (small, inexpensive bulbs to plant in the fall for spring cut flowers, hybrids)

SIBERIAN (*Iris sibirica*, narrow upright foliage and interesting seedpods)

LOUISIANA (tall, strong, marshland plants in many flower colors and with beautiful foliage, various species and hybrids, including the rust-colored copper iris, *Iris fulva*)

YELLOW FLAG (*Iris pseudacorus*, similar to Louisiana types, only with yellow flowers and very invasive)

DWARF CRESTED (*Iris cristata*, six-inch-tall ground cover iris for woodland settings, small flowers)

JAPANESE ROOF (*Iris tectorum*, foot-tall crested iris with glossy foliage and flattened-out flowers)

There are many others, some with many hundreds of cultivars. For more information, contact the Iris Society (www.irises.org).

Leucojum or Summer Snowflake

Leucojum aestivum

Winter and early spring sun

This true survivor is one of the oldest bulbs found naturalized around the South. Its white-with-green-tipped flower, often seen around old home sites, cemeteries, and other neglected garden areas, is so common hardly anyone even steals it anymore. Perfect for naturalizing in lawns and along shrub borders, it will flower even under ancient oaks, as long as it gets a few hours of sun in late winter. By the way, I can find no justification for its book name, "summer snowflake," since it blooms in the spring—but that's what it's called in every garden book.

FLOWER: Eighteen-inch stems topped with two or three or more small, nodding white bells, each petal tipped with a green dot. Holds up well as a cut flower, especially with other early spring flowers such as daffodils, forsythia, or flowering quince.

PLANT: Almost identical foliage to *Narcissus*—narrow, upright green straps. It is very important to not mow or braid bulb foliage before it turns yellow in the late spring or flower bud production is diminished.

INTERESTING KINDS: 'Gravetye' or 'Gravetye Giant' is a robust, taller form. *Leucojum vernum* (spring snowflake) blooms in winter or early spring. A bulb often confused with snowflake is snowdrop (*Galanthus nivalis*), which does best in the upper and mountainous areas of the South where winters are cooler and summers less humid; it has a couple or three strap-like leaves per bulb and usually only one flower per stalk and grows in clumps. The inner flower petals are green-tipped, but the larger outer petals are pure white. It can be grown in pots farther south, but is not for naturalizing in the garden. *Galanthus elwesii* has larger flowers, but it still doesn't like the Deep South.

SOIL: Prefers well-drained topsoil, but grows even in clay or sand that does not have standing water in the winter.

PROPAGATION: Dig and divide bulbs after foliage begins to fall over or turn yellow in mid-spring; replant immediately or keep indoors in a cool dry place until fall planting.

TIP: POTTED BULBS NEED THE SAME BASIC GROWING CONDITIONS as outdoor bulbs, but are portable. For those that need cold winter temperatures (tulips, snowdrops, most daffodils, hyacinths), refrigerate the bulbs a few weeks before planting or plant them in pots, water them, and then refrigerate them—pots and all—until foliage begins to appear. Move to a cool place where they can get a little sunshine, and when their buds open, bring them in to enjoy the flowers and fragrance. After flowering, give them a light dash of fertilizer, keep them moist and in full sun until their foliage browns. Save them, dry, to repeat the process next fall, or discard them as fun but short-lived whimsies.

Liatris, Blazing Star, or Gayfeather

Liatris species

Sun or light shade

Why do flower arrangers pay over two dollars per stem for a flower imported from South American farms when it grows as a hardy wildflower in nearly every abandoned field in the South? One of the most stunning native flowers of North American woodlands and prairies, liatris is an outstanding cut flower and butterfly plant, and a tall "spiky" element in the flower border. It withstands drought, heat, cold, and poor clay soils. Instead of buying it from florists, we should grow it in the front yard! Combine liatris with coneflowers, ornamental grasses, goldenrod, and other naturalistic flowers in a meadow garden.

FLOWER: Narrow stems from three to five feet tall, studded with small curly plumes of lavender or sometimes white, in the summer and early fall. Flowers open from the top of the stem downward, so cutting faded ends can keep it fresh in an arrangement. Highly attractive to butterflies.

PLANT: Hard tuber whose tufts of leaves elongate into multiple flower stems packed with narrow leaves.

INTERESTING KINDS: Spike blazing star (*Liatris spicata*) is taller than most, except for the 'Kobold' cultivar, which is only about three feet tall; *L. squarrosa* has rounded tufts of purple flowers arranged loosely on the stems instead of in solid bottlebrushes of flowers.

SOIL: Thrives nearly everywhere, including hard clay soils, mostly in open woodlands and fields. Prefers dry, poor soils, but is often found along ditch banks that are briefly flooded in winter. Fertilizer increases size, but at a floppy cost.

PROPAGATION: Seed collected in the fall, stored dry indoors until spring, sown heavily, and covered lightly with moist potting soil either directly outdoors or in flats to be transplanted a couple of months later. Or simply lay pieces of the stems, with seeds down, outside in the late fall and cover lightly with good soil; they'll sprout in the spring. Divide in late winter by digging older plants, carefully cutting away chunks with pointy buds from the hard tuber and planting immediately. Also widely available in nurseries and through mail order.

TIP: LIATRIS AND OTHER WILDFLOWERS don't have to look "wild"—to get away with naturalistic plantings in urban settings, fool the neighbors into thinking you know what you are doing. Start by massing lots of each plant in repeated groups. Combine with complementary plants such as ornamental grasses and other city-accepted favorites. For a "human scale" focal point, add a bench, a section of split rail or picket fence, and a birdhouse or two, and your garden will look as planned as anything!

Naked Ladies
Lycoris squamigera
Winter sun, even under deciduous trees

Garden club ladies call them "magic," "resurrection," or "surprise" lilies, but everyone else from Oklahoma and Texas to the Virginias and beyond knows them as "naked ladies" because these long-stemmed pink beauties shoot up out of the ground in midsummer with no foliage at all. My great-grandmother planted a row before her granddaughter (my mother) was born, and to this day we continue to dig and share them, in or out of bloom, with no end to the rapidly increasing bulbs in sight. Their tall winter foliage and summer flowers make them perfect companions to pink or white yarrow, Asiatic jasmine, or English ivy.

FLOWER: Multiple large pink trumpets atop sturdy two-foot or taller bare stems, beginning as early as June, and continuing through July into August. The leggy flowers make a dramatic show even in the middle of a shady summer lawn, where their sudden appearance is nothing short of miraculous.

PLANT: Loose but attractive clumps of medium green straps, one to two inches wide, mostly upright to three feet tall, appear in late fall and persist until spring, when they suddenly turn yellow, collapse, and disappear. Individual clumps make interesting bold accents to an otherwise bare border, or they can be planted for a short winter "hedge" out in the lawn, in sun or part shade.

INTERESTING KINDS: The variety *purpurea* has purplish flowers; *Lycoris sprengeri* is a similar species but shorter, and not as cold hardy.

SOIL: Any well-drained soil. Bulbs are large and can be planted deep—twice as deep as they are in diameter. If your soil is heavy clay, be sure to loosen it a few inches deeper than the bulbs will be planted to allow excess water to drain away from the bottoms of bulbs.

PROPAGATION: Dig and divide clumps of bulbs either right after flowering (don't wait too late or they'll be too far gone and you'll forget where they are) or in the spring as soon as foliage begins to flop and turn yellow. Because roots begin to grow in late summer, replant immediately if possible or store in a cool, dry spot indoors until early fall. Late-planted bulbs may not flower as well the next summer, but will catch up quickly.

TIP: FEED SPRING-BLOOMERS EARLY. Spring-flowering or not, bulbs whose foliage first appears in the fall should be fertilized in the fall, which is the beginning of their growing cycle, when roots and new shoots first start to appear. Feeding after they bloom in the spring means forcing new growth at the end of their season and often promotes lush leaf growth at the expense of flower bud formation. At worst, it can cause bulbs to rot. Feed by broadcasting fertilizer over the entire area so rain can carry it down to roots. Water after feeding to wash potentially leaf-burning fertilizer off foliage.

Spider Lily or Hurricane Lily
Lycoris radiata
Winter sun

One of the most familiar late-summer bulbs is the red spider lily, whose flower stems pop up almost magically overnight, without foliage. The bulbs send up leaves in the fall, which need sunlight in the winter to form the flower buds that will emerge in late August or September. Because these bulbs need sun only in the winter, they make excellent summer understory flowers beneath deciduous trees and shrubs, even in summer-shaded lawns and among ground covers. Often seen in shady, overgrown, abandoned gardens, they are also popular cemetery plants because their foliage appears after mowing has stopped for the fall and ripens before mowing begins in the spring. Spider lily serves as a "marker" bulb for me, helping me remember where my other, little bulbs are planted; and even when I accidentally dig into thickly multiplying spider lily bulbs, very few of them are lost. I use them also with fall chrysanthemums.

FLOWER: Airy clusters of red flowers with long, spidery stamens, atop naked stems up to eighteen inches tall.

PLANT: Narrow, strap-like leaves, about the size of liriope, with a paler green stripe down the center of each, appear in the late summer or early fall and persist until time to mow the lawn in the spring. It is very important not to mow it too early and not to spray with lawn herbicides. Foliage is usually tall enough to poke through English ivy and showy enough to form a winter border.

INTERESTING KINDS: *Lycoris radiata* 'Alba' has white flowers; *L. aurea* (or *L. africanus*) has yellow flowers. A similar bulb is oxblood lily (*Hippeastrum bifidum*), which looks more like a smallish, naked-stem red amaryllis to me. It's a sturdy little pest-proof fall bloomer even in the driest gardens—I see it often in small towns in East Texas.

SOIL: Any well-drained soil that also stays dry in the summer, even with competition from water-hungry tree roots.

PROPAGATION: Bulb division, best done immediately after flowering in the late summer, when you can tell which clumps are flowering the best or when the foliage begins to yellow and die down in the spring. Replant immediately or store dry until fall.

TIP: BULB FOODS ARE BEST FOR BULBS. Like all plants, bulbs need a balanced fertilizer containing nitrogen, phosphorous, and potash, in small amounts. Bone meal alone has only phosphorous, just one of the main ingredients needed for overall plant health and growth. Researchers at North Carolina State University worked with Dutch bulb growers to develop Holland Bulb Booster and other perfectly formulated brands of bulb food. They're expensive, but they go a long way.

Starflower or Ipheion

Ipheion uniflorum

Winter sun, including under winter-dormant deciduous trees

Starflower, one of mid-winter's low-growing fragrant delights, can be kept in a border or allowed to seed into the lawn for a meadow effect that can be mowed once and be gone for the summer. The small old-fashioned bulbs that my great-grandmother planted have persisted for many decades now, multiplying from their original (and still visible) border around a place where a tree once stood; they are now in the lawn where their pale green leaves blend into the grass, but their early spring flowers make a starry, fragrant carpet of pale blue. By summer they are completely dormant, but persist even in the dry soil filled with tree roots.

FLOWER: Dozens of quarter-sized pale blue stars streaked with lighter blue, held just above the foliage, from late January through early March. They impart a fairly assertive violet-like fragrance to the garden.

PLANT: Pale green, grass-like clumps up to about six inches high, early to come up in the fall, and early to go down in the spring. Unlike more "weedy" winter perennials, it blends in perfectly with the lawn and complements liriope and other low border plants.

INTERESTING KINDS: 'Wisley Blue' is a commonly available, bright blue selection. 'Album' has white flowers and 'Froyle Mill' has violet flowers.

SOIL: Must have well-drained soil, especially in the winter, and must remain dry—or super well drained—in the summer dormant period. Perfect under large trees where winter sun can deliver the energy needed by the flowers and multiplying bulbs.

PROPAGATION: Division of bulbs after flowering in the spring. Plant immediately or store dry until fall. If you dig them when they first come up in the fall, they will flop but still bloom and recover well for the next year.

TIP: NATURALIZING BULBS IS A POPULAR CONCEPT, but takes a certain amount of gumption. In a land where the perfectly manicured lawn is considered almost divine, anyone cultivating "weeds" may be considered an unsocial nut. The best way around this is to plant in a pattern, not randomly, as some experts suggest. Strew favorite short-foliage, small-flowering bulbs, such as grape hyacinth, anemone, hardy cyclamen, and starflower, in naturalistic "drifts" and lazy curves, planted thickly enough to look like they're done on purpose. Then dot the area with repeated groups of miniature daffodils or other short bulbs, with bulbs in each group spaced just far enough apart to give the group visibility from the street. Mow the lawn on the high side each spring to give bulbs time to form flower buds for the next season.

Other Great Garden Bulbs

There are many other kinds of bulbs to try—some are all-time favorites of mine, but may not be as reliable or readily available across the entire South. Here are a few worth looking for; you can find much more information on growing them in nearly any all-purpose garden book or mail-order catalog.

Amaryllis (*Hippeastrum* species) (pictured) are perhaps the easiest "big" bulbs to flower— even just sitting on the ground or in pots on a TV. Their strap-shaped leaves and clusters of huge bell-shaped flowers in red, white, pink, and stripes make them popular old-garden and houseplants. The old red kind is ground-hardy in the southern half of the South (USDA Zones 8 and south), but it and all the fancy hybrids are easy to grow in pots or to lift and store dry every fall. *Hippeastrum* × *johnsonii*, called hardy amaryllis, can be hardy to Zone 6.

Autumn Daffodil (*Sternbergia* species) is a short, golden yellow, pest-proof bulb that blooms in the fall (unless something causes it to skip a year, which happens often enough). It performs well in shade or part shade and in rock gardens. The foliage persists until spring.

Calla Lily (*Zantedeschia aethiopica*) is perfectly hardy outdoors, but requires a good bit of moisture to grow and flower well. Excellent as a cut flower, both the white and quite a few yellows and spotted kinds, and is wonderful in containers.

Camassia (*Camassia* species) is a native meadowland bulb that wows gardeners in Europe. It has sword-like leaves and flower spikes up to three feet tall, topped with a loose arrangement of small, starry, blue flowers. It grows and flowers well in boggy gardens or clay soils, even in shade.

Crocus (*Crocus* species and hybrids) has grassy foliage and cup-like flowers that come in myriad colors. Blooms early in the spring and is perfect for rock gardens, formal designs, grouping in the lawn, containers, and forcing indoors. Cheap.

Dahlias (*Dahlia* species and cultivars) have been popular for many years with experienced gardeners. Some are short "shrubs" with lots of flowers; others with incredible foot-wide flowers are tall and have to be staked. These Mexico natives require well-drained soil; plant them in raised beds or containers. Dahlias can freeze, so dig and store indoors or let them dry in their pots for winter storage. Best yet, just treat them as annuals.

Hyacinth (*Hyacinthus orientalis*) is an inexpensive big bang, with foot-tall spikes studded with intensely sweet fragrant flowers in blue, pink, white, or red. They fare poorly in wet winters and torrid summers, but may return for a few years before petering out. Worth planting a few every year for the fragrance alone! Very good for formal plantings and containers.

Montbretia (*Crocosmia* species) is a rampant spreading mass of floppy, sword-shaped leaves with arching stems of vivid orange-red flowers that seem to sizzle in the summer. It is hardy throughout the South. Popular *Crocosmia* cultivars include red 'Lucifer' and deep yellow 'Jupiter'.

Painted Arum (*Arum italicum*) is one of the best winter foliage plants around! This surprising heirloom, most often found in old established gardens where people have swapped plants, fills a huge gap left where summer perennials have gone dormant for the winter. Caladium-like flower spathes are hidden in the masses of upright arrowheads of green leaves in the summer and are followed, after the foliage goes dormant in late summer, by surprising stalks of orange berries. The leaves emerge again in late fall; the foliage of some varieties has variegated veins. A perfect winter companion to hostas, ferns, liriope, mondo grass, and daffodils.

Rain Lilies (*Zephyranthes* species) are summer-bloomers that grace the fronts of flower beds, add interest to mulched areas, and even spread neatly into the natural or meadow lawn. They generally flower after summer rains (hence their common name). The open or nearly closed funnel-like flowers in pure white, pink, or golden yellow, up to four inches wide, extend above the grass-like foliage. Interesting kinds include  atamasco lily (*Z. atamasco*, semi-evergreen, spiky leaves and pink-striped buds that open into pure white flowers), white rain lily (*Z. candida*, pictured, has evergreen leaves and glossy, pure white flowers tinged with pink on the inside), pink rain lily (*Z. grandiflora*, eight-inch stems with pink flowers that are flat in mid-day and close in the evening), and yellow rain lily (*Z. citrina*, with yellow flowers that are fragrant).

Society Garlic (*Tulbaghia violacea*), a strong-smelling relative of chives and garlic chives, is hardy in the lower South (USDA Zone 8 and south) and looks like skinny liriope with tall stems of blue or purplish flowers all summer.

Star of Bethlehem (*Ornithogalum umbellatum*) is in the same league as oxalis because of its tendency to escape into the lawn. But its cool greenness provides a good contrast to the busier spring flowers around it, and its flowers, which are in clusters of pale creamy white, striped green on the outside, are easy additions to daffodil flower arrangements.

Swamp Spider Lily (*Hymenocallis* species) is seen often along roadsides, down in ditches where they are up to their necks in water all winter and spring, but they tolerate cracked blue clay in the summer. Clumps of foliage are topped with numerous white flowers on three-foot stalks. Each white flower has long petals connected with a tissue-like membrane. Tolerates shade and heavy soils.

Tuberose (*Polianthes tuberosa*) is perhaps the most intensely fragrant bulb around—it competes with gardenia in the summer! Tuberose is ground-hardy in the middle and lower South; gardeners in northern areas usually dig the small but fast-multiplying rhizomes in the fall and store dry over winter. Must have well-drained soil. Perfect for potted plant culture, and easy to share.

"MINOR" BULBS ARE MAJOR BEAUTIES. While on plant safaris around the South, I have found many perfectly hardy, NO-maintenance, but underused bulbs that not only grow well with absolutely NO care, they actually seed themselves around the garden (sometimes becoming almost weedy, especially in the lawn). Best bets for these naturalizing bulbs include starflower, lady tulip, true jonquil, Byzantine gladiolus, oxalis, and both wood and grape hyacinth. They grow over the winter, flower in the spring, then disappear—even under the summer lawn.

Windflower (*Anemone blanda*) has daisy-like flowers and fern-like foliage that are perfect for planting at the base of larger winter bulbs or along edges of winter container gardens. Soak the weird little flattened bulbs overnight before planting shallowly and on their edges.

Wood Hyacinth or **Spanish Bluebell** (*Hyacinthoides hispanica*) (pictured) is one of the most enduring old-garden bulbs. Late winter flower spikes over a foot tall are loosely covered top to bottom with open bells of blue, white, or pink, atop tight, foot-tall clumps of dagger-like leaves. Very good in shady old gardens, appearing even through English ivy growing under gloomy old oak trees.

Wood Sorrel (*Oxalis* species) is a plant you either like or you don't, but it's still tough as nails. Whether a weedy lawn pest, a delicate border along the sidewalk, or a filler in low flower beds, the foot-high clumps of light green, or purple, clover-like foliage is topped with masses of small pink, white, or rose trumpets. If you don't like it, at least leave a few clumps for the Easter bunny to hide eggs in.

Keep Your Tropics

I couldn't quite put my finger on what was uncomfortable about my latest trips to South America and Africa. It wasn't the spider I watched eating a bird, or the bat that fluttered onto my bed. Or the killer bees, the alligators in the canal next to my guest home, or the piranhas in the creeks. It wasn't even the luke-warm beer.

And it certainly wasn't the banana and papaya trees—loaded with ripe fruit—in the backyard, mere feet from two coconut palms from which I drank fresh milk right from the fallen coconuts. Heck, who can complain about a pineapple growing in the front yard?

Picture this: bougainvilleas the size of a garage, two-story hibiscus, and miles of canals lined with elephant's ear, sugar cane, snake plant, wild "candle-stick" plants, and flowering lotus. Fragrant frangipanis, towering Norfolk Island pines, and rubber trees dripping with bromeliads and orchids, wrapped in climb-ing philodendrons. Poinsettias ten feet tall and wide, in full bloom.

I sincerely enjoyed hundreds of beautiful gardens planted with gusto, often lined with planters made of tires, practical in a flood-prone land where water from the Amazon Basin stands for months on end, and where clay pots are an expensive premium. The gardens made up for the rest.

But I was still bothered—a lot—by the lack of a season. There are no seasons on the Equator, no planting dates. Spring, summer, fall, and winter roll one after another, with nary a hint of change in the air. You want to plant okra in December? No problem. Want to eat tomatoes fifty-two weeks out of the year? Ho hum.

Forget the lack of window screens, and having to sleep under mosquito nets, slathered with Deet. And don't worry if that bat is a vampire, which is common in those parts. What I wanted was a cool breeze to let me know it's time to slow down. I needed to see daffodils, which won't flower without winter's chill. Give me brilliant red and yellow fall colors, which signal a dormant rest ahead.

Tropical climes can keep their bananas. Give me seasons, so I can mark time.

Grasses
WITH GUMPTION

Ornamental grasses bring the landscape to life! The earliest vivid memory I have of native plants is from a shortcut I took home from kindergarten, along a winding hillside path. At one spot, some wild grasses flowed over the path and were swaying in the breeze and making a rustling sound—which to a five-year-old sounded like the rattlesnakes my mom had long warned me to watch for. Though I could see my house from where I was standing, I was paralyzed with fear, unable to move forward or back, until I took a deep breath and, with a yell, plunged on through to the other side. The experience settled me into a life-long fascination with how grasses look, move, sound, feel, and even smell. Add the taste of corn and oats (both grasses), and all the senses are covered!

Shrub-like and ground cover grasses have been grown in botanical and cottage gardens for many decades. I have a mid-1890s garden catalog with zebra grass on the cover. The U.S. Department of Agriculture's "bamboo introduction station" for the Southeast United States, located near Savannah, Georgia, has nearly every imaginable variety of bamboo and other grasses, and there are members of the American Bamboo Society in every state who know and grow the very best kinds for landscapes. But other than the common use of pampas grass and bamboo, only fairly recently have grasses become more widely accepted as very tough "foils" to other landscape plants—and now they are being used even around fast-food restaurants!

In addition to the other senses, their visual effect is of color, richness, and texture. They come in a wide variety of shapes, colors, variegations, and long-stemmed "flowers" that are long lasting in both fresh and dried cut-flower arrangements. Some grasses grow in tight clumps; others "run" or spread. The plants can be used as specimens, in groups, as a ground cover, in naturalistic masses, and even in containers.

Uses of Grasses

Clump-forming grasses work well with perennials, especially coarse-textured ones like daylilies, canna, black-eyed Susan, hibiscus, and sedum, and as contrasts to "hard features" such as large rocks, benches, or sculpture. Smaller grasses grow well in rock gardens and containers, and larger grasses make good screens and borders.

Though some prefer shade, and a few tolerate moist soils (some even grow in water gardens), most grow best in sunny, dry locations. They put out new growth in the spring, flower in the summer and fall, and have no major pests. Most gardeners leave the foliage alone in the winter, but some cut the old growth back in the late winter to help new growth come out clean and fresh; be sure to do this before new growth begins to come up, or it may look ragged all summer.

Pests

Other than too much water or fertilizer—which cause rampant foliage growth that often "flops" in midsummer—ornamental grasses have few problems. The worst I have encountered are the wasps and large, thumb-sized leaf-footed stinkbugs that love to nest in the thick, cool clumps.

EVEN ORNAMENTAL GRASSES NEED MOWING, at least if you want to keep them neat. There's no **need** to do this, other than for cosmetic purposes—if you don't prune the old growth, new foliage will cover it up by late spring. Once a year, in mid- to late winter, give the old foliage a neat shearing so the new spring growth will come out nice and clean. **Don't burn them**—as tempting as it may be—or risk killing the center of the clump, not to mention losing your eyebrows! Approach grasses from an angle with sharp shears or a fast-running string trimmer, going around and around like eating an ice cream cone, gradually getting down to the main clump.

BAMBOO IS NOT THE THUG that many people think it is. Most gardeners who have problems with bamboo have the "running" kind, generally a species of *Phyllostachys* that includes "fishing pole" bamboo, giant timber bamboo, the beautiful black bamboo, and others. These very cold-hardy bamboos have almost woody underground stems that can shoot in any direction and, when cut, can send new plants up at every joint. They can take over entire landscapes—and gardens of neighbors, too! Other spreading bamboos include the dwarf ground cover *Arundinaria*. Running bamboos can be contained—at least for a while—with trenches, foot-deep edging, and a little luck. Otherwise, herbicides will have to be brought in. Bamboos reportedly do not cross water, so you could plant them next to a stream or build a deep moat around them.

On the other hand, some very beautiful kinds of bamboos stay in slow-to-spread clumps, most of which are not hardy in portions of the South. These are in the *Bambusa* genus, which includes some that get up to ten or more feet high but take many years to spread even a little. Most *Bambusa* species are root hardy in parts of the South, but get killed to the ground by temperatures below the mid-teens.

 Best for Beginners:

- *Pampas*
- *Miscanthus*
- *Striped Cane*
- *Clump-Forming Bamboos*
- *River Oats*

Kinda Tricky:

- *Running Bamboos*
- *Broom Sedge*
- *Japanese Blood Grass*

Best Ornamental Grasses:

The following super-hardy grasses have been commonly grown for many decades by Southern gardeners:

Dwarf bamboo (*Pleioblastus pygmaeus* or *Arundinaria pygmaea*) is a ground cover bamboo to three feet tall, very thick and aggressive, even in dense shade. Must be contained by walks or deep metal or plastic edging.

Fountain grass (*Pennisetum alopecuroides*) forms knee-high clumps of fine-textured foliage with long, narrow, cylindrical "fox tail" flower heads. Note that purple fountain grass, *P. setaceum* 'Rubrum' (pictured on page 74), is strictly an annual in regions colder than Zone 9.

Maiden grass (*Miscanthus sinensis*) is a versatile clump-forming grass with many cultivars, most of which get only four to six feet tall, with dozens of taller flowers opening as tassels and gradually expanding into soft feathery plumes in late summer and fall. Superior in most gardens to pampas grass. Best cultivars include 'Autumn Light' (reddish fall color), 'Cosmopolitan' (erect habit and broad leaves striped with white), 'Gracillimus' (slender weeping foliage with reddish flowers), 'Morning Light' (five-foot clump with white narrow stripes along leaf edges, overall silvery effect and bronzy flowers), 'Strictus' (porcupine grass, with narrow, erect leaves with creamy stripes that run across the leaves), 'Yaku Jima' (compact to four feet, slender green leaves and tan flowers), and 'Zebrinus' (old-garden favorite, broadly arching clumps to six feet, leaves banded cross-wise with yellow). All turn an attractive, completely uniform tan at first frost.

Pampas grass (*Cortaderia selloana*) forms large, roundish, billowy clumps to eight feet or more tall and nearly as wide, with many taller stems of dense, two- to three-foot flower plumes of white or pink in the late summer. Compact form 'Pumila' gets only four to five feet tall.

Ribbon grass (*Phalaris arundinacea*) is a fairly aggressive creeping ground cover to two or more feet high, good border plant or "skirt" for shrubbery. Turns brown at frost. 'Picta' has white-striped leaves.

River oats (*Chasmanthium latifolium*) is a native grass for full sun or moderate shade, with stiff, knee-high, wiry, bamboo-like stems. Topped with numerous arching flower stalks with two dozen or more dangling florets that have been compared to little fish or even "flattened armadillos," which hold up very well in dried arrangements. River oats can self-seed to the point of being invasive.

Striped cane (*Arundo donax* 'Variegata') has very tall stems of coarse foliage that starts out variegated but turns to all-green by late summer; flowering stems may get twelve or more feet tall. May be too aggressive for small gardens and is considered an invasive exotic species in some states; needs room to spread slowly by tough rhizomes.

Other Good Grasses:

Blue lyme grass (*Leymus racemosus* 'Glaucus' or *Elymus arenarius* 'Glaucus') is a showy ground cover of stiff leaves up to two feet tall, the bluest grass of all. Aggressive spreader in moist soils, but more manageable in dry soils or clay.

Broom sedge (*Andropogon virginicus*), a native roadside or abandoned field grass, has upright, feathery flower stalks to four feet tall in late summer persisting through winter. Effective in wildflower or naturalistic plantings, but can be a very aggressive self-seeder.

Feather grass (*Stipa* species) is a knee-high clump of fine-textured foliage, topped in summer and fall with a billowy cloud of yellowish flowers on stems up to six feet tall.

Feather reed grass (*Calamagrostis* × *acutiflora* 'Karl Foerster'), with its upright clump of stiff but slightly arching foliage, is topped in early summer with sturdy flowering stems to five or six feet tall, persisting through winter. Flowers poorly in the lower South.

Japanese blood grass (*Imperata cylindrica* 'Red Baron') features upright clumps to two feet tall with upper portions of foliage a rich, almost blood-red. Spreads slowly but surely, and rarely flowers.

Purple muhly grass (*Muhlenbergia* species), a knee-high clump of slender foliage, is not much to look at until late summer and fall when it's covered with airy, billowy masses of striking pinkish red flowers.

Rumpelstiltskin's Garden

Remember the old fable of the gnome who wove golden garments from common straw? As I wander around my little cottage garden, I realize that it is a "Rumpelstiltskin" tapestry of sorts.

Though it includes scattered collections of rare plant specimens I've coddled from many travels around the horticulture world, my landscape's backbone is of mainstay, nearly zero-maintenance Southern shrubs (nandina, boxwood, hollies, quince, camellia), cherished no-fuss roses rooted from old gardens, many dozens of different hardy bulbs and old-timey perennials (iris, daylilies, canna, sedum), clambering native vines, and reseeding annuals passed around between generous gardeners of all stripes over many years. All have been "selected out" over generations by real gardeners as being useful, hardy, and easy to propagate; they love the South, and create a strong sense of place.

Because my busy family (wife and long-time best friend Terryl, children Ira and Zoe), relaxes in our garden year-round, we've tried to have plants for every season, punctuated with assorted "yard art" to anchor the ever-changing scenery. We've screened parts of our garden from neighbors using baffles of lattice-like fencing, painted teal and pastels to help give a glow of color without being garish. We have strewn a few comfortable chairs on roomy decks, built a waterfall that soothes the city sounds, and now keep a large iron bowl on our deck, crackling with a wood fire on chilly evenings.

And just as we invite colorful birds and other wildlife to delight us with colorful motion and busy chatter, we welcome friends to improve our lives by sharing stories. The plants in this book come from this perspective, and I welcome you into my view of what all a Southern garden should be.

LOW-MAINTENANCE
Lawns

The low-growing, generally flat mat of green plants we call our lawn holds most gardeners in a powerful grip, yet you don't have to be a slave to the whims and fashions of your neighbors. Though its sometimes-obsessive appeal to American gardeners of all stripes and walks of life is astonishing to most people around the world, the lawn has become a deeply ingrained national cultural icon. Advantages and disadvantages to having a lawn aside, you can reduce the amount of time, labor, equipment, water, and pesticides your lawn needs.

A Quick History

Early in our country's settlement by Europeans, open swaths of turf were adopted by a relatively small group of landscape gardeners as a sign of Old World culture and prestige. They were based on elements taken from old European manor "garden park" landscape designs. Most were mowed every month or two with long-handled scythes, or they were grazed by sheep and cattle (kept in bounds by a low ditch called a "ha-ha"). In the 1800s the development of clumsy mechanical cutting machines (often pulled by people), then gas mowers, made the lawn appealing to more gardeners, to whom the wall-to-wall green represented a democratic ideal by which everyone could be proven an equal.

In the early 1900s, newly organized chapters of the Garden Club of America pushed the U.S. Department of Agriculture to develop more uniform lawn grasses, which helped standardize lawn care; soon equipment, seed, and fertilizer companies began promoting the benefits of their products in ways that today would border on brainwashing, with ads suggesting that if you didn't have a nice lawn, you weren't as good or smart or patriotic as your neighbors.

To this day, advice on lawn care—from the size of your mower and edger and leaf blower to the amount of fertilizer, weed killer, and even the color of the grass—is driven by the marketplace philosophy of "more is better." Anyone who argues with this is seen as wacky—even if right.

Benefits

Without question, having a neat lawn is beneficial in several ways. Beyond the physical exercise provided by caring for the lawn (assuming you don't ride your mower) and the obvious leisure activities made possible by a uniform lawn, a thick turf has environmental benefits:

1. A thick turf holds the soil against erosion.
2. Lawns keep dust and pollen down in the summer.
3. A thick turf reduces mud tracked indoors in the winter.
4. Grass shades soil from direct sunshine, which has a dramatic cooling effect.
5. Billions of individual grass plants generate an incredible amount of fresh oxygen while "scrubbing" pollutants from the air.

Plus a neat lawn provides an important design element to the landscape or garden. Its strong shape contrasts with other plants. It can serve as a walkway between flower borders, create a vista to lead the eye to a focal point, and become a crucial "unifying" effect overall.

Labor-Saving Ideas

The lawn's advantages come at a huge cost, requiring gardeners to invest heavily in special equipment, as well as a considerable amount of valuable time and sweaty effort. Some gardeners love their lawns as a hobby; others have them maintained by professionals as a means of proving their social intentions or standing. Most of us, however, simply "mow what grows"—and then only grudgingly.

There are two things you must understand: **There is no such thing as a low-maintenance lawn**—even the most slovenly lawn is the single most labor-intensive feature of any landscape; and **no two grasses are alike when it comes to maintenance needs**—each has distinct requirements for mowing, watering, feeding, and weed control. Find out what kind of grass you have or what kind you want based on your desires and its needs.

Here are a few tips on how a **reasonably neat** lawn can be maintained without becoming a taskmaster; they are ranked in order of importance to the lawn and your neighbors:

- Mow at the right height for your preferred kind of lawn:
  - High for St. Augustine (three inches or the highest setting is best).
  - Medium for centipede, zoysia, and "cool season" fescue and ryegrasses.
  - Low for hybrid bermudagrass.
- Create a distinct edge—dig a small ditch around the lawn or line the lawn with a material such as bricks, rocks, broken pottery, or store-bought edging material—and keep the edge crisp and neat with regular cutting. This creates a dramatic appearance for even a ragged turf.
- Water only when the lawn is about to die from drought.
- Fertilize lightly at least every three or four years, but no more than once a year. Really!
- Weed control is nearly impossible without the use of strong chemicals; if you follow the tips above, your lawn will compete much better with weeds and bad weather.
- Don't look at the lawn too closely, or you will find imperfections that are really not as glaring as you think.
- Look at the big picture, in which even a poor-quality lawn that is mowed regularly and edged occasionally still has a strong visual (and social) impact.

If you think some of these recommendations are kind of far-out, consider how little maintenance—especially irrigation, fertilizer, and weed killers—are used around cemeteries, school yards, country churches, and even your grandmother's old home site: None. Zero. Zilch. Nada. The only people saying you have to do all that "stuff" for a nice lawn are salesmen or suckers! Look around—it's true that you really can just "mow what grows."

But if you want to slightly improve your lawn's appearance and reduce the mowing frequency (weeds need mowing more often than turf), you need more detailed tips on lawn care. For this, contact your county or parish Agriculture Extension Service Office, or get a copy of the Cool Springs Press *Perfect Lawn* book for your state.

Grass in the Shade

If you have over fifty percent shade, you are **out of the lawn business**. Period. In a quarter-century of working closely with home gardeners and landscapers, I have worked with many hundreds of frustrated gardeners who have tried **everything** to re-establish grass where it has died out in the shade, even using solid sodding, careful watering, and fertilizing. I cannot show you a single success story except along the Gulf Coast where winters are mild. Not one.

The solution, even in front yards where grass has too long been the accepted norm, is either a natural layer of leaf mulch, store-bought mulch, or the planting of low-growing ground covers such as English ivy, mondo grass, liriope, periwinkle (*Vinca major*), ajuga, pachysandra (northern parts of the South only), or even moss. There are others, of course, but those are the most commonly used and lowest maintenance.

You can create a landscaped effect by keeping a neat edge between where grass is and is not. Edging materials and low-growing border plants—most especially liriope—can highlight combinations of taller shade plants such as ferns, hostas, and iris, making a nice scene. Top off the effect with stepping stones or a bench, urn, sculpture, birdbath, or other "hard" feature—which creates a focal point that takes people's attention away from your lack of grass.

Create a "Flowery Meade"

Wildflowers are a whole lot more natural in the Southeast than a lawn! And they can easily be used as a foil to the rest of the lawn, with a couple of easy tricks. Think of how golf courses are set up, with a tightly mowed "putting green," a lesser-quality but still-neat "fairway," and the wilder "rough," which is where wildflowers fit into the picture. If you can create this effect by just mowing one area more often than another, it can look purposeful, even if you never plant a wildflower. Just the mowing pattern can look interesting—while cutting your mowing chores dramatically!

Avoid the "wildflowers in a bag" approach, in which a dozen or more kinds of wildflower seed are mixed for a general effect; it rarely works well. Instead, choose several easy, dependable wildflowers, including purple cone-flower, phlox, Queen Anne's lace, coreopsis, liatris, and naturally spreading orange daylilies and daffodils, planted in groups, and then let native grasses and other "weeds" grow up around them for a prairie or meadow effect.

You can set a wildflower meadow off from the rest of the lawn area even more dramatically with a section of split-rail fence, some birdhouses, maybe a sign that says "butterfly crossing." All this together creates a sense of purpose that is as easy to look at as it is easy to manage. Mow on the high side once a year, after frost, to keep taller plants under control while letting reseeding winter annuals and low-growing spring wildflowers and bulbs get the sun they need to flower best.

In the long run, the route toward a low-maintenance lawn is easier than most folks realize, at least physically. But mentally it is hard to let go of that desire for perfection. Plus there are social pitfalls to either avoid or learn to live with. It's your landscape, your spare time. But only you should decide how it affects your reputation!

Sun-Loving Ground Covers

Where a slope is too steep to mow, or you just want to have less grass to mow, choose low-growing, spreading, evergreen plants such as ground cover junipers, liriope, creeping euonymus, orange daylilies, Japanese honeysuckle, and similar plants, massed and mulched to reduce weeds.

Note on Wildflowers

The idea of a wildflower meadow is a romantic one and can be practical in some garden settings where large lawns or borders can be left unmowed. You will need to seed or transplant some plants, whether native or non-native wildflowers, and control some weeds by hand pulling or mowing. Most spring wildflowers are best sown or planted in the fall, and it is much better to select individual plant species than a hodgepodge mixture of wildflower seeds.

Meadows must be mowed once or twice a year to control invasive tall weeds and shrubs. This is usually done right after the first frost of the fall to let spring wildflowers and bulbs come up well, and again in mid-summer to control weeds while not killing fall-blooming wildflowers already coming up. A practical way to "get away" with a wildflower meadow is the careful placement of benches, fence sections, or other "human scale" artifacts, and then mowing paths around and through the area for an edged look.

Mower Care

Get the most out of your power equipment by keeping blades sharp and oil and air filters clean and by changing the spark plug as needed. Every winter, drain the gas tank and run the engine dry to keep fuel from turning into a gummy mess—the leading cause of starting problems in the spring. And believe it or not, string trimmers are designed to be run "flat out"—the engines are more efficient at high speeds.

By the way, keeping mower blades sharp is the easiest trick to a neat, crisp lawn cut, rather than the dingy look created by a dull blade leaving ragged brown grass tips. Get a second blade, so you can keep one on the mower while the other is being sharpened.

Green Thumb Is Official

At last, the "green thumb" has been officially declared a type of intelligence!
As a horticulturist, I was taught that the so-called "green thumb" we've always heard about is merely an indication of certain positive human qualities such as the ability to be observant, pay attention to detail, plan ahead, follow through on projects, and be flexible while working with the vagaries of nature.

But, while studying educational psychology in college, I learned of Harvard professor Howard Gardner's "Theory of Multiple Intelligences" in which he noted and found regions of the brain which "light up" when certain abilities are activated. In addition to the most widely accepted, pattern-smart "logical-mathematical" and language-oriented linguistics aptitudes, he also found evidence of body-kinesthetic (athleticism and control in handling objects, such as surgeons possess), spatial (accurate mental visualizations), musical, interpersonal (awareness of others' feelings and motivations), and intrapersonal (awareness of one's own feelings and goals).

Sounds complicated, those seven kinds of intelligence I learned about. But I always felt that gardeners should be in there somewhere. Look around, and you'll see people who have an obvious nurturing tendency, and that some folks with no formal training in horticulture seem to be gifted with the ability to quickly recognize subtle distinctions in the natural world, and easily relate everyday things to their environment.

And sure enough, now Gardner has found physical evidence of an eighth intelligence, called "naturalist" intelligence, with even its own special brain region that supports it. Simply put, people with naturalist intelligence have the ability to identify and classify patterns in nature, and make predictions based on seemingly random events.

My great-grandmother Pearl, whose garden sported huge collections of daffodils and wildflowers, had a "Bird Sanctuary" sign in her side yard, which embarrassed us as kids because we thought people would think our family weird. But it was she who showed me the difference between black-eyed Susan and purple coneflower, and how caterpillars eat flowers but turn into butterflies without really harming the flowers in the long run. She explained how a bird's wing works, and showed me how to tell if pecans were moldy before bending down to pick them up by stepping on them to see if they were firm or soft.

Naturalists like Pearl are very comfortable outdoors; when on vacation, they watch people, or go to a botanical garden rather than a ball game or opera. They are constantly aware of their surroundings, looking around as they drive, watching weeds and hawks, and braking for butterflies. They observe, touch, and compare even "yucky" things, and often collect stuff — shells, rocks, and flowers (often in mixed cottage gardens, or extensive collections of roses or daylilies or African violets).

They also manipulate things to see what happens; ever-curious plant hybridizers fall into the category of naturalist, as do "giant tomato" or "perfect lawn" gardeners. So do wildflower enthusiasts, bonsai artists, bird watchers, and garden teachers, whose naturalist leanings are coupled with strong interpersonal and linguistic abilities.

Any of this apply to you? Mix in doses of other intelligences, and no wonder gardeners have such different approaches, and levels of success and satisfaction. We may not all be smart—but we sure are intelligent!

Perennials
THAT PREVAIL

Perennials are "hot" in the gardening world, making a trendy come-back in popularity because so many of them simply grow without any care to speak of. From my very first "starts" of heirloom iris and daylilies to my latest "find" of a new wildflower cultivar, I have come to depend on those plants that "come back" year after year to create a never-ending series of surprises—with little or no work on my part.

Unlike trees and woody shrubs, which are also perennial, herbaceous perennials are those that appear to die down part of the year, only to emerge again the following season from roots, stems, bulbs, or rhizomes. The simple term "perennial" is commonly used when referring to herbaceous perennials. And unlike annuals, which grow and flower rapidly from seed, most perennials require two or more years from seed to flower; most gardeners start with mature plants, either bought or divided from other plants. Perennials generally require less maintenance and water than annuals. Many gardeners include flowering bulbs and ornamental grasses in this category.

Once prominent in many landscapes, these enduring plants are being rediscovered for their dependable seasonal effects. Favorite perennials, including many herbs and native wildflowers, have long been shared by gardeners and sold through garden centers and mail-order nurseries. Many are treasured by gardeners as heirloom plants and have proven themselves to be hardy enough to withstand our weather and climate extremes, often with

no care at all. But a good many perennial plants simply do not survive for more than a year or two in our warm, humid climate, just as some of our favorites will not survive long in colder areas of the United States. Still others are exciting new discoveries or hybrids and may take several years to prove themselves in Southern gardens. Only the toughest of them all are featured in this chapter.

Designing Perennial Plantings

While beds and pots of annuals may be replanted with ease, perennial plantings may live for many years and require some planning, and maybe even relocation of existing plants. Perennial flower beds are usually highly visible and should work well into the total landscape design; otherwise, large areas of the landscape may be bare part of the year. Many perennials, like annuals, are effective en masse when they are in bloom, but because of limitations on their blooming period, they are often better used in smaller clumps, where their color and texture can accent other plants. Use small evergreen shrubs, flowering trees, or such hard features as a fence, stone, bench, birdbath, or garden art to enhance a flower garden and "carry" it through all the seasons. One of the easiest design "tricks" is to interplant groups of flowers that have contrasting shapes. For example, daylilies can have their large flowers set off well by the slender spikes of blue salvia and the round flower heads of yarrow. The large leaves of canna and sword-like form of iris plants have a dramatic effect when used in groups among other less-bold plants.

A natural way to begin planting perennials is to create islands of flowers in an open lawn, but because such beds are easily viewed from many sides, they often require high maintenance to keep them attractive. Border plantings along a wall, fence, or hedge can soften the transition between structures and the rest of the landscape or can create alleys of color. Where space is restricted, a simple rectangular bed in front of shrubs or wall can be easily dug and planted. When planting a perennial border against a hedge, fence, or wall, leave a little space between it and its backdrop. This allows for better air circulation, more light penetration, and ease of maintenance from the rear of the bed. Perennial borders often are six to eight feet wide, allowing adequate space for at least a combination of six or more species, front to back, yielding a continual bloom.

To prevent turfgrass from growing into the perennial bed and becoming unsightly, use some form of broad edging or a separating strip. Bricks laid flat, flagstone, bare ground, or a heavy layer of mulch such as wood chips or bark will help keep out grass. Or simply dig a small ditch a few inches deep and wide that can be trimmed when the lawn is mowed, or edged with a shovel when the ground has been softened by a recent rain.

Perennials may be grouped according to color, intermixing plants that bloom at different times for a continual display. Early bulbs may be interplanted with spring yarrow and iris, which usually fade before daylilies and canna begin their season of color. Fall sunflowers and ornamental grasses complete the season. Select plants that have not only attractive, long-lived blooms, but also attractive foliage.

Plant height is a major consideration. In border plantings, the tallest plants are usually placed towards the rear to serve as a backdrop, with a few moved forward to prevent monotony in the design. In island plantings, place tall plants towards the center. Fall-blooming perennials are usually the tallest, making them the best backdrop or accent plants. Most of the middle-height perennial plants are summer bloomers and may occupy the majority of the middle space. Spring-blooming perennials are primarily short plants to be placed toward the front. Emerging foliage and flowers of later blooming plants can also help hide the fading foliage of earlier flowers. Narrow beds with excessively tall plants are usually not effective displays. Whether in borders or island beds, keep the width of a planting about twice the height of the tallest plant.

Site Selection and Soil Preparation

Consider the site before selecting your plants. Although some perennials, such as ferns, tolerate heavy shade, many perennial plants require abundant sunshine. Air circulation is important for avoiding problems; stagnant, warm, and humid air creates ideal conditions for diseases. To perform well for many years, some perennial plants require a good start in properly prepared soil.

Soil preparation for perennials is similar to soil preparation for annuals. But you should devote special attention to perennial bed preparation, because plants may occupy the site for several years with little opportunity for you to correct any problems. When possible, add sand and organic matter such as bark, peat, or compost to soils well ahead of planting time.

A layer of organic matter one to two inches deep, worked into the soil a shovel's depth, is usually adequate. I never add more than three or four inches of soil amendments to a shovel's depth. Since different types of organic matter work and decompose at different rates in the soil, it is best to use a little of two or three kinds of organic matter than a lot of just one kind.

Soil testing provides specific recommendations for fertilizer and lime needs. Since lime lasts for several years depending on the type used, never add lime without a soil test. Perennials need a balance of several nutrients, including nitrogen, phosphorous, and potash; most garden supply stores carry a wide variety of fertilizer mixes. Many fertilizers, such as phosphorus, are best applied and mixed into soils before planting. Keep in mind that phosphorus, including that found in bone meal, lasts for several years and need not be applied regularly.

Propagation

Though most perennials may take a couple of years to flower from seed, many are as easily started as annuals. The quickest way to have blooming plants, however, is by vegetative propagation—by dividing old plants or rooting stem cuttings. Plants produced vegetatively have all of the traits of the "mother" plant. Propagation by division may seem difficult at first, but most gardeners find that dividing crowns and roots and separating bulbs takes very little training and can be mastered quickly. Try dividing monkey grass (*Liriope*) for experience; then move on to daylilies, then iris, and before long, you will have the hang of it.

Perennial plants with shallow roots, or with long, fibrous roots such as daylilies, are easily pulled apart by hand. Thickly intertwined roots may need more forceful separation or cutting with digging forks. Replant only those segments with strong roots and a few intact leaves or crowns. Perennials with taproots, such as baptisia and butterfly weed, can be moved as very young plants, but older, well-established specimens are problematic to move and should be left where they are if at all possible.

In general, it is best to divide perennials during their dormant or "off" season; divide spring bloomers in the fall and fall bloomers in spring. The worst time to divide plants is when they are in full bloom, though some perennials can be divided any time you feel like it. Some perennials may need dividing every few years, or they will slowly crowd themselves into clumps of nonflowering leaves and roots.

Many perennial plants may be propagated from stem cuttings, which does not disturb the plant's roots. Take stem cuttings during the spring or early summer, choosing stems that are mature and firm but not yet hardened and woody. Cut off four- to six-inch segments using a sharp knife or shears, and pinch off the succulent tip and any flower buds to force the cuttings to concentrate their energy on producing roots. Remove the lower leaves that will be below the surface of the rooting medium, but leave a few leaves on the upper part of the stem to provide a source of energy for root initiation and growth.

Because of disease or weather conditions, cuttings often will not root directly in garden soils. But they may be easily started in a pot containing a porous, well-drained rooting medium, such as a one-to-one mixture of perlite and peat moss. Coarse sand and vermiculite are also used as rooting soils. These mixtures will hold moisture and yet allow drainage for air circulation. Root-stimulating compounds, including those that contain fungicides, are available at most garden centers. Using a blunt stick, pencil, or finger, open a hole in the rooting medium and insert the treated cutting. Firm the medium around the cutting, and water it in well.

Many commercial growers use a mist bed to keep cuttings from wilting, but this is usually not feasible on a small scale. You can easily construct a miniature greenhouse by cutting the bottom off a large plastic cola bottle and setting it over rooting cuttings, or by draping clear plastic film over a frame covering the cuttings. Place rooting cuttings in bright light, but not direct sun-

Cut Flowers Also Look Good in the Garden

If it looks good in the vase, it'll look good in the garden – whether you cut them or not. Great no-fuss cut flowers for Southern gardens include the following.
Annuals: *Celosia, Cleome, Coreopsis, Globe Amaranth, Okra* (dried pods), *Black-Eyed Susan, Salvia, Sunflower, Zinnia*
Bulbs: *Gladiolus, Hosta, Iris, Liatris, Lilies, Spider Lily, Naked Ladies, Daffodils, Snowflake*
Perennials: *Daisy, Goldenrod, Hellebore, Obedient Plant, Purple Coneflower, Black-Eyed Susan, Salvia, Ornamental Grasses* (flower stalks)
Shrubs and Trees: *Boxwood, Camellia, Euonymus, Flowering Quince, Forsythia, Hydrangea, Magnolia, Redbud, Roses, Weigela*

shine or the cuttings will overheat. Keep the cap off the rooting bottle, or keep plastic tenting loose, to allow air circulation, and avoid direct contact between the leaves and the plastic. Water daily or as needed, and rooting can occur within three or four weeks. By the time new leaves begin to appear on cuttings, roots are usually formed. Remove the plastic tent, and water regularly until plants are firmly established.

Transplant newly rooted plants into prepared beds or pots, and place those in a bright, protected area until you are ready to set them into your garden or share them with other gardeners.

Planting Them in the Ground

Set perennial plants in their permanent places so that their roots are completely covered with prepared soil, but avoid burying the stem or crown. Place container-grown plants the same depth that they were growing in their pots; place dormant plants dug from the ground at the depth they were growing during the previous season. To encourage side root growth, make a planting hole twice as wide as deep. With bare-root perennials, spread the roots outward as well as downward. For container-grown plants, loosen encircled roots and shake some of the potting soil into the planting hole. Remember to crumble away the top edges of a peat pot to prevent water loss through wicking. Do not let roots dry out, especially during transplanting.

After planting, water the plants thoroughly to force out any air pockets and to settle the soil; then mulch the bed surface with pine straw or bark to keep the soil from drying, crusting, and overheating in the summer and to prevent many weed seeds from germinating.

Wildflowers That Mind Their Manners in Town

We want nature, but we want it tidy. The following native or naturalized plants are "acceptable" in mixed flower beds in town.

Reseeding Annuals:
Coreopsis, Cosmos, Queen Anne's Lace, Black-Eyed Susan, Zinnia

Perennials:
Amsonia, Asters, Daisy, Ferns, Goldenrod, Bee Balm, Phloxes, Obedient Plant, Purple Coneflower, Black-Eyed Susan, Spiderwort, Sunflower, Violets

Trees and Shrubs:
Beautyberry, Buckeye, Hollies, Southern and Sweet Bay Magnolia, Prickly Pear Cactus, Redbud, Sumac, Yucca

Attractive Edibles

Just because you can eat it, doesn't mean you have to; anyone who's ever had a pansy stick to the roof of his or her mouth, has learned the subtle delights of edible flowers. Still, from the sweet, raw-peanut taste of red-bud flowers, to battered and fried daylily buds, there's some mighty good eatin' in the garden. Best commonly-grown edible flowers to try (when no one is looking): basil, broccoli, chives, daylily, Johnny jump-ups, okra, pansy, redbud, rose, squash, and violets. There are many more, of course, including kudzu, but you get the flavor.

BEST VEGETABLES FOR BEGINNERS: (Newer varieties of some vegetables are even attractive enough to include in flower garden spaces.) okra, sweet potatoes, peppers, collards, turnips, radish, corn, tomatoes, cabbage, lettuce.
VEGETABLES WORTHY OF EXPERTS: tomatoes, beets, broccoli, onions, cauliflower, Brussels sprouts, English peas, Irish potatoes, pumpkins.
BEST HERBS FOR BEGINNERS: mint, oregano, basil, garlic, chives, thyme, parsley, dill, pennyroyal, purple coneflower, bee balm.
HERBS WORTHY OF EXPERTS: rosemary, tarragon, sage, fennel, lavender.

Lifetime Companions

All plants look and probably feel better when surrounded with friends, as long as the growing conditions are similar. The trick is to find those that are complementary in texture, color, and season. Example: Spring-flowering azaleas look like green meatballs most of the year, so grow them in the light shade of summer-flowering crape myrtles, skirted with the spikey foliage of iris or daylily or fern, with fall-flowering 'Clara Curtis' mum.

   Great perennials that live for decades, and are compatible with others, include yarrow, soapwort, iris, daylily, daffodils, amsonia, artemisia, liriope, phlox, violets, canna, crinum, hosta, liatris, and snowflake. For the shade, include aspidistra and ferns.

Care and Maintenance

If you do not mulch your plants, lightly work up the soil surface in the spring and early summer to break and aerate compacted soils. This also helps water penetration and makes it easier to incorporate fertilizer. Summer cultivation can damage shallow roots. Early in the season, stake tall plants with wire stands or bamboo canes, being careful not to damage roots.

Apply fertilizers sparingly to plants early in their growing season, after new growth begins to show. If plants are growing well, no additional fertilizer may be needed; otherwise, a second light feeding will be helpful several weeks into the season.

In the fall, cut the old plant stalks to the ground after the leaves have fallen, and mulch to protect crowns and roots from the harsh extremes of mild weather followed by sudden cold spells. Remove any winter annual weeds that may have germinated before applying mulch. Fall is also a good time to divide many plants that may be encroaching on one another.

Hardy Perennials for Southern Gardens

Perennial plants have been enjoyed for centuries, both for their flowers and foliage and for their ability to return in our gardens for many years with little trouble. Although dozens of perennials have long been shared between gardeners, retail garden centers also offer many hardy perennials. By planting only three or four new types of perennials each year, you can quickly build up a showy perennial garden and then divide the plants for your own use or share them with other gardeners.

The following perennials have been proven by "old hand" gardeners to be long-lived winter- and summer-hardy survivors, and they are generally available from garden centers, mail-order or Internet sources, local plant society and Master Gardener plant sales, and newfound gardening friends—whom you will no doubt meet as you begin growing these treasures.

Ajuga
Ajuga reptans
Dense shade to sun

A group of gardeners once joked about starting a "plant chain" in which you send a plant to five people on a list, who will then send you plants, and in turn put your name on their own lists to send out. But we all agreed that if ajuga were sent to anyone on the list, the appropriate punishment would be to get nothing in return but more ajuga! The common name carpet bugleweed hints at how this super-hardy shade plant grows: Ajuga is a ground-hugging mat of foliage and flowers that spreads so relentlessly, from very small starts, that it can take over even large swaths of shaded lawn. But it's okay—the beautiful leaves and spikes of royal blue flowers can turn an otherwise dull landscape into a sea of beauty, especially when it is combined with hardy shrubs, ferns, hostas, and other taller shade perennials.

FLOWER: Numerous spikes up to six inches tall thickly encrusted with half-inch blue "bugles," mostly in the spring and early summer. Good for bees and butterflies, and an occasional hungry hummingbird. The plant is so low growing that a mower or carefully wielded string trimmer can be used to remove spent flowers without harming the ground cover's foliage.

PLANT: Ajuga grows in rosettes of flat or crinkled leaves, each leaf up to three inches long and almost as wide (some cultivars have leaves up to six inches long). Foliage can be solid green, metallic tinted, or variegated and is evergreen in even the most severe winters (even into Nova Scotia!). New plants spread by vigorous runners. Root rot is a problem in heavy clay or poorly drained soils where water stands.

INTERESTING KINDS: 'Alba' has white flowers, 'Rosea' has pink; 'Variegata' is edged and splotched with cream; and 'Burgundy Glow' has green and pink leaves edged with white, with new growth tinged with purple. 'Atropurpurea' and 'Bronze Beauty' are burgundy leaved.

SOIL: Any well-drained soil, even in full sun. Moderate fertility will increase the size of leaves and vigor of runners, but too much can cause succulent growth that is susceptible to rot.

PROPAGATION: Division of plants any time of year.

TIP: GETTING GROUND COVERS STARTED involves very careful soil preparation, mulching, and watering; too little of any of these cultural practices will prevent the plants from spreading quickly, but too much can cause erosion or root problems. The idea is to break up the soil enough for roots to get established, cover the area with just enough mulch to prevent soil compaction from rains, and provide an occasional deep soaking to keep new plants strong and pushing out new runners without rotting.

Amsonia

Amsonia tabernaemontana

Full sun to part shade

The first time I wrote about hardy perennials in my newspaper column, I asked for suggestions from readers to help flesh out a list of great plants. The usual hosta and daylily suggestions came back, but one had a surprise: Amsonia or blue star was one reader's favorite, because it bloomed up a storm every spring, even along railroad tracks and rural ditch banks, and made a tidy addition to a regular flower bed. Yet I had to go to Europe to see our native beauty grown commonly in formal borders and cottage gardens. Now the railway refugee is showing up in major botanical gardens as a spring mainstay and one of the hardiest perennials in the country!

FLOWER: Tight rounded heads of small, blue, star-shaped flowers atop sturdy, erect, knee-high stems in the late spring. Great for cut flowers. Good butterfly perennial in an "in between" season.

PLANT: Many-stemmed dense clump of shoots up to three feet tall, with three- or four-inch willowy leaves the entire length. The roundish mound looks good when combined with daylilies, iris, and other interesting foliage plants and does well in naturalistic settings with woodland ferns. In the fall the almost grass- or shrub-like mound of foliage turns bright yellow, making a very good contrast for evergreen shrubs and emerging bulb foliage.

INTERESTING KINDS: The variety *montana* is more compact, and is the one most commonly seen in European gardens. *Amsonia hubrectii,* named after a Southern naturalist named Hubrect, has soft, extremely thin, needle-like leaves and is one of the most commonly sold varieties today.

SOIL: Any soil—the plant grows naturally along high, dry, hard-as-nails railroad beds and also in ditches of blue mud filled with water all winter and spring.

PROPAGATION: Division of clumps any time of the year, best in fall or winter. Seeds can be collected and sown in the fall in pots left exposed to winter weather; snipping the end off the cylindrical seeds and soaking in water speeds germination, but is not necessary.

TIP: WHY GO TO ENGLAND AND FRANCE to see our own native wildflowers grown in formal gardens? Early European plant explorers went nuts over the beauties of North American woods, prairies, and wetlands, and sent specimens to botanical gardens for evaluation. Those that were the most beautiful and easy to grow, including amsonia, goldenrod, phlox, liatris, black-eyed Susan, sunflowers, asters, spiderwort, and many ferns, became accepted as good garden plants "across the pond." But they are so common here in their native land that we often see them as "weeds" in need of eradication, just so we can plant exotics from Asia, Africa, and South America. Go figure.

Artemisia
Artemisia ludoviciana
Full sun to light shade

When my newlywed brother wanted to impress his mother-in-law (good luck!) with a plant from my horticultural jungle, I told him he could have all the 'Silver King' artemisia he could dig—hoping he'd get it all! The historic plant, which was originally introduced as a "wound wort" or emergency bandage plant, is one of my "top ten" companion plants for other perennials and shrubs—but mine had become so invasive I wanted to get rid of it and start it over in a big pot. It's so tough, I'm sure my brother's gift plant will outlive everyone—including his great-grandchildren.

FLOWER: Insignificant, usually not even noticed. Best ignored or cut off.

PLANT: Generally vigorous, bushy or spreading, medium-height ground cover, with woody stems covered with silver gray or white leaves that are pungent when broken. Many popular varieties of artemisia melt in the humidity of the South, but a handful of them are among the toughest companion plants around. While most plants get only two feet or so tall, some have floppy stems up to three feet long and can spread by underground runners. The soft foliage is simple and lance-like, or sometimes divided into interesting patterns. It's an excellent source of filler material for flower arrangements and an outstanding contrasting foliage companion to iris and other drought-hardy perennials; it can be used around the base of crape myrtles or cascading from a rock wall. Some varieties are invasive; others simply flop over large areas and can be pruned severely.

INTERESTING KINDS: Common 'Silver King' and 'Valerie Finnis' can be invasive. 'Powis Castle' is a fern-leaf hybrid that makes a dense, knee-high shrub whose long stems can flop up to six feet wide, but which is easily tidied up by pruning. 'Powis Castle' is a "designer" perennial that complements nearly every other kind of plant. *Artemisia dracunculus* is the French tarragon herb, but it does not like the heat and humidity of the lower South; many gardeners use the fall-flowering Mexican mint marigold (*Tagetes lucida*) as a tarragon substitute.

SOIL: Artemisias, like most gray-foliaged plants, will not tolerate wet feet; plant in extremely well-drained soils. In areas where rain and humidity are most abundant, plant artemisias in large containers or raised beds.

PROPAGATION: Divide mature clumps, or root stem pieces in sandy potting soil.

TIP: A WEED IS A PLANT OUT OF PLACE, according to some experts, including a rose growing in a corn patch. J.C. Raulston, the late great Southern plantsman, came up with a more garden-friendly definition of a weed: "any plant having to deal with an unhappy human."

Asparagus

Asparagus officinalis
Full sun

Nothing like fresh, home-grown asparagus in season—then having a beautiful "fern" to enjoy the rest of the summer and fall! As new shoots appear in the early spring, cut and enjoy all you can eat until they start getting thin; then leave the rest to send energy down to the crown for next year's crop.

FLOWER: Small, greenish white, not showy at all; red berries form on female plants and are persistent and attractive in the fall and winter before birds eat them.

PLANT: Clumps of many-branched, feathery, medium-green "ferns" from four to five or more feet tall. Fronds are not real ferns—asparagus is in the same family as liriope and lily—but they are not true leaves either; the "needles" on asparagus stalks are really tiny stems filling the role of leaves. Beginning in early April, they quickly shoot up fat, edible spears before branching out for the rest of the summer. Crowns are fleshy tuberous roots like daylilies and get larger every year—some clumps can eventually get five or six feet across. To avoid pests, cut and remove frost-killed asparagus fronds and mulch the bed two or three inches deep with leaf mulch, which enriches the soil as it composts.

INTERESTING KINDS: Old varieties include 'Martha Washington', but modern heat-tolerant hybrids sold as "all male" (which don't waste energy making seeds) include 'Jersey Giant' and others with "Jersey" in the name. Perhaps the best kind is whatever kind you can find locally, especially if found growing in someone's garden where you can vouch for the plant's vigor.

SOIL: Asparagus requires deep, loose soil that is well drained. In the rainy South, this means discarding the old advice about planting in a trench—better to plant shallow and, as the spears grow the first year, gradually add amended soil up to four or five inches over the crowns, creating a raised bed. Mulch heavily to keep crown and roots cool. Fertilize annually with a slow-acting natural nitrogen fertilizer such as cottonseed meal, blood meal, or used coffee grounds.

PROPAGATION: Plant healthy crowns or large transplants, or divide existing crowns in the fall or winter. Do not plant deeply in heavy soils—layer fresh soil above new plants.

TIP: LANDSCAPING WITH ASPARAGUS is a way to have your cake and eat it, too. Though the willowy plants tend to fall over themselves, they make wonderful backdrops for other perennials, especially coneflowers, cannas, and other coarse-textured or large-flowered plants. Instead of having bare ground around asparagus all winter, plant hardy daffodils around and between clumps of asparagus, where they can complement one another. Asparagus is quite graceful when planted along a fencerow.

Aspidistra or Cast-Iron Plant
Aspidistra elatior
Dense to light shade

Cast-iron plant—the name says it all. This common old-garden plant is a mainstay of shaded Southern gardens, from New Orleans to Memphis. As a kid I used to fear falling from my great-grandmother's front porch because of all the cut-off aspidistra stems below; those "punji sticks" could inflict quite a stab.

FLOWER: Insignificant lilac or greenish brown bell-shaped flowers borne on very short stems in the spring, rarely seen because they (and their berries) are hidden by tall, dense foliage.

PLANT: Pointed spearheads of deep, forest-green leaves to two or three feet tall and four inches or more wide, arise once a year in the late winter and early spring from clumps of roots and persist until the following year, only to die down after new growth appears. Severe freezes, especially in the upper South, can brown or kill the foliage, which can be cut off before new growth begins (some gardeners actually spray-paint winter-damaged foliage dark green—and it works!). Aspidistra, which has been used since Victorian days by Northerners as a low-light indoor potted plant, makes a perfect container plant for shaded porches and entries, and combines well in the garden with other woodland plants. It must have shade all year, including winter, or leaves can burn.

INTERESTING KINDS: 'Variegata' is about the only unusual variety found in gardens; it has irregular-width streaks of pale yellow, which can fade to solid green if aspidistra is grown in very rich soils. A similar plant that is hard to find except through specialty mail-order (Internet) nurseries is Nippon or sacred lily (*Rohdea japonica*), which has softer, more narrow leaves, comes in interesting leaf frills and variegations, and has spikes of showy red berries in the fall and winter; like aspidistra, it can grow even under magnolias and holly bushes.

SOIL: Any well-drained soil that stays somewhat dry in the summer will work. Mulches of oak or other hardwood leaves enrich the soil enough for aspidistra to need no extra fertilizer for decades, but potted specimens benefit from an all-purpose potted plant food every year or two.

PROPAGATION: Division of mature clumps, best done in fall or winter so cutting off the foliage won't affect the next year's new growth (if you cut aspidistra in the spring or summer, you won't get any more leaves for the rest of the growing season).

TIP: FANTASTIC WINTER TEXTURE IN THE SHADE can be had with a combination of aspidistra, evergreen holly fern, variegated liriope, ajuga, and lenten rose—all tough plants that do best in dense shade. Where a special spot needs highlighting, add a formal bench or large urn to complement the hardy perennials.

Aster

Aster species

Full sun to very light shade

Forget the "New England" name stuck on asters by English discoverers—asters thrive in the South. These autumn flowers pick up gardeners' spirits in the first few cool days of fall like nothing else, especially when combined with other fall-flowering perennials. And they can grow from woodland edge to the concrete chunks packed along an urban drainage creek!

FLOWER: Many flat, open flower heads of numerous ray petals sticking out from a central disk, up to two inches across, in loose clusters from late summer to late fall. Colors range from white to purple, with lots of pinks, reds, lavenders, and blues. Flowering stems tend to be tall and floppy, but can be pinched or lightly cut back in the late spring and early summer for a bushier, more floriferous show in the fall. The last cutting should be done by early July to allow stems to set buds before frost.

PLANT: Many-stemmed clumps or tall, floppy plants, most with narrow leaves and an airy look that is best combined with other perennials, tied to a wall, or staked. Unbelievably cold hardy, some plants suffer in extremely hot and humid seasons. Moderate fertility and occasional pruning in late spring will help keep the plants more compact, or they can be allowed to flop wherever they want between and over other plants, then cut to the ground after frost.

INTERESTING KINDS: New England aster (*Aster novae-angliae*) and its close relative New York aster (*A. novae-belgii*), both perfectly hardy in the South, include many cultivars: 'Harrington's Pink', 'Alma Potschke' (dark rose pink), 'Hella Lacy' (lavender with yellow center), and 'Purple Dome' are easy to find commercially. Tatarian aster (*A. tataricus*) is a tall, upright fall-bloomer with airy, football-sized clusters of purple flowers and large leaves. One of the toughest of all is the aromatic aster (*A. oblongifolius*), which spreads by underground runners into a three-foot mass of solid purple and yellow every fall—mine has grown for many years in pure clay and absolutely no water at all.

SOIL: Any moderately fertile, well-drained soil, preferably with a fair amount of organic matter worked in. Watering is rarely necessary, but one or two soakings in the summer during bud formation will improve fall flowers.

PROPAGATION: Divide clumps in the fall, winter, or spring, or root cuttings taken in late spring and summer.

TIP: FLOPPY PLANTS GROW WELL TOGETHER in an otherwise orderly garden. Plant tall fall-flowering asters with ornamental grasses, native goldenrod (not allergenic as some people fear), and airy nandina or other evergreen shrub, for an effect that can almost make Texans feel bad about their spring wildflowers.

Bee Balm
Monarda species
Light shade to sun

Bee balm and bergamot are among the first plants new gardeners start giving away, because they just keep on growing—everywhere! Lucky they are so pretty and loaded with hummingbirds, or we'd call them weeds.

FLOWER: Plants are topped for up to two months or more in late spring and summer by clusters of flower bracts that are just a bit too large to put a hand around; individual flowers are long, salvia-like tubes that are irresistible to hummingbirds, bees, and butterflies, and are perfectly edible for humans (spicy-mint, good raw off the plant or in salads and sandwiches). Colors are white to deep burgundy, with pink, lavender, mauve, and scarlet varieties.

PLANT: Multiple-stemmed colonies up to three feet tall, made up of mint-like plants with aromatic leaves two or three inches long and nearly as wide (leaves can also be used to make stimulant teas). Aggressive spreaders, bee balm can become rampant in just two or three years, but is easy to pull from around crowded plants. This woodland and meadow native prefers light shade but will grow in sun if kept moist. Use in wildflower meadows or along creek banks or woodland edges.

INTERESTING KINDS: Bee balm (*Monarda didyma*) is a vigorous native red species, sometimes called Oswego tea because it was used to make a similar beverage by the Oswego Indians of New York State; cultivars include 'Cambridge Scarlet', 'Croftway Pink', and 'Schneewittchen' ('Snow White' or 'Snow Maiden'). Bergamot (M. *fistulosa*) is an invasive native with beautiful pink flowers surrounded with white bracts; spotted horse mint (M. *punctata*) is smaller than the other species but its midsummer flowers are in clusters up the stem, yellow or pink spotted with purple. Very dependable in the butterfly or wildflower garden.

SOIL: Any moist soil, preferably amended at planting time with compost or "woods dirt" to enrich. Light feedings and occasional soakings will keep plants spreading and growing.

PROPAGATION: Root division, transplants, seeds (take a year or two to mature).

TIP: POWDERY MILDEW IS MORE VISUAL THAN ANYTHING, and there isn't much we can do about it. Susceptible plants, including monarda, zinnia, summer phlox, crape myrtle, roses, euonymus, and a few others, are not as bothered by it as we think—they can survive it, even if it distorts leaves and wrecks a few flowers. Even mildew-resistant varieties can get it, and fungicide sprays are temporary fixes at best. Learn to prune a little and live with a little, or plant gray-leaf artemisia or dusty miller nearby to act as a visual complement. When my zinnias get mildew, I put an old concrete chicken nearby—and nobody notices the mildew any more!

Daisies and Mums

Leucanthemum and *Dendranthema* species

Full sun

Forget the arguments over the proper Latin names—daisies and mums begin and end the summer gardening season with large, cheerful flowers perfect for butterflies and flower arrangements. The nearly indestructible plants are grown around country cottages with no care other than an occasional pinch to make them bushier.

FLOWER: Spring-blooming daisies are flat, many-petaled white flowers up to four inches across with yellow center disks; mums are white, yellow, pink, orange, and red and usually flower in the fall.

PLANT: Many-stemmed shrubby plants to two feet tall with narrow, sometimes toothed, medium- to deep-green leaves up to five inches long, which die completely down at first frost. Crown rot associated with heavy rains and high humidity is the main problem facing these plants in the Southeast. Pinch young flower stem tips to encourage more flower branching.

INTERESTING KINDS: Shasta daisy (*Leucanthemum* × *superbum* or *Chrysanthemum superbum*) is the most famous spring daisy, with large white flowers on stems up to three feet tall, and includes cultivars such as 'Becky' and 'Alaska', and the double-flowering 'Marconi' and 'Esther Read'. The much sturdier ox-eye daisy (*L. vulgare* or *C. leucanthemum*) is not as showy but has stiffer stems, with the 'May Queen' variety being the longest-flowering daisy of all. My all-time favorite late fall-flowering mum is 'Clara Curtis', sometimes called 'Ryan's Pink' or "country girls;" its huge light pink flowers spill over flower beds across the South until just before frost. A related plant, feverfew (*Tanacetum parthenium*), has many small white and yellow flowers and an intense "dirty socks" fragrance; it can become quite aggressive, but it is easy to grow from seed. Painted daisy (*Tanacetum coccineum*, also called pyrethrum) does not tolerate the humidity of the Deep South. Florist mums (*Dendranthema* × *grandiflorum* or *D.* × *morifolium*) require a gardener's guiding hand to grow to perfection and are best left to cut-flower experts.

SOIL: Any very well-drained soil of medium fertility. Overwatering and too much fertilizer can cause mums to rot.

PROPAGATION: Divide plants in the fall, winter, or early spring, or set out potted plants any time (being very careful to loosen the potting soil and roots, or otherwise risk watering problems). Seeds are easy to sow, but plants often take a year or more to mature. Stem cuttings taken all summer can be rooted in sandy potting soil and will have visible roots within a week.

TIP: CUSHION MUMS STINK as garden plants; use those showy clumps of garish color as expensive fall annuals and be pleasantly surprised if they survive winter rains and summer humidity. Pinch them back by July 4 to help their leggy stems branch out and flower again before fall.

Daylily
Hemerocallis species and hybrids
Full sun to light shade

"Wherever the sun shines, there is a daylily," says Southern perennial guru Allan Armitage. These most eagerly grown perennials, second in popularity only to daffodils, are the mainstays of the summer flower garden. They are so easy to grow and even hybridize that there are over twenty thousand named hybrids—and hundreds of new ones introduced every year.

Daylilies, which get their scientific name from a combination of Latin words for "beauty" and "day," come in a rainbow of colors (everything but true white and true blue). They survive an astounding range of climate conditions and soil types, are extremely drought-resistant, and have no major insect pests, though recently rust has become a problem in some areas. They flower from late spring until fall and are suitable in every single kind of landscape. No wonder they are touted as America's favorite perennial!

FLOWER: Large, six-petaled flowers (the petals are actually a combination of petals and sepals called "tepals") from two to over six inches across, with the six petals arranged in patterns ranging from circular to triangular, flat or trumpet, thin "spider" to double. Flowers are borne on sturdy scapes (stems) from six inches to six feet tall, mostly in the two- to three-foot range; some varieties have branching scapes with ten to a hundred flower buds. Colors range from pale yellow to blackish red, with everything in between except for pure white and pure blue, and flowers can be single colors or have contrasting "eyes" and throats, bicolor, banded, tipped, or edged ("picoteed"). Most daylilies flower in the morning and fade by late afternoon, but some remain open for up to sixteen hours, and some even flower in the evening.

PLANT: Many flattened fans of long, slender, grass-like foliage grow from a central crown into sometimes large clumps, some of which die down in the winter while others are evergreen or nearly so. Leaves can be six inches to over three feet long, usually arching somewhat.

INTERESTING KINDS: There are way too many kinds of daylilies to mention here. Some of the most common ones include the old orange species (*Hemerocallis fulva*); 'Hyperion', a tall, clear-yellow variety from great-grandmother's day; 'Mary Todd', a free-flowering yellow variety; and 'Stella d'Oro', a foot-high miniature that makes a fine border plant to flower all summer.

SOIL: Daylilies are tough, but will flower more freely if planted in a soil that has been amended with organic matter to a shovel's depth and then slightly raised to keep the crowns from staying wet in rainy seasons. A light feeding as growth begins in the spring will kick off a good flowering cycle. Note that too much water and fertilizer—which is sometimes recommended by expert growers—often sets plants up for diseases. Better to keep plants "lean and mean."

PROPAGATION: Very easy to divide nearly any time of year (even when in full bloom, as done by many collectors who want to know exactly what they are getting). Lift entire clumps, then work apart individual or small groups of fans (prying with a digging fork makes this easier). Growing from seed is a bit of a challenge—sow small, black seeds in potting soil as soon as fat seedpods turn brown and split open, and keep moist; the small, grass-like baby plants can be kept indoors in a sunny window or in a protected area outside and planted in the spring. Most will take another year to reach blooming maturity.

TIP: THE SINGLE MOST COMMONLY GROWN DAYLILY, the old orange one seen growing along ditches, beside country homes, and in cemeteries—and even found in famous botanical gardens—is despised by "society" daylily growers because of its very commonness. In fact, I've never seen anyone get his shorts in a knot quicker than a daylily breeder when someone mentions that old "outhouse" lily! Yet that old "tawny" lily, and the variety kwanso, its double-flowering version, continue to be excellent, readily available, easy-to-propagate, "unkillable" summer perennials for starting new gardeners off on the right foot. They do not cause other daylilies to "revert" to the orange species form, but because they are strong spreaders, do not plant them with newer, less vigorous daylilies or the weenie ones will be overwhelmed.

ANOTHER TIP: DAYLILIES ARE PERFECTLY EDIBLE! Their buds have more vitamins than broccoli and can be eaten the same ways: raw, dipped, steamed, fried, or in soups. Lighter colored yellows and oranges have a less strong flavor. Try chopping daylily flowers into blueberry pancake mix—yum! To learn more about kinds of daylilies and how to choose the best ones for your garden, find tips on growing and even home-hybridizing them, plus how to find friendly, good growers near you, contact the American Hemerocallis Society, www.daylilies.org, or do a word search for the American Hemerocallis Society, whose officers and members are scattered throughout all corners of the country.

NOT TO GET TOO TECHNICAL, but most daylilies have two sets of chromosomes and are called "diploid." Breeders have found ways to double that genetic material into "super" daylilies called "tetraploids" that generally have stronger flower scapes, larger flowers, more intense colors, greater vigor, and sturdier "substance" (thicker foliage and flower petals). Disadvantages include how some of them "melt" in our hot climate. Growing a few different kinds of daylilies will quickly convince you that there are great daylilies in both groups—regular and super!

Ferns
All sorts of weird Latin names
Shade to part sun

Ferns add the most dramatic texture to shaded gardens, creating lush ground covers, complementing woodland shrubs and trees, marking paths, or accenting benches. There are too many to make a thorough list, but a good dozen or so are tough enough to survive on their own in woodsy, partly shaded gardens for many years.

FLOWER: None, since ferns reproduce by spores rather than seeds. Some types have distinctly different male and female (or "fertile") fronds. The fertile fronds of sensitive fern, for example, become upright stalks that look like they're covered with beads when the spores are ripe. Female fronds of other species typically have very conspicuous spore-producing growths on the undersides of leaflets, which often look like insect infestations.

PLANT: Individual leaves arise from shallow, often-hairy root-like rhizomes or a compact crown. While some ferns are very small, most stalks can be up to two feet long with many tooth-like leaflets or finely subdivided, airy fronds to four feet tall and two feet wide. Some ferns die to the ground in the fall, while others are evergreen. All perform best in light shade with occasional soakings, but many are adapted to our worst weather.

INTERESTING KINDS: Of the many ferns for Southern gardens, here are a few of the most interesting and hardy:
Southern Shield Fern (*Dryopteris ludoviciana*)—the most common landscape fern, light-green foliage to three feet tall and a foot or more wide. Deciduous.
Japanese Painted Fern (*Athyrium nipponicum* 'Pictum')—an evergreen clump to eighteen inches, with lower portions of each frond having purplish leaflets, gradually lightening towards the tips in shades of lavender to silvery green. Very attractive.
Maidenhair Fern (*Adiantum pedatum*)—a delicate-looking small fern to eighteen inches, fan-shaped fronds of leaflets are light green on dark stems. Must have shade. Deciduous.
Royal Fern (*Osmunda regalis*)—an airy, deciduous fern four feet tall, eighteen inches wide. Yellow fall color.
Christmas Fern (*Polystichum acrostichoides*)—evergreen fronds two feet tall by five inches wide. New fronds stand upright then gradually arch over to form loose clumps.
Holly Fern (*Cyrtomium falcatum*)—the best evergreen for deep shade, forms a large bird's nest clump two to three feet tall with fronds of many dark-green leaf segments, three inches long and nearly as wide—like holly leaves. May die down in winter.

SOIL: Well-drained woodland soils and natural leaf mulch. Little or no fertilizer is needed for ferns grown in wooded conditions, but a light application of fish emulsion or cottonseed meal helps.

PROPAGATION: Divide or transplant ferns in the fall and winter; keep moist until established.

TIP: FERN FRONDS CAN KILL ROOTS during transplanting; to keep delicate roots from being sucked dry, cut off all fern leaves, then transplant only the roots and rhizomes, getting plenty of the native soil with them. Plant immediately and water thoroughly. Tough, attractive new growth should come up quickly, so you won't be fernless for long.

Goldenrod

Solidago species

Full sun or very light shade

Why go to Europe to enjoy one of our most famous native wildflowers? No Southern garden would be complete without this extremely showy autumn bloomer, which is unfairly blamed for allergies (of which it is innocent). Several named varieties are nonspreading, and the rest are super easy to simply pull up if they get out of hand. A garden with goldenrod looks and feels like home.

FLOWER: Large, branched, generally pyramidal clusters of small, bright golden-yellow flowers, formed atop long, stiff stems up to five feet tall, produced in the late summer to frost; some varieties have narrow, arching, wand-like flowering stems. All can be kept short and full with one or two light pinches to the tips of new growth, which makes the plants bush out with more flowering stems (though pinching will change the shape of the plant a bit). The last pruning should be done by early August to give plants time to set flower buds before fall. An excellent, long-lasting cut flower and wild bird, butterfly, and bee plant.

PLANT: In the winter, goldenrod is a rosette of foliage, which in the spring shoots up one or more tall, usually non-branching stems with narrow leaves up to five inches long. Leaves on many species are rough like sandpaper. Some species are very invasive by way of underground shoots, which are easy to pull once a year to keep the plants under control. Others are low growing and clump forming, not invasive at all.

INTERESTING KINDS: Sweet goldenrod (*Solidago odora*) is tall, unbranched, and non-invasive, and has anise-scented leaves; rough-leaf goldenrod (*S. rugosa* 'Fireworks') has arching stems to four feet tall; *S. sphacelata* 'Golden Fleece' is a compact clump to only two feet tall; and the hybrid cultivar 'Cloth of Gold' begins flowering in July and stays under two feet tall.

SOIL: Any well-drained soil, especially poor roadside or meadow conditions. Can tolerate heavy soil as long as it doesn't stay wet for more than a few hours after a rain. Fertilizer and water tend to make plants leggy and floppy.

PROPAGATION: Very, very easy to pull plants up and transplant (cut them back when moving them while in active growth). Seeds are very easy as well, but plants are highly variable and may take a year or two to reach flowering maturity.

TIP: GOLDENROD DOESN'T CAUSE SNEEZING even though it is blamed for hay fever. Goldenrod's pollen, which is too heavy to float through the air, much less get up your nose, requires insects to pollinate it with its neighbors. The real culprit is ragweed, a large, generic-green shrub-like annual with pollen that floats like smoke in every autumn breeze.

Hardy Begonia
Begonia grandis ssp. evansiana
Sun or shade

When I last visited the headquarters of the American Horticulture Society at River Farm, one of George Washington's properties along the Potomac River, I admired the thicket of hardy begonias spreading along the foundation of the historic house. Old-hand gardeners look down on this unique begonia—which is completely hardy throughout the South—because it's simply so easy to grow. Hardly a reason to not like a flower as pretty as this! It spreads in small colonies into a mass of angel wings topped with airy stems of pink or white flowers, but is so easy to pull up it is no trouble whatsoever if it gets out of bounds. Still, this fun filler plant is difficult to find commercially, other than through mail order. It's best to get a "start" from another gardener.

FLOWER: Loose, airy clusters of half-inch or larger, pink or white, winged flowers with bright-yellow stamens, held above foliage on pale-pink stems. This plant blooms the entire spring, summer, and fall, nonstop, without having to be cut back to force new flower bud formation.

PLANT: Masses of succulent stems grow up to two feet tall with medium-green "angel wing" leaves having pinkish undersides and prominent reddish veins that show through the leaves when backlit. The plants spread readily by the offshoots of tubers and small plant "pips" (bulbils) that form in leaf axils; it is not uncommon to find hardy begonias spreading along the entire length of a house, even between and behind shrubs.

INTERESTING KINDS: 'Alba' has white flowers; 'Simsii' has large flowers. The related wax begonia, a compact bunch of leaves to a foot tall with white, pink, or red flowers held atop glossy light-green or dark wine-green foliage, can tolerate sun or shade. While it is perennial in the lower South, it will come back in the middle South only if mulched and the winter is mild. Houseplant begonias can also be tucked into the garden as specimens for the summer, but need to be potted and brought back inside before frost.

SOIL: Begonias require rich, well-drained soils and medium fertility. They tolerate drought very well, but benefit from occasional soakings to keep them putting out new growth and flowering.

PROPAGATION: Cuttings, rhizome division, or small bulbils produced in leaf axils.

TIP: PRACTICE SAFE GARDENING! When getting new plants from other gardeners, always set them in a trial bed for a few weeks or even an entire season, where you can watch them closely to see if there are insects or diseases—or very hard-to-control weeds—brought in with the plants. It may be impossible to get rid of a weed or disease introduced into the larger garden. And always remember a rule of thumb regarding new plants: The more someone wants you to "take all you want," the more suspicious you should be of its being invasive!

Hibiscus

Hibiscus moscheutos,
and others

Full sun to very light shade

Hibiscus flowers look unreal. But with the exception of the popular potted plant kind (*Hibiscus rosa-sinensis*, a very tender, glossy-slick leaf tropical kind), most hibiscus are hardy in all parts of the South. They are among the last plants to emerge from winter dormancy, but push out with a lush flair that is hard to find in other perennial flowers.

FLOWER: Huge, four-inch to nearly foot-wide, round, funnel-shaped or flat flowers, looking like they came straight from the tropics, appear in late spring through the summer. Dazzling white, pink, wine, and red, sometimes with contrasting throats or edges.

PLANT: Many-stemmed, deciduous shrub-like clumps to six feet or more tall, with large, heart-shaped leaves that are very attractive to insects, which eat holes in them, but don't seem to affect the plant's performance. Prefers wetland conditions, but will grow in moderate garden soils and tolerate light shade. Plants tend to be leggy and floppy, and are best combined with ornamental grasses, cannas, and other bold, tropical-looking plants.

INTERESTING KINDS: Large-flowering "dinner plate" hibiscus, or rose mallow, (*Hibiscus moscheutos*) is the very hardiest species, surviving the winters of the upper Midwest. It includes the regal, six-foot 'Lord Baltimore' and the much smaller Disco series that get only three feet or so tall; Texas star or swamp mallow (*H. coccineus*) is a many-stemmed beauty that is borderline hardy in the upper South, with deeply lobed leaves (which some people claim look like marijuana) and brilliant, glossy-red five-petaled flowers; Confederate rose mallow (*H. mutabilis*) is hardy to the mid-South and has large, soft, medium-green leaves and large, single or double, peony-like fall flowers that change from pure white in the morning to pink, then red as the day progresses.

SOIL: Will grow from ditch bank edges and wetlands to average well-drained garden soils; flowers best with moderate fertility and an occasional watering, but will survive without.

PROPAGATION: Stem cuttings, division of plants, seeds if they're soaked overnight, and you get them before the insects do.

TIP: WHAT'S WITH ALL THE TROPICAL STUFF that gardeners keep trying to have? Bananas, cannas, hibiscus, ferns, elephant's ears, and other big-leaf, big-flowering beauties are easily coupled with large-leaf hardy evergreen plants such as aucuba, magnolia, ivy, and euonymus, to create a lush effect that says "Southern exotic." Because we garden in a nearly year-round climate, we surround ourselves with plants that make us feel special and unique. Other hardy plants with big, bold leaves include camellia, yucca, hydrangea, palmetto, wisteria, and a few tough, large-leaf annuals such as caladium, impatiens, and coleus. By combining these plants with selected artwork or other "hard" features and throwing in the splash of a small water garden, we can wrap ourselves in a garden that takes us far away, yet feels strangely right at home.

Lenten Rose

Helleborus species

Shade

Even the coldest winter wonderland can have flowers. The glossy foliage of hellebores contrasts well with fallen tree leaves, and the clusters of soft-colored flowers, though holding their faces toward the ground, repeat color from nearby plants such as nandinas and provide a welcome relief from the evergreenness of many shrubs. Many selections are available, but even the dowdiest old clump is a treasure.

FLOWER: Several branching stems up to two feet tall hold clusters of downward-facing flowers, each an inch or so wide, starting in mid-winter, but the papery bracts can persist for months, giving a longer-flowering effect. Flowers are white, cream, pink, rose, green, or reddish; often with spots or splashes of deep purple or wine; and centered with many stamens. Because of their downward facing habit, hellebores are best planted on slopes or cascading from retaining walls where their effect is dramatized. Excellent for cut-flower use, if cut ends are seared with a match. Seedpods are elongated and contain viable seed.

PLANT: Clump-forming basal mass of large, lustrous dark-green leaves, each up to two feet tall and divided into fans of up to eleven long, sometimes jagged leaflets. Foliage is evergreen in the worst winters, but will burn in direct sunshine. Slow to establish, but very long-lived, often forming large seedling colonies in woodland gardens. Outstanding companion plant for ferns, ajuga, violets, and between or in front of azaleas, camellias, or other flowering shrubs grown in the shade.

INTERESTING KINDS: Lenten rose (*Helleborus orientalis*) is the easiest to get started, and blooms in mid-winter through spring in a wide range of earthy colors; Christmas rose (*H. niger*) is not as heat-tolerant in the lower South, has less-toothed leaves than Lenten rose, and has white or greenish white flowers that fade to purplish with age; bear's-foot hellebore (*H. foetidus*) has interesting, upright, deeply divided leaves and large clusters of pale-green flowers with purplish margins held well above the foliage and is a great contrast for hostas and ferns.

SOIL: Deep, rich, woodsy conditions that do not stay wet. Adding organic matter to the soil and allowing natural leaf litter to compost around the plants helps keep them healthy. Does not tolerate extremely acidic soils, so add a little lime to the planting site and broadcast fresh agricultural lime over the area every few years.

PROPAGATION: Divisions can be made of mature plants but are slow to reestablish, or plant a few "store-bought" plants and allow them to sow their own seed into surrounding wooded areas.

TIP: LEAF LITTER FEEDS THE SOIL beneath trees by composting right on top of the ground and getting eaten and carried deep into the soil by earthworms. What a great deal!

Mexican Petunia

Ruellia brittoniana

Full sun or light shade

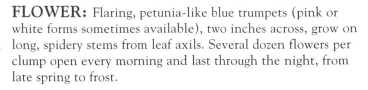

Not long ago, ruellia was found only around rural cottages, where it had been shared between gardeners for many decades for its dependable all-summer flowers; now it is a popular botanical garden wonder that attracts butterflies, hummingbirds, and evening hawk moths. Considered by some Master Gardeners to be invasive, most gardeners find it easy to control with edging material or by sharing with new gardeners. Stems stuck in vases of water will have visible roots within a week—which is good, because although the shrubby perennial is becoming more widely grown, it is still sometimes hard to find at local garden centers.

FLOWER: Flaring, petunia-like blue trumpets (pink or white forms sometimes available), two inches across, grow on long, spidery stems from leaf axils. Several dozen flowers per clump open every morning and last through the night, from late spring to frost.

PLANT: Many-stemmed shrubby summer perennial, three feet wide by three or four feet tall (sometimes taller in the shade). Each stem is covered with narrow, dark-green leaves opposite one another at knobby nodes. The plant is killed to the ground at first frost, but returns with a vengeance the following spring. Needs mulch in the northern areas of the South or should be rooted and carried indoors for winter. This spreading perennial is best suited to perennial borders where there is room to spread or in large containers or beside water gardens.

INTERESTING KINDS: 'Chi Chi' (pink), 'Katie' (compact, slow-spreading dwarf form).

SOIL: Any, even around dry roots of small trees. Prefers well-drained soil, but will grow even in shallow containers in water gardens.

PROPAGATION: Stems with at least one or two leaf nodes inserted into moist potting soil or a vase of water root quickly, all summer. Or divide thick clumps any time of year (cut back tall plants if dividing in the summer).

TIP: GIVE AWAY YOUR EXCESS when you have a beautiful plant that grows a little too well. When asked to help determine which tough plants to include in this book, several members of a statewide group of Master Gardeners wrote that ruellia should not be included—because it's too vigorous. But gardening friend Ralph Sowell of Jackson, Mississippi, wrote "I've been growing and propagating Mexican petunia for about six years. It takes no care! I grow it in sun, shade, and 'in between.' I have made more than fifty families very happy by giving them plants that I root. Everyone loves the plants. If you plant them in pots, they won't increase." This approach is a lot more positive than that of the naysayers!

Mint

Mentha species

Full sun or light shade

Mint helps the medicine go down, brightens the breath, and masks bad odors near the trash bin. And once started, it can be almost difficult to get rid of. I grow a hardy "spearmint gum" mint in a crack in my back driveway—a wall of fragrance when the kids or I walk by.

FLOWER: Small, lavender or pinkish white, salvia-like blossoms on stems above foliage, fragrant and edible but usually not showy enough to enjoy at the expense of foliage, which generally shuts down while plants are in bloom.

PLANT: Invasive underground rhizomes sprout masses of round to oblong leaves up to an inch and a half long and half as wide. Upright stems of some species are a foot or more tall. Leaves are aromatic with oils, which makes them extremely fragrant when crushed or after a good rain. The oils are the main source of mint flavors, as well, and can be a mild stimulant when steeped in hot water for tea; mint is a major ingredient in cold medicines and cough syrups. Most mints need to be trimmed back occasionally to keep them covered with fresh foliage, or they tend to get woody and leggy. Their invasive roots can find every crack and crevice.

INTERESTING KINDS: With well over five hundred different mints to choose from, the most popular (and readily available) include the following assortments. In the peppermint group are black-stem peppermint (*Mentha* × *piperita vulgaris*) with very strong fragrance and vigorous—really invasive—habits, and lemon or orange mint (*M.* × *piperita* 'Citrata'), which is not aggressive and makes great tea. The spearmint group includes the heavily scented true spearmint (*M. spicata*), curly-leaf mint julep mint (*M. spicata* 'Crispa'), and ginger mint (*M.* × *gracilis*). *Mentha suaveolens*, apple mint, is not very fragrant, but 'Variegata', pineapple mint, is beautiful and fragrant when fresh.

SOIL: Mints love moist soils, so any well-drained soil that gets occasional watering will do fine, such as under the air conditioner drips, near a water faucet, or along the drip line of a house. Feed lightly with natural fertilizers such as cottonseed meal or even old nitrogen-rich coffee grounds.

PROPAGATION: Root pieces in water, or simply dig chunks up, roots and all, and transplant. If moving in the summer, cut foliage back severely and move just underground stems and roots—don't worry, the plant will jump right back!

TIP: MINT GROWS TOO WELL for some gardeners, who find that it gums up raised beds and gets around even metal edging. Better to restrain it in a large container—but expect it to find a way out of the hole in the bottom of the pot!

Mondo Grass
Ophiopogon japonicus
Dense shade to part sun

My great-grandmother planted mondo grass under a dogwood that her husband planted under old oak trees on a steep slope, and it has been mowed like a lawn and held the slope for well over half a century—in dense shade, over a hundred yards from the nearest water faucet.

FLOWER: Inconspicuous spikes of pinkish white, bell-shaped flowers held close to the ground, usually hidden in foliage; showy when mondo grass is mowed close like a lawn. Berries are metallic blue and held on the same short spikes.

PLANT: Low-growing, arching, fine-textured (thin) leaves that are very dark blue-green, produced in soft clumps that spread rapidly by way of runners that can grow six inches or more out from "mother" plants before sprouting the following spring. Foliage will bleach out in hot sunshine. Mondo grass, which can be used as a lawn substitute in the shade (see Tip below), cannot be kept in bounds except with regular edging of the soil around its roots—it can run along, grow into, and actually help split open cracks in a sidewalk! Roots form small tubers that are simply storage parts for food and moisture, helping it survive incredibly dry summers.

INTERESTING KINDS: Hard-to-find variegated kinds are available, and a giant variety (*Ophiopogon jaburan*) gets nearly two feet tall and looks like liriope (see liriope entry); *O. planiscapus* 'Nigrescens' is a very slow-spreading, nearly black variety with pink flowers that makes a stunning combination with low-growing perennials and small bulbs. Landscapers use 'Nanus', a tightly tufted, two- to three-inch-tall dwarf mondo grass, between stepping stones and pavers (it makes a great addition to small pots of mixed plants, as well).

SOIL: Any well-drained soil; mondo grass grows well around tree roots and between stones. Poor drainage or excess moisture causes leaf tips to burn and sometimes can lead to crown rot.

PROPAGATION: Divide mature clumps any time of the year. To get ground covers established, keep plants in small clumps of three or four crowns, plant six inches apart, and mulch in between with oak or other hardwood leaf mulch that keeps the soil cool and loose and woodsy. Expect the clumps to "just sit there" the first summer, but to really jump the following spring.

TIP: THE PERFECT WEED in shady lawns, mondo grass quickly colonizes flat shady areas, even under dense, mature oak trees. The good news is that when mowed three or four times a year, it becomes a perfectly neat lawn substitute where grass won't grow. Bonuses: It is evergreen with small spring flowers, and tree leaves are all the food it needs!

Monkey Grass or Lily Turf
Liriope species
Heavy shade to moderate sun

No question, this is the border plant of choice for Southern gardeners, but it makes a tough potted plant, as well. I have pots of different kinds of liriope, all several years old, which get not one drop of water from a hose—ever—and look fine.

FLOWER: Simple stalks up to a foot or more tall, clustered with small, hyacinth-like, blue, pinkish lavender, or sometimes white flowers in the summer; mature clumps can produce two dozen or more very showy flower stems above the foliage. Excellent for flower arrangements. Blue-black berries up to a quarter inch in diameter may persist into fall.

PLANT: Narrow, grassy foliage a foot or so tall emerges in the spring; leaves are evergreen, but may start looking ratty by late winter. Cutting off the old foliage is not necessary, but is a common practice that neatens plants and reduces leaf spot diseases; this should be done before new growth pushes up in the spring, or nipped leaves will look ragged the rest of the year. *Liriope muscari*, which can root if set right on top of the ground for an extra few inches of impact, is outstanding as a dense border plant; it also makes a fine summer-flowering perennial, singly or in small groups as accents, and in mixed-plant containers, where its evergreen effect helps carry a composition through seasonal changes. *Liriope spicata* has narrower leaves and spreads rapidly as a shady ground cover.

INTERESTING KINDS: Cultivars of *Liriope muscari* include 'Monroe White', whose white flowers are especially showy in the shade; 'Silvery Sunproof', which prefers sun and has white variegation that turns yellow in the shade; and 'Variegata', with creamy white edging. Other self-explanatory cultivars include 'Majestic', 'Evergreen Giant', 'Silvery Midget', and 'Big Blue'.

SOIL: Any well-drained soil, even heavy clay (plant high in these conditions to avoid rot) and dry sand. Moderate fertility will enhance root growth, which affects the following year's leaf and flower production. No water is needed—ever.

PROPAGATION: Dig mature clumps, cut straight down, and separate individual crowns (a piece of the "body" that includes some leaves and some roots). New plants fill out with new growth the spring following division and quickly become solid clumps, which can be divided every two or three years and still retain their clump shape.

TIP: MONKEY GRASS EATS MAGNOLIA LEAVES when used as a drought-tolerant ground cover or border; it's a common botanical garden trick to reduce raking chores. Instead of packing flat where they land, magnolia leaves that fall on liriope turn on edge and compost straight into the ground. And the blue flower spikes are a bonus in the summer shade of the magnolia tree.

Obedient Plant
Physostegia virginiana
Full sun to part shade

Here's a plant to give to all your neighbors—one so pretty they can't believe you want to pull and pull and pull and then give it all away! This native plant is almost irresistibly beautiful and loaded with hummingbirds and butterflies. But it simply won't stay put, leading everyone who grows it to comment on how it is not very obedient at all.

FLOWER: Inch-long, tubular flowers produced in the summer by the dozens and blooming a few at a time from the bottom of straight spikes up to the top. Individual flowers are "hinged" so they can be swiveled to point in any direction and stay that way (hence the plant's name). The species is lavender to pink, with cultivated varieties concentrating on deeper colors or white flowered forms, and more compact flower heads. Excellent cut flower that can last a week or more in water.

PLANT: Spreading mass of individual stems up to three feet or more tall, with long, pointed, deep-green leaves opposite one another on distinctly square stems. Plants may flop under the weight of the flowers after a rain, requiring staking or interplanting with fall asters or other supportive plants. Plants can be cut to the ground after flowering. The biggest gardener gripe is how quickly the plants can spread and colonize a flower bed, but my experience is that the excess is very easy to pull.

INTERESTING KINDS: 'Summer Snow', 'Bouquet Rose', and the rose-pink 'Vivid' are easily found; 'Variegata' has pink flowers and white-edged foliage.

SOIL: Any well-drained soil of moderate to even low fertility. A native plant that needs little or no extra care.

PROPAGATION: It's so easy to dig and divide plants any time of the year that there's no real reason to propagate any other way.

TIP: SOME PLANTS GROW SO WELL and spread so rapidly that you simply have to get out once every year or two and pull part of them up. In most cases—obedient plant, goldenrod, ruellia, phlox, asters, and perennial sunflowers come to mind—they are easy to pull with one hand while you are drinking coffee with the other. All I do is wad them up and drop them right back where they were pulled so they compost and recycle into the soil. Doing this after a good rain or watering is less a chore than it is therapy. Plus, if you pot a few up, they provide gifts for unsuspecting new gardeners—who are eager to get new plants before they realize how invasive they are! Think of them as great starter plants for children, too.

Phlox
Phlox species
Full shade to full sun

Spring wouldn't be right, and neither would summer, without phlox. Among our most eye-catching native perennials, these extremely popular Southern garden flowers have been mainstays in European gardens since the mid-1700s. Different species are so distinct they almost seem unrelated, yet all are tough and easy to grow. But then, hey, they're native!

FLOWER: Five-petaled stars up to one inch across of white, blue, pink, lavender, purple, or red (sometimes with contrasting "eyes"), produced in masses on stems above foliage from late winter through late summer (depending on species). Lightly fragrant, incredibly showy, and great for butterflies.

PLANT: Multiple-stemmed plants that generally die down in the winter (though some woodland species have their dormancy in the heat of summer), which, depending on the species, can be creeping woodland ground-huggers or meadow beauties up to five feet tall, with deep-green leaves that are generally oval or oblong. Powdery mildew is a problem on many kinds, and there isn't a lot to be done about it other than thinning out new growth so that what is left has better air circulation and avoiding irrigation (which these plants detest anyway).

INTERESTING KINDS:
Woodland phlox (*Phlox divaricata*), also called wild sweet William and blue phlox, is a low-growing (under fifteen inches), spreading forest plant, usually evergreen except in severe winters, that flowers in March and April. It creates airy masses of medium true-blue flowers, with enough fragrance on a warm day to fill the entire woods. Perfect complement to naturalized daffodils, ferns, and the unusual native trillium and mayapple that appear at the same time. Its cascading habit also makes it a great winter-hardy potted plant and flower border edge, or accent in a rock garden. Cultivars include 'Fuller's White', 'Louisiana', and pale blue 'Dirigo Ice'.

Creeping phlox (*Phlox stolonifera*) is smaller and more compact than woodland phlox, well under a foot tall, with more rounded leaves. It spreads well even in dry woodland soils, and it flowers in masses of white, blue, pink, or purple. Cultivars include 'Bruce's White', 'Sherwood Purple', lavender blue 'Blue Ridge', and pink 'Home Fires'. All do best in light shade except in the upper South where some sun is tolerable.

Moss pink or **thrift** (*Phlox subulata*) is as garish as a plant can be, cascading from hillside gardens and rock walls. Its tiny, needle-like leaves disappear into the background most of the year—until they cover themselves with solid sheets of pink, blue, or white flowers in late winter and early spring. Propagate by sticking small bits of stem right into the ground. This very low-growing phlox absolutely requires low fertility and drought, and grows best in hot sun in perfectly well-drained soils, making it ideal for tucking into retaining walls, rock gardens, and massed along slopes. Cultivars include 'Scarlet Flame', 'Coral Eye', 'Snowflake', and 'Maiden Blush'.

Downy phlox (*Phlox pilosa*) is another creeper that stays about a foot or so high, but comes in some sturdy cultivars perfect for container or border edging. Best bets include 'Chattahoochee' (a hybrid, blue with a wine eye), 'Eco Happy Traveler' (deep pink), and 'Ozarkana' (fragrant, light pink with a red eye).

Summer phlox (*Phlox paniculata*) is the "tall boy" of midsummer, sprouting sturdy multiple stems up to four or five feet tall, topped with football-sized panicles of garish pink or white, purple, lavender, or red. Some cultivars are touted as mildew resistant; powdery mildew is generally a problem best dealt with by thinning stems in the spring and providing good air circulation or by hiding the bulk of the plant behind a small picket fence or daylilies. There are many cultivars, including 'Mt. Fuji' (white), 'Bright Eyes' (pink with rosy centers), and 'Robert Poore' (iridescent purple magenta).

SOIL: Most phloxes grow best in well-drained, moist soils of moderate fertility, but tolerate great extremes in nature. Occasional watering will improve their leaf color and flowering abilities.

PROPAGATION: Divide plants in the fall or winter, or root stem cuttings in the summer; some are so easy to root that all you have to do is stick small cuttings in the ground and they will root and begin to spread almost immediately. Dividing plants every three or four years will keep plants full and growing well, while increasing your plantings in other areas. With the exception of *Phlox drummondii*, which is a seed-grown annual, other phloxes grown from seed may take a year or more to reach flowering maturity.

TIP: WILDFLOWER MEADOWS ARE MESSY-LOOKING unless you add a few "human scale" features to make them seem less wild. It is perfectly acceptable to use native wildflowers such as phlox, goldenrod, liatris, and purple coneflower in "normal" flower gardens—after all, every flower is wild somewhere! An entire formal English-style flower border, with tall plants to the back and smaller flowers to the front, can be created using only Southeastern natives. Also add a section of fencing, an attractive bench, an arbor, some birdhouses, artwork, and wide mowing paths as points of reference to help visitors think you know what you are doing.

Purple Coneflower

Echinacea purpurea

Full sun to light shade

Only a flying saucer from the planet Gaudy would be painted pink and orange, just to drive preening designers nuts. That, and purple coneflower, perhaps the hardiest native perennial of them all. Found growing in prairies and along road-sides, it is nearly indestructible in home gardens—unless you try to pamper it with good soil, fertilizer, and lots of water, which simply cause it to grow too tall, flop over, and die.

FLOWER: Each flower is a dramatic combination of a thumb- or golf ball-sized, bristly orange or black central cone (described as shaped like an old beehive), and long, thin, pink or white ray petals held above multiple-branching flowering stems. Some varieties have drooping petals; others stick straight out. The "noses" persist well into the winter and are favorite sources of nutty seeds for goldfinches and other small winter resident birds.

PLANT: Basal rosette of dark-green, pointy-oval, sand-papery leaves are evergreen through some winters, then shoot slightly leafy flowering stems up to three or more feet tall in the spring and summer. Plants spread slowly with a few underground rhizomes, but seed themselves around generously. Coneflowers do fine by themselves, but look better in combination with hard features or other summer flowers and ornamental grasses (remember, they are prairie natives).

INTERESTING KINDS: Native plant enthusiasts obsess over yellow forms and some kinds with scraggly pink ray flowers; endangered forms, including the Tennessee coneflower (*Echinacea tennesseensis*), a low-growing mound with an interesting greenish pink cone and rays that stick straight out, are becoming commercially available through specialty mail-order nurseries. Most gardeners go for the big bold varieties, including 'Magnus', 'Bravado', and the rosy-purple 'Bright Star'; white flowering forms include 'White Swan' and 'White Lustre'.

SOIL: Any well-drained soil, even heavy clay and roadside grit. Low fertility is not required, but lots of nitrogen at one time can cause lanky growth and root problems. Water only when direly needed!

PROPAGATION: Easy and fast from seed collected and sown in midsummer or early fall, may flower the next season. Also very easy to dig and transplant small seedlings in the winter.

TIP: COLLECTING CONEFLOWER SEEDS can be easy or hard, depending on how closely you watch your garden. When blooms with central cones and "ray" flowers (purple coneflower, black-eyed Susans, sunflowers, zinnias) fade, seeds are already forming but may not be ripe for a few days. Wait until all the ray petals are completely brown and dry, then snip the cones from stems and put them in a paper bag where they can continue to dry without shattering seeds everywhere. The seeds of purple coneflower are light colored; the black bits are chaff.

Rudbeckia or Black-Eyed Susan
Rudbeckia fulgida 'Goldsturm'
Full sun or very light shade

This plant is what I call unkillable. The first perennial I set out on my newly bare, hot, dry, pure-clay hillside—a "horticultural hell" where I had just killed all the grass and hauled in huge Arkansas boulders—was a perennial I had seen flowering profusely in a pot at a Texaco gas station in North Carolina, in broiling hot sun and reflected heat. And it was covered with butterflies. Fifteen years later, mine are still thriving, flowering from June to August with no care whatsoever, and I have dug and shared many small plants from around its base.

FLOWER: Typical black-eyed Susan three inches or so across, with a dark chocolate-brown cone surrounded with many stiff yellow ray petals sticking straight out. Each flowering stem, up to about two feet high, is many-branched, with so many flowers in June and July and into August that a lizard could walk from one side of the mounded plant to the other without bending a petal. A few flowers "spritz" into fall. Brown cones are packed with small nutty seeds, loaded with nutrition and plant fat for birds migrating into the area for the winter. Close inspection often finds tiny crab spiders lurking in the petals awaiting a tasty gnat or aphid before it can do any damage to the plant.

PLANT: Flat basal rosettes of pointy-oval leaves that are up to four inches long and half that wide with prominent veins. Flowering stems are sparsely leafed, providing a deep-green backdrop to the intense flowers. After flowering, the plant dies back to the ground where small offshoots can be found growing from the base on short runners.

INTERESTING KINDS: Several different rudbeckias are available through specialty mail-order nurseries, including cut-leaf coneflower with deeply lobed leaves (*Rudbeckia laciniata* 'Hortensia' or 'Golden Glow' is a popular old "pass-along" plant with double flowers, 'Goldquelle' is more compact and spreads less aggressively); there are others as well, which are more or less hardy.

SOIL: Any hot, dry soil, but prefers a well-drained soil with some organic matter content (prairie soils are naturally filled with grassland debris). Fertilizer helps promote sturdy new plants, but no water is needed other than perhaps once in the depths of a prolonged dry spell.

PROPAGATION: Easy from seed, easy to divide small plants from the base of mature clumps.

TIP: HEAT-LOVING PERENNIALS ARE PERFECT POTTED PLANTS for patios, porches, and along walks and pools where full sun and all-night residual heat can wilt even the hardiest. Purple coneflower, rudbeckia, liatris, and soft-tip yuccas are good choices for those conditions.

Salvia

Salvia species
Full sun to light shade

One of my earliest horticulture jaunts across the South was in search of blue flowers for the summer— and I found them in salvias, several of which are perfectly hardy perennials that complement other garden plants while attracting butterflies.

FLOWER: Generally long, tall spikes of blue, purple, or white, two-lipped trumpets either spaced singly above one another or packed densely into one solid spike of color. Most of the hardy salvias are summer flowering, some only in the short days of fall (they may bloom in the spring after a mild winter in the lower and middle South). Even the dark-blue salvias make fantastic butterfly and hummingbird plants.

PLANT: Spreading masses of stems bear leaves up to four inches long and sometimes nearly as wide, often very fragrant (sage, the widely used culinary herb, is a hardy salvia). Counting the flower stalks, salvias can range from a foot or less tall and over three feet wide to over five feet tall and wide. Pinching new growth of taller varieties makes them more compact, as will cutting them back after they begin to fade from the first flush of blooms.

INTERESTING KINDS: Common sage (*Salvia officinalis*) is a somewhat short-lived perennial with highly fragrant leaves and many forms, including variegated; bog sage (*S. uliginosa*) is a very hardy, upright airy plant to about six feet with narrow, fragrant leaves and spikes of pale-blue and white flowers all summer, tolerates dry soil or wet but can be invasive by underground runners; violet sage (*S. nemorosa* and the similar *S.* × *superba*) is a spreading plant with narrow, erect flowering stems to nearly three feet tall covered with many violet-blue or purple flowers all summer. Cultivars of a similar hybrid, *S.* × *sylvestris*, include 'East Friesland', 'Rose Queen', 'Blauhügel' ('Blue Hill' or 'Blue Mound'), and 'May Night'. Brazilian sage (*S. guaranitica*) is my favorite for its wide leaves and five-foot stems topped with spikes of deep- or clear-blue flowers that are loaded with hummingbirds; it "moves" around my mulched garden by runners, but is not invasive.

SOIL: Any well-drained soil, best with a good amount of organic matter added. Overwatering can rot the roots of some and can lead to crown rot on culinary sage, which grows well in containers and raised beds. Salvias tolerate drought, but mulches of pine straw or shredded bark can keep soil cool and moist.

PROPAGATION: Stem cuttings taken in the spring or summer root readily. Division of plants is easy with the types that spread rapidly.

TIP: BEST BUTTERFLY PERENNIALS include, in order of bloom: yarrow, phlox, purple coneflower, rudbeckia, salvia, liatris, sedum, and goldenrod. And lantana is even better, where it is a hardy perennial.

Saponaria or Soapwort

Saponaria officinalis

Full sun or part shade

"Kiss me at the gate" is an old name for several hardy perennials, including saponaria or soapwort, which gets its most common name from how easy it is to make a soapy lather from the leaves and stems—which was a very practical consideration in the not-so-long-ago days of "lye soap or no soap." It is also called bouncing bet because many decades ago sprigs of it were used to rinse empty beer bottles by barmaids, who were commonly called "bets" or "betties." My great-grandmother grew it, and her original clumps are still alive, as are the ones I dug for my own garden. One potful has been on my driveway for several years with no care other than the occasional green water tossed out of the dog bowl. Bonus: Because of its soapy taste, neither deer nor slugs will mess with soapwort. Rock soapwort (*Saponaria ocymoides*), which has cascades of red, pink, or white flowers, has poor tolerance for the heat and humidity of the middle and lower South.

FLOWER: Single or double pink and white, almost waxy tubes that flare out with five large petals, produced in clusters at tips of branches from late spring through fall. There is no fragrance, but the flowers are very showy. I have never seen butterflies or hummingbirds on mine, which I have grown for many years.

PLANT: Low-growing, to two feet tall, prostrate and spreading ground cover with roundish oblong leaves up to three inches long. Leaves are glossy-slick and absolutely evergreen in all parts of the South (and even into Vermont). The single-flowering species uses underground runners to get into every crack and crevice, will grow along house foundations and even railroad tracks, and is often found naturalized along river banks where "washer women" planted it for impromptu clothes washing. The double-flowering kind generally does not run but does spread by floppy stems a yard or more in every direction. Use soapwort in a rock garden, beside a gate or mailbox, or as a ground cover "skirt" for ornamental grasses.

INTERESTING KINDS: 'Alba' is a single-flowered white cultivar; 'Rosea Plena' is a pale-pink double; 'Rubra Plena' has nearly crimson double flowers that fade to pink.

SOIL: Any well-drained soil will do, and the plant can even tolerate flooding part of the year or extreme drought.

PROPAGATION: Dig and divide plants, getting pieces of underground stems, or root stem cuttings in the summer.

TIP: LAYER LONG-STEMMED PERENNIALS by throwing soil over stems that have been first bent or slightly wounded and held down to the ground; roots will form at the bend or wound during the summer, and you can cut and remove the rooted plants in the fall.

Sedum
Sedum species
Full sun or light shade

My high school best friend's mother had a concrete urn filled with sedum, exposed to brutal summer sun and heat, and icy winter freezes, and never watered or fed; twenty years after she died, the sedum is still gorgeous. And I have a boot planted with gold moss sedum that's been on my front porch for four years now. These are mere hints of what sedums can do, given some well-drained soil and left alone.

FLOWER: Tight, broccoli-like heads or loose panicles of starry flowers in white, yellow, gold, red, or pink produced on fleshy stems which are sturdy and upright or trailing, that can be green, burgundy, or purplish. Excellent butterfly and bee plants.

PLANT: The two main kinds of popular sedums are low-growing, ground-hugging, or cascading forms with many stems and small leaves, and larger, upright, leafy-stemmed specimens up to two feet tall. All have fleshy, succulent stems and leaves that bruise and break easily, but all are cold hardy throughout the South; foliage on some turns red in the winter. Most sedums grow best in full sun, with little water and fertilizer, or they lose their hardiness.

INTERESTING KINDS: Trailing sedums include gold moss sedum (*Sedum acre*), with tiny pale-green leaves and showy yellow spring flowers, which roots rapidly and grows nearly on thin air; stone orpine sedum (*S. reflexum*), with bluish green needle-like leaves; and the clump-forming *S. kamtschaticum*, which comes in an array of leaf shapes and spring flowers of yellow, red, or a combination. Finally, there is the tough Southeastern native whorled stonecrop (*S. ternatum*), which tolerates shade and has round leaves in a whorl around six-inch stems topped with starry white flowers in the spring. Upright sedums include showy stonecrop, *S. spectabile* and *S. telephium*, now renamed *Hylotelephium spectabile* and *H. telephium*. Popular hybrids include pinkish 'Autumn Joy' (seen in every garden in the South), rosy-pink 'Carmen', ruby-red 'Ruby Glow' and 'Sunset Cloud', and the really pretty dusty-purple 'Strawberries and Cream'. Other upright sedums are 'Atropurpureum', with outstanding bronze-red foliage, and the dark-burgundy 'Vera Jameson'.

SOIL: Any well-drained soil, in raised beds, rock gardens, and containers such as cemetery or porch urns, strawberry pots, and hanging baskets. Give them tiny amounts of fertilizer at a time, if any.

PROPAGATION: Stem cuttings, division of mature plants, and leaves planted "attachment end down" from which new plants can grow.

TIP: ROCK GARDEN SOILS MUST DRAIN WELL or roots can rot. Blend equal parts topsoil, coarse or sharp sand, and organic matter (peat, compost, potting soil, or finely ground bark). Do not add lime if acid-loving plants will be included in the planting. Mulch to keep the soil in place.

Spiderwort
Tradescantia virginiana
Full sun to deep shade

My great-grandmother said it best, writing in 1914, during a visit to her own grandmother's garden, of "the wild tradescantia that grew on each side of the gate, remembered because my mother all dressed up to go to church followed the custom of the day and gathered a large bouquet which she carried in her hand and among the red roses were the delicate blue tradescantia with their long bright green streams of leaves." This is the spiderwort that some "accomplished" gardeners try so hard to get rid of, but which is one of the all-time great native wildflowers— so important a discovery that it is the namesake of John Tradescant, the most famous English plant explorer. Some weed!

FLOWER: Distinct, three-petaled blue, white, pink, or purple flowers, up to an inch and a half across, produced in small clusters atop knee-high stems. Flowers open just for one day, but there are many dozens per stem so the plants appear to be in full bloom for weeks on end; direct sunshine causes them to close, so the best flowering is on cloudy or overcast days, or when the plants are in some shade. Each flowering stem has several long, dagger-like leaflets that hang down, giving a spidery effect.

PLANT: Slow-spreading, clump-forming grass-like evergreen to one or more feet tall, sometimes with arching leaves. Cutting the plant to the ground only makes it come back stronger.

INTERESTING KINDS: 'Innocence' is pure white; 'Red Cloud' is nearly red; 'Bilberry Ice' is pale lavender with a deeper blush; 'Zwanenberg Blue' is deep blue; 'Purple Dome' is purple; 'Purple Profusion' is a one-foot mound of narrow, wine tinted, bluish leaves, with long blooming stalks of purple flowers. A close relative to spiderwort is purple heart (*Tradescantia pallida* 'Purple Heart' or 'Purpurea', or *Setcreasea purpurea*), a semi-hardy ground cover with vivid, bright-purple foliage that is best treated as a sun-loving potted plant in the upper South.

SOIL: Any soil at all, from dry roadsides to nearly wetland conditions, although well drained is best. Little or no fertilizer or supplemental water is ever needed for spiderworts.

PROPAGATION: Very easy to divide any time of the year. Cutting back leggy plants during active growth is a good idea anyway, in preparation for division. Self-seeds so readily some varieties may become weedy and seedlings need to be pulled before they get established.

TIP: "WORT" MEANT "PLANT" in olden days and often connoted an herbal or medicinal use. Spiderwort flower heads have a spidery look, so it's a "spider plant." And by the way, it is reported that spiderwort will change colors in the presence of nuclear emissions. Not that knowing this does anyone any good—best advice, if you notice this effect, just keep gardening because by then it will be too late to do much else!

Sunflower
Helianthus species
Full sun

I was very happy with the three-dollar pot of perennial sunflower I bought—it flowered perfectly well, even in my hard clay, just like I was told it would. Then I noticed that the very same kind of plant was flowering at the same time in every roadside ditch and hedgerow in the South—for free!

FLOWER: Daisy flowers with an often dark central disk of flowers edged with many long golden-yellow ray florets, one to three inches across, arranged in loose clusters atop tall, many-branched flowering stems in early to mid-fall. Not fragrant, but very showy and attractive to butterflies and moths, and later, seed-eating birds.

PLANT: Perennial sunflowers are generally many-stemmed with leaves up to four inches or more long, narrow or rough oval, ranging in height from around four feet to over eight feet. Taller fall bloomers need staking to prevent flopping under the weight of many autumn flowers, especially when the rains set in. Some gardeners simply cut the plants at knee height in the early summer, which causes more compact growth with more branches and flowers. Some can be quite invasive through seeds and underground running roots, but it's generally easy to pull the excess once a year and prune the rest.

INTERESTING KINDS: Narrow-leaf or swamp sunflower (*Helianthus angustifolius*) is a popular fall-flowering "tall boy" for even ordinary garden soils; it shoots up to eight or more feet tall and is topped from late September through early November with many sprays of two- to three-inch, bright yellow-orange daisies with dark centers. Leaves are long and narrow, and the plant is easy to control by pulling the excess in the summer. The more compact, wider-leaf *H.* × *multiflorus* gets only about five feet tall and flowers from summer to fall, often with double flowers. Jerusalem artichoke (*H. tuberosus*) is a rapidly spreading hedge-forming perennial with large leaves (up to eight inches long) and bright yellow flowers in the fall; its tubers, which are prolific reproducers, are perfectly edible and even sold in grocery stores.

SOIL: Any soil, well drained or not; most perennial sunflowers grow in both swampy conditions and meadows, sometimes even on high, dry hillsides. Moderate fertility increases vigor unnecessarily, leading to "lodging" (flopping) later.

PROPAGATION: Seed sown in the spring, or fall or winter division of multiple-stemmed plants. Tubers of Jerusalem artichoke are easy to store and plant.

TIP: LITTLE BIRDS LOVE LITTLE SEEDS produced by coneflowers, sunflowers, rudbeckias, goldenrods, and other summer- and fall-flowering perennials. Don't rush to cut dead flower stems down until birds have first had a chance to glean the seeds.

Violet
Viola odorata
Shade, winter sun

Some weed! Northern gardeners hate violets because they spread into the lawn. But perennial violets are summer plants "up there," while in the South they are mostly winter beauties that pose little problem to the summer lawn. Their green leaves, fragrant flowers, and happy disposition make them a "must" for gardeners with shaded landscapes.

FLOWER: "Pansy" flowers up to two inches across, produced in masses on very short stems in late winter and early spring in the South. Very fragrant, and long lasting as cut flowers. Usually deep purple-blue, but sometimes found in pink and white forms. Flowers are perfectly edible.

PLANT: Low-growing dense clump of deep-green, heart-shaped or split leaves most prominent in the winter when other plants are dormant (violets thrive in cool weather better than hot). Plants spread by somewhat aggressive stolons and seed production under shrubs and escape into adjacent lawn areas. Yet because they are mostly winter-active, violets really don't cause much harm to summer lawns, which are dormant in the winter.

INTERESTING KINDS: Sweet violets have a few improved cultivars with larger flowers and more variety of colors, including 'Royal Robe' (an old purple favorite, a cultivar of *Viola cucullata*), 'Royal Elk' (purple with long stems for cutting), 'Charm' (small white flowers), and 'Rosina' (pink flowers). The Southeastern bird's foot violet (*V. pedata*) has deeply cut leaves that resemble a bird's foot, and its flowers are pale-violet to purple; it is not as easy to get established, but once it gets going will become better established by seeding itself around. There are other violets better suited for cooler climates.

SOIL: Any well-drained, loose soil that is high in organic matter—like that found naturally under deciduous trees and shaded lawns; moisture in the summer is not critical, nor is a lot of fertilizer, though flowering will be improved with a mid-winter feeding.

PROPAGATION: Seed, division of plants, transplanting seedlings from other areas of the landscape in fall and winter.

TIP: VIOLETS AREN'T THE ONLY WOODLAND "WEED" IN TOWN, at least not when you consider the truly weird plants that have been brought from the woods to our shaded winter gardens. Species of wild ginger (*Asarum*) have thick, leathery heart-shaped leaves all winter, some of which have fantastic variegation; wake robin (*Trillium*) has exotic, three-leaved umbrellas with elegant flowers right in the center; mayapple (*Podophyllum*, also called wild mandrake) forms colonies of short stems, each topped with one leaf or two large, overlapping, shield-like leaves hiding a single flower; Jack-in-the-pulpit and green dragon (*Arisaema*) and their relatives with eerie, hooded flowers and divided leaves. Woodland gardens can be strange places in the late winter and early spring.

Yarrow
Achillea species
Full sun

Yarrow is another plant I have tried to give away, without enough success. The old white kind, introduced by early colonists, was used to wrap bad wounds (hence another common name, "wound wort"). The most common Southern yarrow is the spring-flowering pink kind so often seen blooming in old or country gardens where plant swapping has determined what grows best.

FLOWER: Small flowers held in large, flat, compact clusters up to four or five inches across, atop sturdy stems from two to three or more feet tall. Common variety is white, but many cultivated forms include yellow, golden, pink, cerise, and red; some make superb cut flowers, even when dried.

PLANT: Forms a clump of stems up to a foot or more tall and half that wide, with ferny, fragrant, evergreen, finely divided, soft leaves. New growth begins to billow up in the late winter, providing a convenient and attractive support for floppy daffodils (a great interplanting combination, by the way). Most yarrows spread aggressively into every nook and cranny possible, to the point where one begins to wonder if a mistake has been made in choosing the plant to begin with. Digging and roguing out excess plants is a temporary solution at best. Yarrows sometimes have trouble coping with excessive rainfall and high humidity, leading to crown rot.

INTERESTING KINDS: Common yarrow (*Achillea millefolium*) has the most fern-like leaves and is hardy into Alaska; its flowers, which do not last as long as cut flowers, come in an astounding array of colors and include cultivars such as 'Rose Beauty', red 'Colorado', and golden-yellow 'Fireland'. The best cut-flower yarrows are fernleaf yarrows (*A. filipendulina*), with large heads that dry well when hung upside down after coming to full maturity; all fernleaf yarrows are yellow or gold, including 'Coronation Gold'. Hybrid yarrows include yellow 'Moonshine', mixed-yellow 'Anthea', and pink 'Appleblossom'.

SOIL: Any well-drained soil, best with some organic matter mixed in. Water only during the worst droughts and then deeply but only occasionally.

PROPAGATION: Divide mature clumps, or transplant small plants that have "gotten away" from the main clump.

TIP: NATIVE OR NATURALIZED? Some of our best-known roadside and meadow plants, including yarrow, dandelion, Queen Anne's lace, and roadside daffodils and orange daylilies, were introduced by European settlers and are known as "naturalized" wildflowers. Only plants growing in North America before Christopher Columbus' "discovery" are considered true "native" wildflowers. Non-native plants that are taking over and threatening the natural order of things, including kudzu, honeysuckle, and water hyacinth, are called "invasive exotics."

Other Good Perennials:

Banana (*Musa* species) is a large, clump-forming tropical plant with fleshy stems and huge leaves, root-hardy if mulched except in the upper South, where it should be dug and stored over winter.

Boltonia (*Boltonia asteroides*) is a tall, airy native aster with many small white or pinkish flowers in late summer and fall, best as a "filler" with other fall-flowering perennials or in wildflower gardens.

Butterfly Weed (*Asclepias tuberosa*), a knee-high mass of orange flowers in midsummer, makes an excellent native butterfly plant. *Asclepias incarnata* is a pink-flowered relative. *Asclepias curassavica* blooms all summer but is only hardy in the lower South.

Cardinal Flower (*Lobelia cardinalis*) is an outstanding native hummingbird plant with four-foot spikes of cardinal red flowers in late summer. Outstanding perennial for shaded or moist gardens.

Dianthus (*Dianthus* species) offers many kinds of "pinks," including perennials with compact mounds of green or bluish grass-like foliage and fragrant spring flowers, such as cottage pinks. 'Bath's Pink' is super heat and humidity tolerant.

Four-o'-Clock (*Mirabilis jalapa*) is an antique evening-blooming perennial with many branching stems three to five feet tall and wide, and sweetly fragrant trumpet-shaped flowers in red, white, yellow, or pink. Outstanding hummingbird and butterfly plant, flowers well in shade. Easy from seed.

Gaura (*Gaura lindheimeri*), is an airy summer and fall perennial to four feet tall or more, free-flowering white blossoms fade to pink, very good for butterflies and extreme drought conditions and poor soils.

Indian Pink (*Spigelia marilandica*) is a woodland native with two-foot spikes of showy two-inch trumpet flowers in red and yellow in the late spring. Outstanding shade perennial and cut flower.

Ironweed (*Vernonia* species) has clumps of five- to seven-foot leafy stems with brilliant purple flowers in late summer and early fall. Outstanding butterfly native; perfect at the back of the border; wet or dry soils.

Joe-Pye Weed (*Eupatorium purpureum*) (pictured), a many-stemmed native to eight feet tall, features showy whorls of lance-shaped leaves topped with a loose cluster of dusty rose in late summer. Excellent for butterflies and damp soils. 'Gateway' is only six feet tall with purplish stems and flowers.

Lantana (*Lantana camara*) (pictured, next page) is the best butterfly perennial, not root-hardy in the upper South but still widely planted as a spreading, shrubby annual. Masses of yellow, pink, or red flowers all summer.

Lythrum (*Lythrum virgatum*) has upright stems of pink to six feet tall. Tolerates many conditions but can become invasive—even the "sterile" cultivars—in wetland areas. Outstanding for butterflies.

Peony (*Paeonia* species and hybrids) is best in the upper and middle South only; most fail to bloom after mild winters; early-bloomers such as 'Festiva Maxima' and many single-flowered kinds do all right if planted shallowly and protected from afternoon sun. Tree peonies also need chilling periods at low temperatures and are slow growers.

Peruvian Lily (*Alstroemeria* species and hybrids) is a shade loving cut flower hardy to 0 degrees Fahrenheit. Spreads rapidly even in dense shade. Flowers in the summer, then foliage dies down as new foliage comes up in the fall.

Purple Heart (*Tradescantia pallida* 'Purple Heart' or *Setcreasea pallida*) is an old-garden favorite for its creeping masses of long purple leaves. Winter hardy except in the upper South, where it's a great container plant.

Red Hot Poker (*Kniphofia uvaria*) features flowering stems three to five feet tall packed with drooping red or yellow tubular flowers, above clumps of grass-like foliage. Requires well-drained soil.

Russian Sage (*Perovskia* species), airy, waist-high clumps of gray-green foliage topped in spring, summer, and fall, has billowy stems of lavender-blue flowers; extremely heat and drought tolerant. 'Blue Spires' has violet-blue flowers.

Stokes' Aster (*Stokesia laevis*) is a low-growing clump to two feet tall with long, smooth leaves similar to liriope, only wider. Teacup-sized aster-like flowers in late spring and summer are blue, purple, or white. Several great cultivars are available. Tolerates all soils, including wet ones.

Trillium (*Trillium* species) are woodland natives; each rhizome produces a six- to eighteen-inch-tall stem topped with three leaflets and a single, three-petaled flower of pink, white, yellow, maroon, or purplish red in spring.

Verbena (*Verbena* species) is a spreading ground cover of solid masses of spring and summer flowers covered with butterflies. Most perennial species are not totally hardy in the upper South.

Veronica (*Veronica spicata*), the most heat-tolerant speedwell, is two feet tall with showy spikes of white, purple, lavender, or blue in the spring. 'Sunny Border Blue', a hybrid, is popular in the South.

Wild Ageratum or **Mist Flower** (*Eupatorium coelestinum*) is a spreading mass of many stems to two feet tall, topped in the fall with fluffy clusters of powdery blue flowers. Vigorous native spreader that can be difficult to control; outstanding for butterflies and edges of naturalistic or meadow gardens.

Fast-Reference Lists for Perennials

Heavy or Wet Soils
- Amsonia
- Aspidistra
- Canna (Bulbs)
- Cardinal Flower
- Ironweed
- Joe-Pye Weed
- Louisiana Iris (Bulbs)
- Lythrum
- Stokes' Aster

Late Summer and Fall Flowers
- Asters
- Boltonia
- Canna (Bulbs)
- Daylily
- Dwarf Goldenrod
- Four-o'-Clock
- Ironweed
- Lantana
- Obedient Plant
- Purple Coneflower
- Mexican Mint Marigold
- Ruellia
- Salvia
- Soapwort

Culinary Herbs
- Mint
- Oregano
- Rosemary
- Sage
- Thyme
- Garlic (Bulbs)
- Mexican Mint Marigold
- Parsley
- Dill
- Chives (Bulbs)
- Garlic Chives (Bulbs)
- Lemon Balm

Butterfly Plants
- Canna (Bulbs)
- Coreopsis
- Goldenrod
- Ironweed
- Joe-Pye Weed
- Lantana
- Liatris
- Lythrum
- Bee Balm
- Phlox
- Purple Coneflower
- Rudbeckia

- Salvia
- Sedum
- Verbena
- Yarrow

Shaded Gardens
- Ajuga
- Peruvian Lily
- Aspidistra
- Ferns
- Hosta
- Iris (Bulbs)
- Liriope
- Lobelia
- Mondo Grass
- Phlox
- Indian Pink
- Violet

 Best for Beginners:

- Daylily
- Mexican Petunia
- Artemisia
- Ajuga
- Ferns

- Liriope
- Sedum
- Yarrow
- Four-o'-Clock
- Daisy

Kinda Tricky:

- Astilbe
- Peony

- Cushion Mums

The Plant-Society-a-Day Garden

While I have no problem with every plant society on Earth thinking that its favorite plant is the best of all—seeing everything else in Eden as a mere "companion"—it is possible, even practical, to have a "plant society a day" in your own garden.

There are roses, of course, though most of us have learned to avoid mostly-fussy hybrid teas. My favorites are the non-stop, "gardener friendly" heirlooms, including old timers such as 'Old Blush' and 'Cecile Brünner' (the old sweetheart rose), and not-so-antique 'The Fairy' and 'Red Cascades'. America's Floral Emblem isn't hard to grow if you choose easy varieties.

Iris come in every color of the rainbow, but the most commonly grown is the old-timey, white-flowering "flag" introduced to America early in the 1600s as "orris root" (its rhizomes were used as an herbal fixative). Even when out of bloom, its year-round spiky foliage makes it a vital "backbone" plant for flower beds. And there are many dozens of dependable daffodils, including the two dozen that my great-grandmother grew, which are still flowering after all these decades of neglect; every winter I anticipate the fragrance of paper-whites and sweet yellow jonquils that lend bouquet to my winter camellias (again, survivors from my great-grandmother's garden).

By late spring, daylilies are loaded with fat buds atop sturdy scapes. I have a few hybrids from special friends, and really admire the long-blooming 'Stella d'Oro' miniature. Still, my favorite is the old double orange 'Kwanso', grown for eons as a nutritious food (more vitamins than broccoli!). It grows for me, you, anybody, anywhere, with absolutely no demands. None.

Then there are the herbs, which, though I do cook with fresh basil, garlic, fennel, rosemary, and mint, I mostly use as "just good plants" with perennials.

Let's see, that's six plant societies represented: rose, iris, daffodil, camellia, daylily, and herbs. Throw in wildflowers (coreopsis, henbit, black-eyed Susan, purple coneflower, phlox, goldenrod, and on and on, providing beauty and food for wildlife through every season), and my garden's fit for a plant society a day.

Then there are the hibiscus, dahlia, African violet, and gourd societies (yes, there's even one for them). If we'd start a Compost Club, and a Faded Poinsettia Society—there's gotta be millions of honorary members—and a Friends of Half-Hardy Plants (motto: Good Luck!), I'd be covered. The goal: a plant society a week. Better yet, a Companion Plant Coalition!

Porch
PLANTS

Most of us learned at an early age how to grow simple plants in pots, from the first time a school teacher showed us how to put a bean seed in a milk carton. We learned to give it a little sunshine, some water when it got dry, and a little "plant food" to help it grow.

Then it usually died, which set us up for expecting failure with adult plants, from poinsettias and African violets given to us as gifts, to floppy paper-white narcissus, to all those macramé hanger plants that were such a craze in the 1960s and 1970s. And when we or a family member came home from the hospital with one of those mixed pots of baby tropical plants— usually a heart-leaf philodendron, a small palm, a mother-in-law's tongue, and a prayer plant—the prayer plant quickly gave up the ghost.

Then without realizing it, we began learning about tough plants, because that mother-in-law's tongue (known botanically as *Sansevieria*) survived, and the heart-leaf philodendron vine began spreading all around the window. Those simple plants taught us that some potted creatures actually thrive in the low-light, low-humidity, cool-temperature spaceship environments we call home.

This chapter highlights some of the toughest, easiest to grow, longest-lived potted plants found across the South in homes of the rich and the poor, the horticulturally literate and the ungifted non-green-thumbers. They are seen in airports, malls, and offices and on country cottage front porches growing in a huge array of pots, including china vases and old paint buckets.

Environmental Needs

Location, location, location! Most of these potted plants are tropical in origin and can thrive if provided three basic conditions: good light, humidity, and protection from freezing.

Light requirements range from direct sunshine through a clear window to low light that is still easy to read by. No need to get technical—just remember that while some plants will survive for months in very dim areas, most do best either right in or right beside a bright window.

Humidity is not as important for these plants as for, say, ferns or African violets or orchids. At the very least, make sure the plants are not kept in the direct draft from an air conditioner or heater, both of which pull water from the leaves of plants more quickly than they can replace it via roots and stems. Cluster plants close together to create a humid "microclimate."

Temperature is not as crucial for this selection of plants. Though they prefer the same temperatures we do, they will tolerate down to 30 degrees Fahrenheit for a few hours at a time.

Cultural Needs

Good location aside, how you take care of your plants can determine the difference between their thriving and merely surviving. Water, fertilizer, and occasional repotting are about all these selections need, though an occasional bout of pests may need to be dealt with.

Watering "as needed" is the rule of thumb. Too wet is worse than too dry. To know when plants need watering, stick your finger in the potting soil or lift the pot to check for weight. Never water just on a regular schedule, because variations in environmental conditions, plant type, pot size, potting soil type, and the amount of fertilizer used will cause plants to grow at different rates and need water in varying amounts.

Fertilizer is plant food, and most of these plants need very little at a time. Some can grow for years on just water alone—but that's being abusive.

My rule of thumb is to use a good timed-release fertilizer (the long-lasting fertilizer beads) once in the spring, then occasionally hit the plants with a light shot of liquid plant food containing "trace minerals" (iron, zinc, calcium, etc., listed on the side of the container).

Always use plant foods at one-half the recommended strength—the directions on the containers indicate the absolute highest application amounts the manufacturer can legally get away with, which is simply not necessary for good plant growth. Really. Overfeeding causes many problems.

Repotting should be done when plants have been in the same worn-out potting soil for years or when the plant has gotten too big for its pot.

Pests, including spider mites, mealy bugs, and scale insects, can be annoying, but can usually be controlled by pruning out the infested leaves and spraying with insecticidal soap or misting three or four times with a fifty-fifty alcohol and water spray.

 Best for Beginners:

- Airplane Plant
- Rubber Tree
- Snake Plant
- Heart-Leaf Philodendron

- Asparagus Fern
- Chinese Evergreen
- Devil's Backbone

Kinda Tricky:

- Boston Fern
- African Violets
- Orchids
- Palms
- Weeping Fig

- Bromeliads
- Prayer Plant
- Jade
- Kalanchoe

Asparagus Fern

Asparagus densiflorus

Full sun to moderate shade

One of the hardiest, most drought-tolerant potted plants around, this "false fern" is a member of the lily family, closely related to edible asparagus. Though its long cascading "fronds" make it an ideal companion to other tropical plants, it is mostly grown as a hanging basket or pillar plant.

Tiny, needle-like leaflets give the arching stems a light-green billowy effect. Occasionally, this plant produces small white flowers and a few scattered red berries. It roots from hard white tubers, which help the plant get through long periods of drought, but most gardeners simply cut them off during repotting because they just take up potting soil and root space.

Of the over three hundred members of the *Asparagus* genus, the most commonly grown potted plant asparagus fern is 'Myersii' or foxtail fern, in the Sprengeri group, which produces many dense, nearly cylindrical spikes of darker green leaves. Asparagus ferns will have greenest foliage in part shade and will tolerate light frosts if left out too long in the fall. They can also make interesting summer ground covers outdoors.

Begonia

Begonia species and cultivars

Bright indirect to moderate light

There are too many kinds of begonias to go into here, but the most common ones seen on windowsills around the South are the cane-type "angel wing" kinds, grown as much for their foliage as their flowers. I have an old friend whose mother roots them in water and shares them with all her children, friends, grandkids, and anyone else who wanders by.

Angel-wing begonias have multiple upright stems, each up to four or five feet tall, with bamboo-like joints sporting pairs of leaves shaped, well, like angel wings, with rounded "shoulders" tapering to points. Leaves are sometimes glossy green, often with light-tan or pale-pink spots. Flowers are produced in large clusters and range from pure-white to medium-red, with some pinks and oranges. Long, heavy stems can break, or be pruned, with new flowering stems produced from lower leaf joints; stem cuttings root readily for starting new plants.

Interesting varieties include pink-flowering, large-leaf 'Dragon Wing', which tolerates full sun (with water), and 'Irene Nuss', which has red-and-green leaves and huge clusters of coral pink flowers.

Chinese Evergreen

Aglaonema species

Medium to low light

Expect to find Chinese evergreen thriving in offices and airports where all other plants have slowly wasted away in the low light and low humidity. And expect every single cutting you take to root, even in just water; in fact, I have had rooted cuttings live in the same jar of water for years.

Small, canna-like plants usually have several sturdy upright stems; old clumps can easily have dozens of stems, forming a large basketful of foliage that spills over the edges of pots. Each stem is topped with narrow, sword-like leaves up to a foot or more long and four or five inches wide. Each leaf is smooth and glossy (which enables it to tolerate low humidity) and is usually variegated; 'Silver King' and 'Silver Queen' are two popular old variegated varieties of *Aglaonema nitidum*. Flowers look like small greenish white callas, sometimes ornamental but most often hidden in foliage.

Chinese evergreens make superb specimens in ornate pots or can be used in smaller pots placed on top of the potting soil of larger plants for a ground cover effect. Water only when very dry.

Croton

Codiaeum variegatum var. *pictum*

Full sun—the more the better

Go to the tropics, and find this African native beside nearly every doorstep, in the hottest, sunniest part of the yard. In our own temperate-climate homes, put it in a south or west window and leave it there for years, with only an occasional pruning to thicken it up with new leaves and stems.

The wavy, foot-long, leathery leaves, sometimes wide like a rubber tree or very narrow and curly, are glossy and splashed in every imaginable combination of green, yellow, orange, pink, purple, red, and bronze—the more sun it gets, the more color it has. It grows best in a sunny greenhouse where humidity is high, but needs to be kept out of air conditioner or heater drafts indoors or placed between larger plants and a window where a humid microclimate is often found. Mealy bugs may be a problem but can be killed with three or four mild alcohol/water mistings a few days apart.

Plants with similar foliage effects include "sun" coleus and copperleaf (*Acalypha wilkesiana*).

Devil's Backbone
Pedilanthus tithymaloides ssp. *smallii*
Full sun to light shade

In the tropics, this densely stemmed tropical shrub is grown even in cemeteries—and it can get to waist high or taller, and three feet across, in frost-free parts of California, Florida, and southern Texas. Sometimes called "red bird cactus" because its red flowers resemble birds in silhouette, this milky-sap succulent is most famous for its crooked stems, which zigzag at each leaf joint. Because of its extreme tolerance of neglect, devil's backbone is one of the hardest potted plants to kill—except with kindness, or freezing.

The most common forms have plain green leaves, pointed ovals produced singly at each leaf joint. But quite a few selections feature green-and-white variegated foliage, which often turns bright pink when the plant is grown in a full-sun window.

A stem piece can root easily even if left on a table top for months until it almost shrivels to nothing; in fact, most succulents actually root better if they are allowed to dry a few days after cutting, to give the cut stem a chance to heal over to prevent rotting in moist potting soils.

Dracaena
Dracaena species
Bright to moderately low light

No office would be complete without a "corn plant" or "dragon tree." From the time they were first hauled out of African jungles, several kinds of dracaena (dra-SEEN-ah) have been among the most popular potted plants, because they can be pruned to thicken back up when they thin out from low light and low humidity. All are extremely easy to root from stem cuttings in moist potting soil.

The common corn plant (*Dracaena fragrans*) is often sold as tiered, multiple-stemmed specimens, with each stem up to three inches in diameter and topped with a large whorl of long, curving downward leaves, each up to three feet long and four inches wide. 'Massangeana' is just one of several cultivars with a broad yellow stripe down the center of each leaf. When a corn plant produces an airy flower scape—rare indoors, but it happens—its intensely sweet fragrance can run people out of the house.

Madagascar dragon tree (*D. marginata*, *D. cincta*, or *D. concinna*) has much thinner stems, long and twisting or arching, and many thin leaves up to two feet long but only a half-inch or so wide, usually with a narrow margin of purplish red. 'Tricolor' has gold stripes in addition to the red and green. Ribbon dracaena (*D. sanderiana*) is a small white-variegated dracaena with whorls of six- to eight-inch, knife-like leaves, often sold as terrarium or even aquarium plants. The popular "Chinese good luck bamboo" is simply a ribbon dracaena leaned at different angles during production, which produces a twisted or spiral stem.

Dumb Cane
Dieffenbachia species
Bright to medium light, tolerates low light

Know someone who talks too much? *Dieffenbachia* (dee-fen-BACH-e-uh) is the plant for him. Well, not really—swallowing even a small amount of the plant's sap, even accidentally while chewing a fingernail after handling the plant, can paralyze the voice box, leaving a person unable to talk for hours—which is painful and not a nice thing to do.

These striking, upright plants have thick stems topped by wide, pointed, canna-like leaves up to three feet long and a foot wide. Most common varieties have striking white, yellow, chartreuse, or cream variegation, from pale speckles against a dark green background to broad stripes and nearly solid white spots covering most of the leaf. Small pots usually are stuffed with several plants, giving a multiple-stem effect, and can be divided into individual plants, sometimes just one, two, or three to a pot for more "elbowroom." Tall plants can easily be cut back severely—to just a few inches tall—to force strong new growth near the base; the cut-off portions are easily rooted.

Moving dumb cane suddenly to bright light can cause leaf scorching, but the new leaves produced will adjust to the growing conditions. Overwatering is worse than prolonged drought for dumb cane.

Dwarf Schefflera
Schefflera arboricola
Bright to moderately low light

This tidy little indoor shrub, much tougher than the large schefflera, has leathery, deep green, hand-sized, many-fingered leaves, and is as durable as indoor plants can be. A law school classmate of my wife's bought one at a parking lot "truckload" sale and did everything in his power to kill it, before leaving it with us when he moved back to Wisconsin. Since

then I have rooted several branches in water and given them away. It tends to get branchy and quite leggy in low light, but pruning thickens it right back up.

Sometimes grown as several plants in one pot with braided trunks, there are also variegated kinds on the market including 'Gold Capella' which has deep green, shiny oval leaves with contrasting intensely yellow variegation.

Scheffleras are very tolerant of a wide range of growing conditions, even down to near-freezing or over a hundred degrees. However, a well-drained potting soil is a plus, since overwatering may cause roots to rot in low-oxygen conditions, especially in the winter or in dark areas where plants don't dry out as quickly.

Moses in the Boat or Moses in His Cradle

Tradescantia spathacea

Full sun to moderately low light

This purplish burgundy clump-former is so drought-tolerant and low-care that it's often seen planted on graves or as edging in the tropics. It gets its name from the boat-like flower bracts stuffed with small, three-petaled flowers. This old, old heirloom "pass-along" plant is grown in a huge variety of containers, which must be brought indoors during freezing weather.

Each short stem, up to six or eight inches tall and usually produced in bunches, is covered with a whorl of sword-shaped leaves up to six or eight inches long. Most are solid green on the top, with a maroon or burgundy underside; 'Vittata' ('Variegata') is reddish with yellowish green stripes. The plants tolerate very low humidity, high or low light intensities, and extended drought, making it a very tough plant that can survive the neglect of a variety of gardeners.

Moses in the boat can be used as a small potted specimen, ground cover under larger potted plants, or outdoors as summer edging. Propagate by carefully prying or cutting loose individual stems from the "mother clump" and repotting.

Night Blooming Cereus

Selenicereus grandiflorus and other species

Very bright to moderate light

Even though this cactus relative is one of the ugliest things ever put into a pot, the old "pass-along" plant has been shared for many generations, partly because it simply won't die. Many gardeners have memories of sitting up late at night to wait—hopefully—for it to come into flower; if you miss it, it's gone—the flowers are limp and wasted by early morning.

Several species have cylindrical or angular stems, but the most popular has a cascading mess of long, flat, leathery, serrated leaves, each producing more scraggly leaves in an almost random pattern. The plant is durable—from broiling in a hot window to gathering dust in dim corners—and roots easily from leaf cuttings stuck directly into potting soil.

Its fat, pointed flower buds, produced on long, supple stems from serrated leaf tips after a period of drought (or neglect), open slowly at night into fist-sized trumpets of narrow petals, many protruding stamens, and an interesting spidery pistil. It is usually fragrant in a thin sort of way, not heavy or musky like other tropical night-bloomers. One of mine had nearly two dozen flowers open at one time (I have a faded photo to prove it), but most flower just one or two at a time. The flowers are completely wilted by early morning.

Peace Lily
Spathiphyllum species
Moderate to deep shade

The large, dark leaves and pure white flowers of this extremely shade-tolerant calla lily relative cause it to be nearly overused as an indoor plant. It is everywhere, especially in airports, malls, and office buildings, and will even fill the void of a summer-dormant fireplace hearth. It will "talk" to you by wilting when it needs watering. One thing it will not tolerate is hot sun, so always make sure it is only near, not in, a south or west window.

A typical peace lily plant has several dozen leaves that arise directly from the soil, each a broad sword of extremely deep green on a stiff stalk. Each flower, also produced on an individual stem at or above the top of the foliage canopy, is a white, leaf-like spathe partially cupped around a central flower spadex.

It is a favorite gift plant, but should in every case be repotted when received; because its commercial production involves lots of greenhouse watering, growers use a potting soil that drains too quickly for convenience to home gardeners. For continuous new growth of both foliage and flowers, fertilize lightly every few waterings.

Pencil Cactus
Euphorbia tirucalli
Full sun to bright light

This plant is sometimes called "milk bush" because of its thick shrubby growth and milky sap. So many gardeners have gotten their "start" of this tall, twiggy oddity from other gardeners that it may be the most passed-around potted plant in the country. Not a cactus at all (it's in the same milky-sap family as the popular poinsettia), it is named for its thin, cylindrical stems, which look like lots of green pencils stacked end-to-end. The green stems are thornless and usually leafless; the leaves are tiny green things that last only a short while, hardly noticeable, and there is enough chlorophyll in the stems to keep the plants going with no foliage at all.

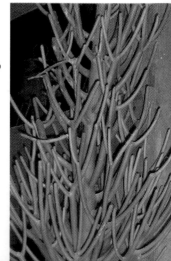

Like its close relative crown of thorns and other members of the *Euphorbia* genus, pencil cactus must be allowed to dry completely between soakings or its thick stems will rot. Also, like its milky-sap cousins, its sap can irritate the skin of some gardeners and even cause severe eye irritation, so be sure to wash your hands after cutting on the plant, especially when making lots of cuttings to root in a well-drained potting soil.

Philodendron
Philodendron species
Bright to medium light

Grown for their glossy leaves, this diverse but durable genus of tropical vines and subshrubs are among the most common houseplants in the country. Many are survivors from a "hospital basket" of mixed plants and are kept alive for decades on little more than an occasional watering. I have one rooted in a cola bottle of water, left over from my son's hospital birth back in 1986!

Very few gardeners ever see a philodendron flower, which is a creamy white, calla-like spathe hidden within the foliage canopy. The foliage is glossy, slick (almost rubbery), and durable even in low humidity. Most grow best in bright but indirect light.

Split-leaf philodendron (*Philodendron bipinnatifidum*) has huge, elephant-ear leaves, deeply divided almost to the midrib, produced from a stocky, shrub-like trunk with incredibly strong aerial roots used for support. It and a near relative (*Monstera deliciosa*, which often has holes in the leaves like Swiss cheese) can get six or eight feet tall and nearly as wide, with leaves up to three feet long. 'Xanadu' is a super-tough "dwarf" form used in mass plantings or as a potted specimen for low-light, low-humidity, breezy spots.

Heart-leaf philodendron (*P. scandens*) and spade-leaf philodendron (*P. domesticum*) are fast-growing vines that attach to supports with smaller aerial roots. Their leaves are glossy and deep green, and the vines can wrap around an entire kitchen window from a small pot on the sink. 'Royal Queen' is a spade-leaf with deep red foliage. Many other cultivars are available.

Pothos or Devil's Ivy
Epipremnum aureum
Bright to medium light

As the strikingly bright, long-lasting foliage of the pothos vine climbs or cascades, it creates a tropical contrast you'd expect to see in a real jungle. This plant often outlives its gardener, moving from one generation to another by stem cuttings.

The rarely flowering vine has a tough, stiff stem that wraps and attaches with stubby aerial roots. Depending on the amount of humidity and care, its thick, glossy green leaves, usually splashed or marbled with large yellow blotches, can easily surpass a foot or more long and more than half that wide, with mature leaves sometimes deeply cut. The yellow is more pronounced in bright light.

Best used as a hanging basket plant, as a climber or cascading "trailer" planted with a taller plant, or even as a summer ground cover at the base of landscape trees, in sun or shade.

Relatives include heart-leaf philodendron (*Philodendron scandens*) and arrowhead vine (*Syngonium podophyllum*).

Rubber Tree
Ficus elastica
Full sun to moderate light

I have had a rubber tree, which I named "Big Jim," since the mid-1970s. It has survived many moves before, during, and after my college years and gets watered maybe ten or twelve times a year, fed once a year, and pruned back to bare trunks whenever it gets too big. And it just keeps on growing. Its sticky, milky sap, which can irritate eyes, is what rubber is made from.

Pruning these usually single-trunked trees forces new stems to come out right at the cut, which thickens the plants into indoor shrubs of broad, thick, foot-long leaves of green, sometimes variegated or tinged with red. New growth is usually sheathed in a red covering that quickly sheds.

Unlike its cousin the weeping fig (*Ficus benjamina*), which is fairly tough but drops its leaves at the slightest provocation (even turning it halfway around to get more light), rubber trees tolerate lower light and humidity than any other indoor potted tree. Interesting relatives include fiddle-leaf fig (*F. lyrata*), creeping fig (*F. pumila*), and the edible fig (*F. carica*).

Snake Plant or Mother-in-Law's Tongue
Sansevieria trifasciata
Very bright light to very low light

Talk about tough—this succulent from Africa can grow in an ashtray on top of the TV! And go months without water—really! I have collected many different kinds of *Sansevieria* (sans-see-VAIR-ee-uh); some are still alive after minimal care for over thirty years—in the same pots. I even have one that my grandmother grew in a big paint bucket lined on the outside with aluminum cooking foil.

The plants thrive in moderate light, but tolerate full sun or dark corners, as long as they are not over-watered. Rhizome-like runner stems can be divided, and you can even cut leaves into small pieces, which root to form new plants.

Common cultivars include variegated ('Laurentii') and dwarf ('Hahnii'), but many more species and varieties are available from collectors and through Internet companies, including kinds with long, pointed, carrot-like cylindrical leaves, and some with wide leaf blades that look like beaver tails.

Spider Plant or Airplane Plant
Chlorophytum comosum
Nearly full sun to moderately low light

One of the most popular hanging basket plants, from Africa, spider plant grows as a sprawling clump of long, narrow, arching, grass-like leaves, either solid green or variegated. It sends out two- or three-foot flowering stems, also arching up and then back downward, covered with half-inch white flowers and ending in miniature plantlets, each of which can be cut off and quickly rooted into a new plant. 'Variegatum' and 'Vittatum' have broad white stripes on leaves and plantlets.

Spider plants can be used as fast-multiplying hanging baskets, ground covers in other potted plants or in shaded summer flower beds, and as easy "give-aways" to get kids started on gardening. They are often combined with other contrasting plants such as ornamental sweet potatoes and impatiens. The plants need repotting every couple of years or so, during which they can be divided into more plants. Slice off the starchy tuber-like root appendages, which simply take up potting soil space.

Other Good Potted Plants

African Violet (*Saintpaulia ionantha*) - Popular flowering plant with many thousands of cultivars and even its own plant society; easily grown in medium light with high humidity.

Aluminum Plant (*Peperomia obtusifolia*) - Many-branched foliage plant with crinkled variegated leaves; best used under other plants for shared humidity.

Arrowhead Vine (*Syngonium podophyllum*) - Philodendron-like vine with narrow, arrowhead-shaped leaves, usually variegated. Tolerates very low light.

Bird of Paradise (*Strelitzia reginae*) - Clump of many upright canna-like leaves, with fantastic orange and purple flowers; needs bright light and rootbound conditions to flower.

Boston Fern (*Nephrolepis exaltata*) - One of many popular ferns, requires medium light and protection from heaters and air conditions which dry them out too quickly.

Burn Plant (*Aloe vera*) - Old standard potted plant with several "fans" of narrow, slightly toothed succulent leaves (sap is a good salve for cuts and burns). May flower in bright light.

Calamondin Orange (X *Citrofortunella microcarpa*) - One of several small potted citrus plants that do best in very bright light indoors. Fragrant flowers, edible fruit.

Cast Iron Plant (*Aspidistra elatior*) - Normally used outdoors in the South, but also a very good indoor potted plant for low-light areas.

Crown of Thorns (*Euphorbia milii* var. *splendens*) - Multiple-stemmed upright shrub with thorny stems and milky sap, topped with bright red, pink, or white flowers.

Fiddle-Leaf Fig (*Ficus lyrata*) - Large indoor tree with huge leaves, up to two feet long and half as wide, with prominent veins.

Grape Ivy (*Cissus rhombifolia*) - Vining plant with grape-leaf-like leaves.

Holly Fern (*Cyrtomium falcatum*) - Large leaflets give a holly-leaf effect, very good for both outdoors in the shade, or low light indoors.

Ivy (*Hedera helix* cultivars) - Outdoor plant with many cultivars, including forms with small or large leaves, green or variegated.

Jade Plant (*Crassula ovata*) (pictured) - Thick, shrubby plant with fat succulent leaves on stubby stems. Prefers dry conditions.

Kentia Palm (*Howea forsteriana*) - One of several popular indoor palms, which tolerate medium light. Low humidity and spider mites are often problems.

Norfolk Island Pine (*Araucaria heterophylla*) - Large tropical tree with needle-like leaflets on whorls of stems every few inches up the very straight trunk. Needs bright light, often outgrows its space.

Rex Begonia (*Begonia rex*) - Begonia with many variations in leaf colors and patterns, usually densely hairy and showy. Easy to root leaves in water; requires humidity and medium light.

Sago Palm (*Cycas revoluta*) - "Birds nest" growth habit, many dark green fronds arise at one time around a thick, stubby "trunk." Does best in very bright light.

Ti Plant (*Cordyline terminalis*) (pictured) - Dracaena relative with narrow stems and brilliantly colored, pink, magenta, or orange variegation. Easy to root.

Umbrella Tree (*Schefflera actinophylla*) - One to many trunks topped with large leaves of many oval leaflets. A large indoor tree that can remain in the same pot for years, with pruning for size control.

Wax Plant (*Hoya carnosa*) - Cascading or climbing vine with thick, oval leaves, often variegated, with clusters of flowers that look like they are made of wax. Tolerates drought and low humidity.

Zebra Plant (*Aphelandra squarrosa*) - Upright small shrub with many stems of striking variegated leaves, topped with exotic yellow flowers. Requires high humidity.

Felder's Personal Potting Soil Recipe

I did research on various potting soil mixes in college and came up with my all-purpose blend that holds up a long time, keeps plants upright in the pots, stays moist without staying wet, and holds nutrients so they don't wash out too quickly. It is easy to make and inexpensive; I mix it on the driveway and store it in a plastic garbage bag.

Ingredients: One part cheap potting soil and one part finely ground pine bark mulch. That's it. The bark allows good water and air penetration; the potting soil holds moisture and nutrients. Sometimes I put a few rocks in the bottom of pots to help keep top-heavy plants from tipping over.

Quintessence in the Garden

Ever find something that is so "just right" it can't be improved upon? There's a word for a perfectly apt object: quintessence.

Such an item usually does only one thing, but does it so well it would be hard to replace. Pencils are replaceable; the hand-held pencil sharpener is quintessential. A spatula can be used for scraping windshield ice, but it's mostly for hot skillet stuff—hard to cook without one. Others would be smoke alarm, vacuum cleaner, hair brush, coffee filter, toilet plunger, TV remote control, and phone answering machine. And the mouse on my computer. Whether simple or complicated, you could get by without them, but they'd be missed (or need to be reinvented).

There is also quintessence in the garden: wheelbarrows, night lighting, leaf blowers, and other labor-saving tools that we take for granted. Then there are the multi-purpose things we use, from five-gallon buckets and red wagons to balls of twine and chicken wire; often these simple tools have no moving parts, other than a gardener.

Then there is the little stuff that falls somewhere between necessary and just plain handy, like crunchy perlite that does nothing but lighten potting soils, and an opposable thumb (hard to show pride, without hooking a thumb under an armpit). Some we really don't need, but they do a job well while working on the simplest level.

Ideal tools which embody the principles of simplicity and rightness include garden hose, watering can, bulb planter, pecan picker-upper, hose-end water valve, water wand, leaf rake, pincushion sprinkler, flat metal file, self-locking plastic cable ties, and, for flower arrangers, a metal "frog" and a stack of green oasis blocks.

Garden accessories that go to the heart of gardening without adding clutter to our lives are hummingbird feeder, wind chimes, rain gauge, outdoor thermometer, weather vane, hose hanger, tiki torch, and porch swing.

I suppose there are living things that have carried the essence of the gardening spirit through many centuries, that are the epitome of a garden but don't become the taskmasters. My short list would include gourds, shade trees, seeds of all types, butterflies and bees, rosemary, hot peppers, and a handful of universally-grown flowers: orange daylilies, daffodils, iris, violas, and old roses.

These are a mere smattering of "just right, almost can't garden without, everyone needs, and anyone can" use items that do only one thing, but do it so well they'd be hard to garden without. In other words, they're quintessential!

STEADFAST
Shrubs

Want to REALLY have a low-maintenance landscape that looks good EVERY MONTH OF THE YEAR? Your choice of shrubs and small trees, and how they are planted that very first time, can make or break the landscape.

Long-lived woody shrubs, vines, and trees create the basic framework around which other flowers revolve. They are the "bones" of the garden, providing year-round focal points, lines, hedges, masses, and security. Plus, when compared with annuals and perennials, and especially the lawn, these long-lived plants are generally as close to low maintenance as anything.

This chapter is packed with one gardener's choice of shrubs, observed over decades of personal experience, after lecturing hundreds of times in small towns and big cities about the importance of using garden plants that are beautiful, useful, and tough enough for our soils and climate, and that give a special "sense of place" unique to any other place on Earth. There are many other good shrub choices, but these keep rising to the top of the heap for durability and beauty—and include even some of the "edgier" ones that many garden designers once turned away from as "old-fashioned" or common.

The secrets to success with tough woody plants are simple: Choose good plants, place them in appropriate conditions (sun or shade, wet soil or dry),

dig a wide hole, and loosen the roots when planting. Adding soil amendments means just that—adding to, not replacing, your native soil. Mulches, deep soakings, and light feedings can help get plants established so well they can survive— even thrive—for decades with little or no attention. Really.

148

Winter Texture Is Easy

Keeping in mind the ideal textural combination of "spikey, roundy, and frilly," you can have an interesting winter landscape by combining several kinds of shrubs and trees for contrasting forms and foliage. My favorites include the bright green,

teardrop-shaped arborvitae contrasted perfectly with the burgundy winter foliage and red berries of heavenly bamboo (*Nandina*); throw in a soft-tip yucca, and an airy, tree-form yaupon holly, and you'll have an eye-catching combo! Even crape myrtles, sumac, or althea look better when underplanted with ground cover junipers, dwarf yaupon, or dwarf nandina. Don't forget

that some shrubs bloom in winter and early spring—a texture bonus in the "off" season—such as witch-hazel, sweet olive, mahonia, and camellia (pictured), some of which are also ever-green. Mix and match at a garden center to see what works for you.

 ## Best for Beginners:

- Nandina
- Althea
- Hollies
- Soft-Tip Yucca
- Spirea

- Abelia
- Flowering Quince
- Forsythia
- Ligustrum
- Shrub Roses

Kinda Tricky:

- Azaleas
- Hybrid Tea Roses
- Japanese Hollies

- Euonymus
- Red-Tip Photinia
- Elaeagnus

Shrubs for Fragrance

Mid-winter delight: riding around on a moderately-warm day, and smelling sweet olive, elaeagnus, or winter honeysuckle—all of which bloom with sweet bouquet in mid-winter. Early spring brings sweet shrub, hardy orange, then super-sweet cleyera and ligustrum, before magnolias kick in, and roses take us right into fall.

Abelia

Abelia × grandiflora

Sun or shade

The earliest memories of many gardeners are of watching the butterflies and hummingbirds flutter around this dense, evergreen, long-flowering shrub. Winter hardy even into Boston, it is tough enough to be commonly grown in Southern cemeteries, in full sun or fairly dense shade. Often used as a medium-sized foundation shrub, it also makes a great roundish specimen at the back of flower beds, especially where butterflies and bees can work the flowers without being too close to people.

Plant winter bulbs underneath the south side of abelias where they can get the sunshine they need to continue flowering for years. Or highlight its faint bronze and pink tinge, which comes from both leaves and flowers, near a Japanese red maple and pink, summer-flowering naked ladies (*Lycoris squamigera*).

FLOWER: Clusters of small, three-quarter-inch white to pink tubular bells, produced from mid-spring to frost on new growth, are surrounded with pink sepals, which persist after the flowers fall off even into the winter, almost like small pink blossoms.

PLANT: Evergreen or semievergreen shrub, three to six or more feet tall and wide, with graceful arching branches, covered with small glossy pointed oval leaves of green with a bronze cast in the fall. Easily sheared for thickness or thinned and allowed to grow into a leggy fountain with bronzy fall colors.

INTERESTING KINDS: 'Francis Mason' is compact and dense with pink flowers and variegated leaves; 'Golden Glow' has yellow foliage; 'Prostrata' makes a dependable ground cover for slopes. The hybrid 'Edwin Goucher' is a dwarf, airy, pink-flowering abelia. Chinese abelia (*Abelia chinensis*) is a sturdy shrub with larger leaves and large, thick clusters of flowers—the best of them all for butterflies.

SOIL: Any well-drained soil, moist or dry. Tolerates city conditions very well.

PROPAGATION: Cuttings made in the summer, or division of older shrubs in winter.

TIP: IT'S EASY TO HAVE COLOR in the spring, but can you name eight summer-flowering shrubs? Hydrangeas could be on the list, but aren't—though their dried flower calyxes persist into the summer, they actually bloom in the late spring. And figs are flowers, but not grown as such. How about good shrub roses and, of course, crape myrtles? Add the long-flowering abelia, butterfly bush, chaste tree, pomegranate, gardenia (which needs winter protection in the upper South), and the very old-garden althea or rose-of-Sharon. And that's without counting semi-woody oleander, native elderberry, and small flowering trees such as mimosa and 'Little Gem' magnolia.

There is no need to have only spring color in shrubs when we have such good choices of hardy, low-maintenance flowering shrubs for the South's summer and fall as well!

Althea or Rose-of-Sharon
Hibiscus syriacus
Sun or shade

A drunk driver once ran over my great-grandmother's old althea (which most of us pronounce AL-thea), and it came right back with new flowering growth. That's one tough shrub if it can be pruned with a pickup truck! This old-garden plant graces many older neighborhoods out of sheer persistence. Interesting varieties are all over the place, but are hard to find commercially because the plant doesn't look like much in a pot. Once set out, though, it quickly becomes a focal point from summer to fall for its prolific large flowers and even in the winter when its long branches are tipped with light-brown seed capsules—which some people enjoy as winter interest.

FLOWER: Single or double, open, bell-like typical hibiscus flowers up to four inches across, in white, pink, red, lavender, pale blue, sometimes with a contrasting "eye" or flower streaks, all produced in late spring through fall on new growth, even in the shade. Flowers are great bee attractors. Some gardeners prune off the slightly showy dried seed capsules (which have many seeds, producing unwanted seedlings).

PLANT: Upright, vase-shaped shrub to ten feet or more with medium-sized, lobed leaves that sometimes turn golden in the fall. Sooty mold (black, sticky, fungus-like growth) is often a problem on altheas grown under insect-drippy shade trees, but does not harm the plant or reduce flowering by much. Pruning the shrub can thicken it up, but the best shape is open and upright. Only moderate thinning is needed, which will also increase the size of flowers on the unpruned parts of the shrub. Althea is easily trained into a single trunk by removing excess branches, or train it as an espalier against a wall or fence.

INTERESTING KINDS: There are many great old cultivars, but the National Arboretum has introduced sterile (seedless) kinds that have much heavier flowering, including 'Minerva' (ruffled lavender pink with reddish eye), 'Aphrodite' (rose pink with deep red eye), 'Diana' (pure white), and 'Hélène' (white flowers with deep red eye). The popular 'Blue Bird' is more lavender in the South's heat.

SOIL: Any well-drained soil, especially dry, even under trees. Moderate fertility if any.

PROPAGATION: Seedlings may be transplanted, or foot-long cuttings rooted any time of year.

TIP: SOME SHRUBS AND TREES ARE WEEDY in that they self-seed all over the place. Althea, mimosa, sweet gum, Chinese tallow-tree, and many oaks can be regular pains to pull from flower and ground cover beds. The best thing to do is to just put on a pair of gloves and pull them while they are small, which is most easily done a day or two after a good rain, when the ground is soft and yielding.

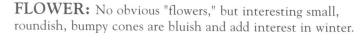

Arborvitae
Thuja occidentalis
Full sun to part shade

Talk about cemetery plants— arborvitae ("tree of life") is an old standby that never seems to die. It used to be a super-popular shrub for foundation plantings, but older forms grow very large and wide, and because they cannot be pruned significantly without killing branches, they fell out of favor. New compact, dwarf, and even golden varieties are among the choicest flower bed accent plants, long used in European gardens and now in the Southeast as well. A well-placed arborvitae adds eye-catching "instant oomph" to the rear of a perennial border year-round.

FLOWER: No obvious "flowers," but interesting small, roundish, bumpy cones are bluish and add interest in winter.

PLANT: Striking forms, most are pointed "teardrops" but some are round or irregular. Brilliant emerald or golden frond-like fans of tiny scale-like leaves are produced tightly on the ends of old growth, resulting in practically no leaves in the centers of the shrubs. If part of a branch dies, it opens a view right into the densely twiggy interior, and not much can be done to get it to thicken back up—arborvitae, like other conifers, cannot be pruned severely or branches simply die. Older arborvitae shrubs lose their pyramidal or conical shapes and sometimes should simply be removed and replaced. Bagworms are the larvae of moths that cover themselves in rustic tents of dead foliage and crawl around to eat arborvitae foliage; hand pick them or spray with a biological worm spray.

INTERESTING KINDS: 'Emerald' is a dense, narrow cone to about fifteen feet tall and four feet wide; 'Globosa' remains tightly rounded to about three feet high and wide ('Little Gem' and 'Little Giant' are very similar); 'Rheingold' is cone-shaped, slow-growing, and bright golden, only four or five feet tall; 'Woodwardii' is an old-fashioned globular arborvitae that grows very slowly up to around eight feet. 'Degroot's Spire' and 'Brabant' are narrow and columnar. There are many, many others.

SOIL: Any well-drained soil; wet soils may lead to root rot.

PROPAGATION: Buy new plants from cash-and-carry outlets, or find great variety through mail-order nurseries.

TIP: WASPS LOVE EVERGREENS and often build fairly large papery nests in the inner coolness of the foliage. When getting ready to prune thick hedges or even to work around arborvitae or other dense shrubs, take a moment to carefully nudge them with pruning shears and be prepared to run if a few sentry wasps appear! If you discover the general area where the nest may be, use caution and gently waft an aerosol insecticide their way from a safe distance or from the protection of a car with windows nearly rolled up; straight-shooting hornet and wasp jet sprays often burn foliage, so use those only as a last resort.

Azaleas
Rhododendron species
Shade to part sun

What Southerner can forego having azaleas alongside the house or in drifts through the shaded landscape? Though they are almost irresistibly beautiful when in flower, they look like big green meatballs the rest of the year; still, if planted well, they can thrive with little or no care.

FLOWER: Showy, flattened funnels, single or double, or "hose-in-hose" (like one flower stuck inside another), in red, pink, white, orange, mauve, purple, and spotted or streaked combinations. Usually blooms over several weeks in early to late spring, with some kinds repeating a bit in the fall.

PLANT: Informal rounded mounds from three to eight feet tall and wide, usually evergreen, with pointed oval leaves from one to three inches long produced in whorls at branch tips and along stems of new growth. Tip pruning after flowering and into midsummer can help produce thicker plants.

INTERESTING KINDS: Of the many kinds of evergreen azaleas, two are the most popular: Southern Indian hybrid azaleas, large flowering shrubs that are not cold hardy in the upper South, including such popular old varieties as 'Formosa' (rosy purple), 'George Lindsey Tabor' (light pink), 'Pride of Mobile' (watermelon red), and 'Fielder's White' (with chartreuse throat). And compact, more cold- and sun-tolerant Kurume azaleas (*R. × obtusum*, *R. kaempferi*, *R. kiusianum* cultivars), which include 'Christmas Cheer' (bright red), 'Coral Bells' (pink), 'Snow' (white), and 'Hinodegiri' (purplish red). Other hardy azalea types include Gumpo or Satsuki hybrids, and the super-cold-tolerant Kaemferi and Glenn Dale hybrids (yellow-pink 'Fashion' and 'Geisha', which is white with red stripes).

SOIL: All rhododendrons must have well-drained soil, preferably partially blended with peat moss and finely ground pine bark mulch for acidity and better internal soil drainage. Will not tolerate heavy clay, wet, or alkaline soils. Sun tolerance is directly associated with a wide, cool, mulched root system. Moderate fertility and only an occasional deep soaking will keep azaleas healthy; too much of either can increase susceptibility to disease and winter damage.

PROPAGATION: Rooted cuttings taken in midsummer, or stems can be layered during the summer. Or just buy new ones as needed (always take flowers with you to make sure you get the exact kind you want if you are matching to existing azaleas).

TIP: "TRUE" RHODODENDRONS and "wild honeysuckle" are also popular in the South, but have a tough time dealing with poor soils and drought. Evergreen "rhodies" like you see along mountain streams must have perfectly well-drained soils, shade, and summer irrigation; even then, some get root rot. And the native deciduous azaleas seen along river banks with pink, white, orange, red, or purple flowers, which are often intensely fragrant—*R. canescens* (pink or white), *R. austrinum* (golden yellow to scarlet), and over a dozen others—perform fine if planted in a woodsy soil under shade trees and watered during summer droughts.

Beautyberry
Callicarpa americana
Moderate shade to full sun

Every fall, carloads of gawkers stop by my garden to stare at the beautyberry, a native of Southern woodlands and fields where forests have been cut, sometimes called French or Spanish mulberry by garden club ladies. Its long arching stems, made thicker by my pruning the plant fairly hard in mid-winter, are studded at every leaf joint with stunning clusters of purple berries. It's also one of the best butterfly and berry-eating bird plants of my garden. And being a native to our woods, it simply needs no care at all to survive and thrive even in miserable soil. By the way, the edible berries, though extremely bland, were once used as filler for Native American "pemmican," a combination of dried meat, berries, nuts, and melted fat.

FLOWER: Three-inch clusters of pinkish lavender flowers appear on either side of leaf joints as new branches elongate from late spring to midsummer, usually not very showy because they are almost hidden in the foliage. Many butterflies and bees visit them for nectar and pollen. Most attractive are the golf ball-sized clusters of bright magenta-purple fruit, which begin to "color up" in midsummer and persist right into the fall or later, unless birds eat them first.

PLANT: Medium-sized roundish shrub to six feet tall and nearly as wide, with long, arching branches covered loosely with hand-sized oval, light-green leaves produced evenly along stems. The toothed leaves usually drop in the late summer, revealing the colorful berries. Since flowers and fruit are produced on new growth, heavy pruning in the winter will keep these leggy plants somewhat in bounds, but it is not necessary to prune at all.

INTERESTING KINDS: 'Lactea' is a white-berried variety. Chinese beautyberry (*Callicarpa dichotoma*) has finer-textured leaves and slender branches that sweep to the ground, with violet berries. Much more refined than the native species, Japanese beautyberry (*C. japonica*) gets up to five feet tall and wide with good fall leaf colors of orange and reddish purple.

SOIL: Any well-drained soil, even very dry woodland soils, with moderate fertility; can grow in wet soils also.

PROPAGATION: Because most varieties are hard to come by in commercial garden centers (they look deceptively scraggly in pots), either order some from a helpful garden center or through mail order. Seedlings around older plants are very easy to transplant, and cuttings root well.

TIP: BOGGY SOILS NEED NOT BE DULL when you consider shrubs that actually love low, wet soils. Start with a large wax myrtle (*Myrica cerifera*), add an evergreen Florida anise (*Illicium floridanum*), and a beautyberry (*Callicarpa americana*), surround that with two or three sweet shrubs (*Calycanthus floridus*), and let the shrubby ground cover Virginia sweetspire (*Itea virginica*) run. You'll have year-round color, texture, and a bona fide one hundred percent native woodland bog garden.

Boxwood

Buxus species

Full sun to moderate shade

When my cluttered cottage garden seemed bare in the winter, a landscape architect told me to stop whining and just plop in a few boxwoods in groups— little green meatballs that gave year-round structure to the hodgepodge. The same shrubs can provide instant formality to a row of pots, even in the winter.

FLOWER: Small and rarely noticed, but sometimes slightly fragrant.

PLANT: Round, deep-green shrubs from two feet to ten or more feet tall and wide, used for borders, pots, formal gardens, foundations, hedges, or as a round specimen. Fingernail-sized leaves, sometimes pointed or notched on the end, are produced in pairs (small-leaf hollies are produced singly). Slow and dense, growth often shades out lower limbs until they are completely bare; sometimes older plants have to be cut back hard to get them started again. Shearing in the late winter and a couple of times in the summer will keep them neat.

INTERESTING KINDS: English boxwood (*Buxus sempervirens*), often called American or common boxwood, is the hedge seen planted around historic antebellum homes and, if allowed to grow into tree-form, can get fifteen or more feet tall. Some landscapers call *B. sempervirens* 'Suffruticosa', which grows very slowly to around four feet tall, the true English boxwood. The most common modern-day boxwoods are varieties of little-leaf boxwood (*B. microphylla*), which generally stay under five or six feet if left unpruned, but are very easy to keep compact; popular varieties include the variety *koreana*, which is small and slow-growing and much better suited for colder mountain or upper South areas; the variety *japonica*, which tolerates heat and humidity well; and 'Compacta', which can stay under two feet tall.

SOIL: Requires a well-drained soil that never stays wet. Mulches, especially around new plants, protect shallow roots from drying out or overheating, and "feed" the soil with organic matter as it decomposes. Fertilize boxwoods very lightly in the spring, and water only during periods of severe drought.

PROPAGATION: Very fast from cuttings made in the summer and rooted in potting soil and sand. Also very widely available as potted and balled-and-burlapped plants in garden centers.

TIP: TO SHEAR OR NOT TO SHEAR, which removes stem tips only, is a question facing many gardeners whose shrubs get tall and "leggy" and grow up over the window ledges. Rule of thumb: The more you cut, the more compact and dense the new growth will get. Boxwoods, hollies, privet, and other hedge or foundation plants should be sheared in late winter through early fall to let new growth have time to "harden off" before winter. Do not shear spring-flowering shrubs in late summer or winter!

Camellia
Camellia japonica and *Camellia sasanqua*
Part shade to sun

Many gardeners are surprised to learn that "all the tea in China" is made from the leaves of the little-grown *Camellia sinensis*, a large, cold-hardy evergreen shrub that has small white flowers in the late summer and early fall. But everyone in the South should have at least two kinds of camellias—*C. sasanqua* and *C. japonica*—in their gardens, for flowers from fall to spring, sun or shade. Once established, these old-garden favorites will prove why they are called "rose of winter."

FLOWER: Large, showy, open "roses" up to five or more inches across produced in the fall, deep winter, and early spring. Either single or double, camellia flowers are red, white, pink, blotched, or striped—with over three thousand different cultivars from which to choose, there is one for every Southern garden! Most have no fragrance at all and are frequently grown near sweet olive, whose fragrance fills the winter garden. Bud drop can be caused by too much fertilizer or severe summer drought; buds failing to open is usually caused by sudden winter weather fluctuations.

PLANT: Tall, roundish evergreen to ten or more feet tall, with pointed oval leaves up to five inches long. Leaves may scorch in hot sun and are susceptible to scale insects, which cover the undersides of leaves and can be controlled with an application of dormant oil on a mild winter day. Pruning is best done after flowering, mostly to thin "clutter" or wayward branches.

INTERESTING KINDS: The common old camellia (*Camellia japonica*, often simply called japonica, pictured at left) has large leaves and large flowers in the winter and spring and is not cold hardy in the upper South or mountains, but can survive if planted in a protected area and mulched heavily; sasanqua camellia (*C. sasanqua*, pictured at right) has smaller leaves and flowers, blooms in the fall and early winter, and is less cold hardy; many others include hybrids made with the smaller-flowering, super-cold-hardy *C. oleifera*, which can take very low temperatures, well below zero. *Camellia reticulata* has among the largest flowers of all camellias, but is a lanky shrub with poor cold tolerance. *Camellia* × *hiemalis* is a dependable small shrub with low, spreading branches and a long flowering period.

SOIL: Camellias are one of the few shrubs that require an acidic soil, created by adding peat moss and other organic amendments to native soil in a wide planting hole that is well drained. Mulch is crucial to keep roots cool and moist in the summer, especially around young plants. Deep soakings every few weeks the first two or three summers will usually get camellias established enough to grow on just rainfall from then on (many old camellias around the South haven't been watered for decades). Light feeding in the early spring is more than enough.

PROPAGATION: Seedlings are very slow to mature, taking up to five or more years to flower; it's better to take cuttings in the summer, rooting them in a sandy soil in a shaded area. Or simply buy or order varieties you want from a reliable camellia nursery or grafted beauties from a local camellia society.

TIP: THERE IS ONLY ONE GOOD SHOT at soil preparation for camellias and other large shrubs. For fast growth and long life, dig a three- or four-foot-wide hole, at least a shovel's depth, mixing the native soil with peat moss and finely ground chipped bark (two parts native soil to one part amendments). Loosen the potting soil a bit and spread the roots out, set the top of the new plant's root system a little higher than the soil around it to allow for settling, then backfill with the amended soil. Water thoroughly, cover the planting area with mulch, and water again when the soil gets completely dry—watering too often can rot roots. Feed lightly and water only during hot dry weather the first two seasons. Then leave them alone to get tough!

POPULAR CAMELLIA VARIETIES: There are too many camellia cultivars to even begin listing, and many of the astounding new varieties introduced since the 1950s (including the super-hardy hybrids from the 1990s) are hard to find at individual garden centers. But the following camellias have proven themselves by surviving in low-maintenance garden conditions for many decades. Many can still be found in "grandmother's garden" and are certainly worth seeking out.

Camellia japonica: 'Pink Perfection' (pink), 'Professor Charles S. Sargeant' (red), 'Debutante' (light pink), 'Betty Sheffield' (red and white), 'Elegans' (deep pink with very showy protruding yellow stamens, sometimes called 'Chandler'), 'Alba Plena' (white), 'R.L. Wheeler' (large rose-pink semidoubles), 'Vulcan' (fiery red).

Camellia sasanqua: 'Yuletide' (red), 'Apple Blossom' (white blushed with pink), 'Jean May' (pink double), 'Mine-No-Yuki' (white), 'Sparkling Burgundy' (rich, ruby rose peony form), 'Cleopatra' (very cold hardy, rose-pink, semidouble), 'Tanya' (deep rose-pink, single, tolerates much sun).

Camellia oleifera hybrids: 'Snow Flurry' and 'Polar Ice' (white), 'Winter's Charm' (pink), 'Winter's Star' (lavender), and any of the April series.

Camellia × *hiemalis:* 'Shishi-Gashira' (rose-red semidouble blooming from fall to spring), 'Showa-No-Sakae' (large soft-pink double), 'Chansonette' (vigorous spreading shrub with large double pink flowers).

Cleyera
Cleyera japonica
Full sun to moderate shade

I think of cleyera in two ways: my cleyera, which is tall enough to shade my front deck, hang wind chimes in, and for my children to climb in looking for old bird nests, and so fragrant in the spring it almost makes us dizzy; and my neighbor's cleyeras, which are planted three feet apart and constantly kept clipped into such cramped little gumdrops they never have a chance to make flower buds. These inexpensive shrubs are often set out way too close together for fast screens and foundation shrubs, when what they really need is elbowroom from competition (although they can grow in very dry soils even close to thirsty oak trees).

FLOWER: Clusters of creamy white, half-inch, very fragrant blossoms appear in late spring and make quite a show when they fall to cover the ground. Berries are not as attractive, but make great bird food (though they often end up as litter on my deck).

PLANT: Fast-growing, easily pruned evergreen shrub that can grow up to fifteen or more feet tall if unpruned. Commonly planted in rows or groups as foundation plants, often only two or three feet apart, where they quickly become a pruning maintenance problem. Thumb-sized leaves appear in whorls at the ends of twigs, and have an almost rubbery feeling, dark on top and light green beneath, with reddish leaf stems. New growth is usually shiny copper-bronze. Easy to prune into small evergreen trees.

INTERESTING KINDS: 'Tricolor' has yellow-and-rose variegation. Cleyera is sometimes referred to in landscape manuals as *Ternstroemia gymnanthera*, but no one in their right mind would prefer that name over just plain "cleyera."

SOIL: Any well-drained soil. Cleyera is in the same family as the camellia, so it can tolerate highly amended soils, but will grow just fine even when planted in heavy clay—as long as surface water does not pool around plants for more than a few hours after a rain. Mulches help young plants get established. Wide holes help roots spread more quickly, leading to faster shrub growth.

PROPAGATION: Seeds, stem cuttings in the summer, or just buy the plants small—they're cheap and fast growing.

TIP: THAT "SOUTHERN TOUCH" IN LANDSCAPES comes from shrubs with big or shiny leaves, which create a subtropical feel that is especially important in the winter, when our favorite flowering plants drop their leaves and we find ourselves staring at neighbors from December to April. Some of the best for overlooked winter or shade texture come from hollies, cherry laurel, aucuba, cleyera, privet, and indica azaleas, as well as evergreen ground covers such as English ivy, holly fern, aspidistra, and Asiatic jasmine.

Deutzia

Deutzia scabra

Sun or shade

As a kid trying to avoid chores, I used to hide behind and beneath my grandmother's "fuzzy deutzia" without really appreciating what a fragrant plant it is. Botanic gardens use deutzia effectively as a "disappearing bridge plant" to provide important color and flower texture in the time between when the main show of azaleas and wisteria is over and when roses and summer perennials come into their glory. After that, they disappear into the backdrop of other more substantial summer shrubs. Deutzia is an excellent understory shrub to use between trees and showier foliage plants.

FLOWER: The ends of every branch of this shrub sprout partially upright sprays of small pinkish white clusters, mildly fragrant, after azaleas and other mid-spring shrubs have made their showiest splash. Flowers are formed on the previous year's stems, but appear on long twigs as leaves come out in spring.

PLANT: Small to large deciduous shrub six to ten feet tall with arching branches of oval, sharply toothed leaves up to three inches long. Rough to the touch, leaves have curious little "uplifts" in each cut in the leaf margin. Shrubs are many-stemmed, with larger cane-like trunks sporting attractive shred-ded exfoliating bark, which gives a craggy old look to mature plants. Pruning is best done by simply culling out older or taller stems close to the ground, rather than shearing the entire shrub.

INTERESTING KINDS: Fuzzy deutzia (*Deutzia scabra*) is a large old-garden specimen, up to fifteen feet tall with arching branches; it has pink cultivars ('Pride of Rochester' has double, frilly, pink-tinged flowers). Showy deutzia (*D.* × *magnifica*) has very showy white flowers and gets six to eight feet tall and wide. Slender deutzia (*D. gracilis*) has slender stems three to six feet tall that are easily pruned into a small hedge or accent behind statuary, with small, bright-green leaves and pure white flowers; its dwarf form 'Nikko' makes an outstanding ground cover to about three feet tall with burgundy fall colors when grown in the shade. New cultivars with names like 'Pink Charm' and 'Strawberry Fields' are very hard to find commer-cially, but give an idea of the variety that is becoming available thanks to plant explorers and observant nurserymen.

SOIL: Any well-drained soil, even heavy or dry sites under trees.

PROPAGATION: Roots incredibly easily nearly any time of the year and is very easy to divide in the fall or winter by digging up outer stems from clumps.

TIP: HOW MUCH IS TOO MUCH MULCH? The rule of thumb for organic (leaf- or bark-based) mulches is to use exactly enough to completely cover the ground, then add that much more to allow for settling and decomposition. Always spread evenly, never pile high on trunks or at the base of shrub stems.

Elaeagnus
Elaeagnus pungens
Sun or shade

Have a school bus you want to hide? Not much would beat elaeagnus, whose single greatest problem is that gardeners usually plant them closer than six or eight feet apart. In fact, these are commonly planted too close together, too close to other plants, and too close to buildings, resulting in never-ending, monthly pruning chores. Any time I see them being pruned into little gumdrops around public buildings, I want to curse ignorant landscapers who set them out too close for fast effect at a huge profit, only to cause maintenance nightmares for decades to come. Yet when planted with elbowroom, they make outstanding screens, erosion controls, highway plantings, and specimens, especially where their delicate early winter fragrance can be enjoyed.

FLOWER: Hidden in dense foliage, slender, half-inch white tubes appear in the fall and early winter with a sweet, gardenia-like fragrance, followed by nearly inch-long winter fruits that are prized by birds, many of which nest or rest in the shrubs all summer and winter.

PLANT: Very large, mounding, naturalistic evergreen to fifteen feet high and wide, with hundreds of long, willowy, moderately thorny stems that give an almost too-ragged look to the entire shrub. Leaves are mottled green above, silvery beneath, giving an interesting olive-tree appearance from a distance. Best planted where they can "do their own thing" without being bobbed into oversized meatballs. When planted in the shade, their long canes actually grow to be vine-like and can be loosely tied together to form an arbor-like portal into another part of the garden.

INTERESTING KINDS: Variegated cultivars are very showy, but may not be as winter hardy in upper or mountainous areas of the South: 'Aureavariegata', or 'Maculata', has green leaves with golden yellow centers; 'Aurea' and 'Variegata' have golden edges to green leaves; 'Sunset' has bright-yellow foliage. The Russian olive tree (*Elaeagnus angustifolia*) is a deciduous tree that grows much better farther north; the legendary "gumi" (or "goumi") bush (*E. multiflora*), including several forms such as 'Crispa' and variety *ovata*, is smaller (to six or eight feet), flowers in the spring, and has attractive scarlet, edible fruit an inch in diameter.

SOIL: Any well-drained soil, including severe slopes and seasides, with only moderate fertility.

PROPAGATION: Very easy to root pieces of branches in the summer.

TIP: IF YOU MUST PRUNE ELAEAGNUS, don't simply shear the outer surface or it will sprout back with an immediate vengeance. Instead, reach a few inches into the interior (check first for wasps!) and cut so that new growth will have to come up and out of the existing shrub; sometimes making a few thinning cuts like this is all the pruning elaeagnus needs.

Euonymus

Euonymus japonicus

Full sun or shade

Few shrubs polarize garden designers more quickly than golden euonymus and its kin. Put it by a brick wall, and it clashes; place it against gray wood or near other gold variegated plants such as aucuba, and it's a brilliant focal point. Hate its insects or diseases, or simply prune to force clean new growth. But it's one tough shrub.

FLOWER: Small cream-colored flowers in the spring are not showy at all.

PLANT: Bushy evergreen shrub to eight or more feet tall with many branches from a single trunk, covered with leathery, oval-round leaves generally less than three inches long, solid deep green or variegated in golden yellow or silvery-white. On varieties with golden variegation, the new spring growth comes out almost chartreuse, a very interesting combination with red or white azaleas nearby in full bloom. Growth is leggy in the shade, but still brightens gloomy corners. When sheared, these bulky shrubs make excellent hedges or specimen plants, or they can be pruned into small trees or espaliered to show off their curvy trunks; they also make great container plants, winter and summer.

INTERESTING KINDS: Golden euonymus ('Aureomarginatus') is nearly solid golden yellow; gold spot euonymus is green with a single large yellow blotch in the center of each leaf (may be less garish than the solid yellow); 'Grandifolius' is a compact, deep green, globe-shaped variety that is very easy to prune; 'Silver Princess' and 'Silver King' have green leaves with silvery or white variegated edges. Box-leaf euonymus ('Microphyllus') is a unique, small version with narrow leaves that are in perfectly opposite pairs, making an "X" when viewed straight down from the end of a stem; it comes in a splashy green-and-white variegation. There are severely upright euonymus varieties, as well. One of the most common "wild" euonymus is a semi-climbing shrub with a difficult name, *Euonymus kiautschovicus*, which often can be seen growing several feet or even yards up older tree trunks in dense shade; its flower clusters are good for bees and butterflies, and it has showy red fruits in the fall.

SOIL: Any soil at all—moist, dry, hard clay, or sand.

PROPAGATION: Super easy to root from short stem cuttings in the summer or fall.

TIP: NO NEED TO HATE THE PESTS of euonymus—they're easy to control. The popular shrubs are very susceptible to small, crusty scale insects, which attach to the undersides of leaves and stems and can sometimes completely defoliate the plant, and powdery mildew fungus, but all are very easy to control with hard pruning and an application of dormant or summer oil.

Flowering Quince
Chaenomeles speciosa
Sun or shade

This indestructible shrub is literally the first to flower, sometimes before Ground Hog Day in February. It grows in sun or shade; tolerates every extreme of soil, temperature, or neglect; and makes a super cut flower for bringing much-needed color into the winter home. It can be pruned with a pickup truck and still come out blooming. Excellent for hedges and perfect for underplanting with daffodils and ground covers (which help lure the eye from the quince itself, which is not very showy in the summer and fall).

FLOWER: Large, flattened, apple blossom-like flowers up to two inches across in a common scarlet, but also pink, white, orange, and salmon. Produced in small clusters tightly held against bare stems in January, February, and March, even in the coldest winter. May not bloom as prolifically near the coasts in mild winters. Very attractive to bees on warm winter days, excellent cut flowers, especially when cut in bud and "forced" in water indoors. Small, lumpy, green-to-yellow, apple-like fruits are practically inedible, but make good pectin for jellies.

PLANT: Long-lived hedge or specimen plant has many thin but strong branches, sparsely thorned, which shoot upwards for six feet or more from a small basal clump; some forms have twisted, curly stems. Leaves, which often have smaller leaf-like "stipules" wrapped partway around their base, are up to three inches long, oval and serrated, and emerge somewhat bronzy in the spring and often shed early in the fall. Not a handsome shrub, except when in full bloom when nothing else is. Prune by thinning older stems close to the ground (easy enough to do when bringing in flowering stems for indoor use), or completely cut the shrub nearly to the ground every spring to force strong new flowering shoots to grow over the summer.

INTERESTING KINDS: 'Apple Blossom' (white and pink, lots of fruits), 'Contorta' (white or pink with twisted branches, makes a good bonsai plant), 'Coral Sea' (coral pink and tall), 'Minerva' (cherry red), 'Red Ruffles' (ruffled red, almost thornless), 'Snow' (white), and 'Toyo Nishiki' (tall, with pink, white, pink-and-white, and red flowers all on each stem, good fruits).

SOIL: Literally any kind, anywhere, except in wet areas. Needs no fertilizer or water for years.

PROPAGATION: It's easy to root cuttings or to divide small plants from the base of older clumps.

TIP: BRING SPRING INDOORS by cutting branches of early spring blooming shrubs and trees and place them in water in a warmish room in the house (although, the hotter the room, the shorter they will last). Flowering quince, forsythia, cherry, pear, and flowering almond can all be forced to bloom a little ahead of schedule.

Forsythia
Forsythia × intermedia
Sun or shade

"Golden bells" is an apt descriptive common name for this old-fashioned winter flowering shrub. Commonly planted as hedges in older parts of town or as a large specimen shrub, or even interplanted with flowering quince, spirea, and other spring bloomers for a "garden bouquet," this nearly indestructible shrub never fails to perform in mid- to late winter. Its long stems also make great indoor arrangements when cut in bud or flower and placed in tall containers of water for "forcing" in mid-winter.

FLOWER: Inch-long trumpets in bright to golden yellow, produced in clusters at leaf joints from one end of the stem to the other. Entire shrub looks like yellow fireworks. Flower buds are cold hardy to below 0 degrees Fahrenheit, making this one of the most dependable bloomers in our fickle climate; may not flower well along our coastal areas because flower buds require several hundred "chilling hours" (below 50 degrees Fahrenheit, but above freezing) to form properly. No problem in the middle to upper South.

PLANT: Fountain-shaped deciduous shrub with long, stiff, arching branches arising from a fairly narrow basal clump, with pointed, slender oval leaves up to four inches long produced in pairs. Few gardeners expect the large shrub to get eight feet tall by six feet wide; luckily, forsythia can be pruned by thinning old canes close to the ground or cutting the entire shrub to a few inches tall to force strong, arching, new growth to shoot up over the summer and fall. To rejuvenate a forsythia that is unsightly and to achieve the fullest fountain effect, prune a third of the old stems to the ground every year for three years; your patience will be rewarded. The plant itself, with its arching form and medium-green leaves, fits in well with other shrubs and makes a good backdrop to a flower border.

INTERESTING KINDS: 'Lynwood' or 'Lynwood Gold' (standard in garden centers), 'Fiesta' (grows to under five feet with deep-yellow flowers, followed by green and yellow variegated leaves that last all summer), 'Spring Glory' (pale-yellow flowers), 'Gold Tide' (spreads rapidly by suckers, grows to only two feet tall).

SOIL: Any kind at all, even cemetery soils, sun or shade. Plants that are pruned heavily should be fed lightly in the spring, but no water is ever needed after the first season in the ground.

PROPAGATION: Division of crowded clump in the fall or winter, or stem cuttings taken in the fall or winter.

TIP: ROOT DECIDUOUS SHRUBS THE EASY WAY, as has been done for centuries by country folks who had less than a lick of horticultural training. Simply take mature stems (near, but not right on, the ends of recent branches), and stick them most of the way into a sandy-soil flower bed. Do this in the fall or winter, and the plants will root by late spring.

Hollies

Ilex species

Full sun to dense shade

Hollies provide the evergreen "bones" of foundation designs, hedges, specimens, and accents around which all the other plants flow through the seasons. Tough and versatile, they come in an astounding range of species, types within each species, and cultivars within each type. The biggest problem with most is usually in site selection—putting them too close together or under windows or other spots where they have to be pruned.

FLOWER: Tight, inch-wide clusters of small, yellowish white flowers appear first thing in the spring on the ends of the previous year's growth—which is why, for berry production, you should not prune hollies heavily. Most hollies also have separate male and female plants, meaning you can't have berries without both kinds of plants present and bees to spread the pollen. Holly berries can be insignificant clusters of black or very showy wads of bright red, perfect for winter effect or holiday décor or for impromptu tabletop arrangements.

PLANT: Depending on plant type, either mounding, upright, or tree-form, usually evergreen with leaves ranging from boxwood-like to three or more inches long, with or without sharp spines, in a range of shades from dusty gray-green to lustrous forest green to dark blue-green. Hollies can be pruned tightly into solid balls or boxes, hedges, foundation plantings, or allowed to grow into interesting forms. They can also be "rejuvenated" by cutting severely in the late winter or early spring—almost to the ground—and within a month or so new growth will come out, which in turn can be tip-pruned to thicken it up.

INTERESTING KINDS: Native hollies include several tree-like kinds, including American (*Ilex opaca*), yaupon (*I. vomitoria*), dahoon (*I. cassine*), and possum haw (*I. decidua*). Other great groups of hollies are shrubby Chinese (*I. cornuta*) and Japanese (*I. crenata*), and the more tree-like lusterleaf (*I. latifolia*). There are several other similar species, and many very popular hybrids between species.

SOIL: Any well-drained soil; if planting near a house, try to get out past the drip line that stays too wet in the winter and spring.

PROPAGATION: Stem cuttings can be taken in midsummer, rooted in bright but indirect light and high humidity. Some hollies have root suckers or seedlings that can be transplanted.

TIP: MOST HOLLIES ARE DENSE and hard to grow anything beneath; your best bet for a "skirt"—or even as a ground cover that actually "eats" holly leaves—is liriope, whose summer stems of bright lavender-blue or white flowers bring attention to the trunks of tree-form hollies.

Felder's Holly Picks:

These represent only the most "mainstream" hollies, but they are usually easily found and very dependable:

AMERICAN: Big woodland trees with very spiny leaves; over three hundred cultivars; favorites include 'Howard' and yellow-fruited 'Callaway'.

DAHOON: Great small understory tree for between pines, with heavy, long-lasting berry set on females and typical yellow-green leaves (normal for the species).

LUSTERLEAF: Best evergreen tree holly for dense shade, largest leaves of all the hollies (up to six inches long and three inches wide); intolerant of heavy wet soils or sunny, windy sites.

CHINESE: Popular foundation and "parking lot" shrubs with dense, durable, glossy bright-green leaves with or without spines or scarlet red berries (which are the largest and showiest of all the common hollies); easy to prune into low to medium hedges or to train as tree-form. Cultivars include 'Burfordii', a stout large evergreen with a single spine (even the smaller-leafed dwarf Burford can get large with time); 'Rotunda', dense low mound with very spiny leaves well suited for burglar-proofing or foot traffic control; and 'Carissa', a low-growing single-spine 'Rotunda' variation.

YAUPON: Multi-branched airy native evergreen with gray stems and loose berries, perfect as a specimen or "baffle" (hedge where you want a feeling of privacy that you can still see through); 'Pendula' is a striking weeping form; 'Will Fleming', a narrow, needle-like, fruitless accent to eight feet or more; 'Nana' and 'Stoke's Dwarf' are compact round evergreens grown as foundation and other hedge-type shrubs, usually sheared into small gumdrops.

JAPANESE: Roundish, dark-green boxwood-like evergreens from four or five to fifteen feet tall with dark foliage that tolerates shearing very well. Popular as foundation shrubs but very susceptible to root rot in heavy soils or when planted under roof eaves, which causes sudden "browning out" in midsummer; best general cultivars include 'Helleri', 'Compacta', and 'Convexa'.

DECIDUOUS: (pictured at right) Airy, small trees with outstanding winter berries on bare branches.

HYBRIDS: 'Nellie R. Stevens', a popular cross between hardy Chinese and heat-intolerant English (which are best suited for the upper South), very prolific berry producer with deep-green foliage; 'Foster', well-known loose Christmas tree shape with long, dark-green leaves and bright clusters of berries, used as a specimen or large container plant, may not be cold hardy in upper or mountain areas of the South; 'East Palatka', yellow-green small tree with few spines per leaf; 'Savannah', upright small tree with several spines per leaf but great berries; 'Hume #2', dark-green, almost spineless leaves with heavy berries, very popular for cutting.

Hydrangea

Hydrangea species
Sun to moderate shade

Tradition dictates that every garden have a "hy-geranium"—but your choice of which kind to use is wider than many gardeners think. Soil preparation is the key to long life and flowers.

FLOWER: Large round or flat lacy heads of smaller flowers in white, pink, red, blue, or purple produced above foliage in the late spring and summer. Flower clusters have showy, petal-like sepals, which remain after "real" flowers fall, gradually fading in color. Most species flower on old growth, so severe winter pruning or hard freezes can prevent flowering (see Tip below). Blue or pink flowers on old-fashioned French or garden hydrangeas (*Hydrangea macrophylla*) are caused by soil acidity: For pink flowers, add lime to the soil under shrubs; for blue, add sulfur or liquid "soil acidifier" (liquid sulfur).

PLANT: Medium to large deciduous shrubs with big bold leaves usually serrated along margins. Some make small specimen trees; others are for hedges or borders and need "skirting" with liriope, mondo grass, or other evergreen ground cover. Pruning can make or break a hydrangea's form and flowering (see Tip below).

INTERESTING KINDS: Old-fashioned French or garden hydrangea (*Hydrangea macrophylla*, the latter word meaning "big leaf"), is four or five feet tall and wide, and grows in either sun or shade with good initial soil preparation; oakleaf hydrangea (*H. quercifolia*, pictured) is a shade-loving woodland native with deeply lobed leaves on fuzzy twigs, with attractive shaggy stems and large clusters of white spring and early summer flowers that fade to pink ('Snow Queen' and 'Snow Flake' have large, pure-white flowers; the latter is double flowered); peegee hydrangea (*H. paniculata* 'Grandiflora') is a tall shrub with showy white flower clusters in the summer; smooth hydrangea (*H. arborescens*) is another native medium-sized shrub with summer flowers ('Annabelle' is a hugely popular, heavy-flowering cultivar, very hardy); climbing hydrangea (*H. anomala*), a shrubby vine that climbs with short, clinging aerial rootlets on walls, has roundish, heart-shaped leaves and flat clusters of white flowers.

SOIL: Must have well prepared soil with generous amounts of organic matter blended into native soil in a planting hole that is much wider than deep. Thick leaf mulch will keep roots cool and moist. Light fertilization and only occasional deep soakings are all that the shrubs will need later.

PROPAGATION: Division of multistemmed plants or stem cuttings taken in the late winter or summer.

TIP: WHACKING ON HYDRANGEAS wrecks French or oakleaf hydrangeas. In the late winter, thin old or tall stems and lightly cut the remaining ones back, leaving some of the previous year's growth to sprout into flowering branches. Or immediately after flowering, cut entire shrubs back by two-thirds. For summer bloomers, simply thin unwanted branches.

166

Junipers

Juniperus species

Full sun to light shade

Junipers are as versatile and important as hollies for their wide variety of shapes and landscape uses, from ground covers in hot dry sites to foundation shrubs, hedges, screens, and even as striking specimens. They prefer drought and resist even severe freezes for decades.

FLOWER: Not significant on conifers; some species have attractive cones or light blue "berries" in the fall and winter, perfect contrasts to foliage (certain juniper berries, by the way, are used to flavor gin).

PLANT: There is a form for every garden, ranging from low, spreading ground covers to upright trees, with every kind of mound or spike shape in between. All are evergreen with tiny needle-like foliage, some stiff and prickly, some soft. Several ground cover varieties develop an attractive purplish or reddish winter tinge. Junipers cannot be pruned hard or they will die (see Tip below), and many are susceptible to spider mites (for which, really, there is no practical control even with regular spraying), and bagworms (caterpillar larvae of moths that cover themselves with portable bags of dead leaves; hand-pick bagworms or use a safe biological worm spray early in their June or July feeding cycle).

INTERESTING KINDS: Ground cover junipers, which grow from six inches to two feet high and spread many feet in each direction, include these common ones: Japanese garden juniper (*Juniperus procumbens*), shore (*J. conferta*), parson's (*J. davurica*, an excellent choice for the South), 'Bar Harbour' (*J. horizontalis*), Andorra creeping (*J. horizontalis* 'Plumosa'), blue rug (*J. horizontalis* 'Wiltonii'), and savin (*J. sabina* 'Tamariscifolia'). Popular shrub junipers: pfitzer (*J. chinensis* 'Pfitzeriana', to six feet and spreading, some varieties have golden or silver-blue new growth), Hollywood (*J. chinensis* 'Kaizuka', striking upright shrub to twenty feet with thick, irregular growth), Gold Coast (*J. chinensis* 'Gold Coast', three feet by five feet with lacy, yellow foliage), blue point (*J. chinensis* 'Blue Point', a narrow, upright specimen to about eight feet tall), skyrocket (*J. scopulorum* 'Skyrocket', a very narrow, tall spike to fifteen feet tall but only two feet wide). And of course there is the great eastern red cedar (*J. virginiana*), the most durable evergreen tree ever.

SOIL: Any well-drained, even gravelly or extremely acidic or alkaline soil. Spreading out the roots when you plant junipers, mulching, and watering only during extreme dry spells is all they need to get started.

PROPAGATION: Difficult and slow from cuttings, it's best to just buy the ones you need.

TIP: CUTTING JUNIPERS KILLS THEM unless you lightly shear new growth for thickness. If you prune back to where no needles remain on a stem, it will usually die all the way back to its point of origin. It's best to just thin cluttered or wayward branches and limbs on aging junipers and let Nature take her course.

Kerria

Kerria japonica

Full sun to moderate shade

The old "yellow rose of Texas" isn't a rose at all— but it sure looks like one when it flowers, and it is in the rose family. Introduced to America in the early 1800s, kerria is often found in older gardens and is still a graceful addition to a lightly shaded shrub border beneath tall trees. And it's easy to share.

FLOWER: Solitary buttery-yellow apple blossom-like single or very double rose-like blooms, one to two inches across, appear in leaf joints in late spring, often "spritzing" through the summer and early fall.

PLANT: Upright, many-stemmed arching shrub, six to ten or more feet tall, with many non-invasive suckers appearing around its narrow base. Leaves up to two inches long are yellow-green, sharply pointed and almost triangular, heavily serrated or toothed and with prominent veins. Stems have a slight zigzag habit, angling slightly at every leaf joint, and remain light green all year, making the plant an excellent specimen planted against a fence or evergreen backdrop. Prune by thinning old canes close to the ground, from which they will shoot back up with flowering vigor.

INTERESTING KINDS: 'Pleniflora' is the most common form, with large, frilly, double flowers on large, rambling, arching plants; 'Shannon' has large single flowers on vigorous shrubs; 'Kin Kan' has interesting yellow-striped stems and single yellow blooms; 'Variegata' or 'Picta' is variegated with white-edged leaves; 'Alisa' and 'Albescens' or 'Albiflora' have white flowers.

SOIL: Any well-drained soil, including very dry under trees and in competition with nearby shrubs.

PROPAGATION: Division of suckers nearly any time of the year except during very dry periods, but can still be done if plants are cut back to foot-high stubs and allowed to resprout in new locations. Mulch will help get plants established.

TIP: SURVIVORS FROM GRANDMOTHER'S GARDEN don't have to be "old fashioned" when they are used well in contemporary landscapes. Many heirloom shrubs are making a real comeback because of four trends: They are historic or full of memories of bygone people or places; they provide unusual but valuable flowering or foliage alternatives to the "same old, same old" mass-production meatballs and gumdrops that we have been lulled into depending on by fast-food designers, contractors, and growers; they are generally pest resistant or they would have disappeared decades ago; and they have proven themselves to survive in ordinary or even abandoned garden conditions, thriving on rainfall alone—making them ideal for the twenty-first century and beyond.

Dependable examples include kerria, spirea, camellia, althea, chaste tree, forsythia, snowball bush, philadelphus, weigela, flowering quince, flowering almond, butcher's broom, sweet shrub, sweet olive, and deutzia. Oops! Did I forget azaleas? But who needs them, with all those others to step in?

Leatherleaf Mahonia

Mahonia bealei

Shade or part (morning) sun

The dreariest dark corner of a garden is made instantly fantastic with the unusual shape of evergreen mahonia, whose architectural form and startling winter flowers stand out against a north or east wall or when viewed through a shaded bay window.

FLOWER: Multiple short (to six inches) racemes of yellow erupt from the tops of shrub stems in mid- to late winter when little else is showy. Sometimes fragrant, often attractive to bees on warm winter days. Flowers are followed by hanging chains of light blue berries that fall before summer if not eaten by birds. The flowers are better and the fruit more persistent when the plant gets some morning sun.

PLANT: Mahonia has many upright, slightly spreading, rarely branching stems arising from a central crown. Stems are usually three or four feet, but can get up to six or ten feet tall, each topped with an unusual whorl of leaves over a foot long, each with up to fifteen broad, leathery, holly-like, spiny-toothed leaflets nearly three inches long; the effect is reminiscent of a grotesque, coarse cross between nandina and holly. Fantastic plant for shady gardens (including in the winter, or leaves may scorch), especially where the striking plant is set as a specimen against a wooden fence or bare wall. Prune by thinning tall or old stems close to the ground, from where they will resprout.

INTERESTING KINDS: Oregon grape holly (*Mahonia aquifolium*) spreads freely as a ground cover or mass planting and has several cultivars, including the very low-growing 'Compactum' and 'Orange Flame' which has orange-bronze new growth. *Mahonia X wagneri* 'King's Ransom' has purplish red winter color and good flowers. Chinese mahonia (*M. fortunei*) and cluster mahonia (*M. pinnata*) are not as hardy in the upper South but make great container specimens for protected porches and patios.

SOIL: Any moist soil, even heavy, if drainage is good (where water does not stand around the roots for more than a couple of hours after a heavy rain). Moderate fertility will encourage lush foliage.

PROPAGATION: Divide multiple stemmed crowns or just buy what you need and be done with it.

TIP: BIRDS GET DRUNK on berries of pyracantha, magnolia, and other landscape plants if the berries have frozen, thawed, and then fermented. Whether or not that causes alarm to gardeners, it can be a real problem if the stupefied birds can't move enough to stay warm or out of reach of roaming cats.

Still, many great tree and shrub berries are safely enjoyed by mockingbirds, cedar waxwings, blue jays, towhees, cardinals, robins, sparrows, finches, doves, and even woodpeckers, many of which won't come to a traditional bird feeder loaded with seeds. Best bets for birders: pyracantha, mahonia, holly, sumac, magnolia, crabapple, wax myrtle, ornamental pear, cherry laurel, beautyberry, elaeagnus, nandina, ligustrum, and elderberry.

Ligustrum or Privet

Ligustrum japonicum

Sun or shade

Want a fast evergreen screen, cheap? Don't mind pruning for the rest of your life? Ligustrum or privet is the way to go. Plant 'em well, then run for your clippers.

FLOWER: Small, showy, very fragrant white flowers on the ends of the previous season's growth in mid-spring; some people claim to be allergic to the cloyingly sweet flowers, but often are reacting to wind-blown tree pollen. Late summer fruits are small, fleshy, and nearly black, highly attractive to birds, and can be a nuisance when dropped on cars.

PLANT: Upright, spreading, large evergreen shrubs or small trees, with oval leaves from one to over three inches long. Because all tolerate heavy pruning, they are commonly sheared into tight specimens or hedges; this usually removes flowering growth and requires several clippings a year. They may also be allowed to grow naturally into umbrella-like, spring-flowering trees with practically no maintenance. Whiteflies can be a nuisance in the summer and early fall, but there's no practical control other than using an insecticidal soap spray to smother larvae and adults.

INTERESTING KINDS: Japanese ligustrum (*Ligustrum japonicum*), the most popular fast shrub for foundations and hedges, has big leaves that are glossy deep green above and pale green underneath and can grow to ten or more feet tall; 'Variegatum' and 'Silver Star' have white variegated foliage. *Ligustrum lucidum* 'Recurvifolium' has unusual twisted leaves. Golden ligustrum (*L.* × *vicaryi*) has golden-yellow foliage and performs best in full sun. Glossy ligustrum or Chinese privet (*L. lucidum*), often sold as Japanese ligustrum, can easily reach twenty-five or thirty feet tall, which makes for a real pruning chore if mixed with other kinds of privet. Chinese ligustrum (*L. sinense*), commonly called privet (the traditional plant used for switches in bygone days—ouch!) has small, dull-green leaves and can become an invasive thug if seedlings are not kept pulled from nearby flower beds; it also has a variegated and a hard-to-find weeping form. Amur privet (*L. amurense*) is the common privet of Northern gardens and cities, often deciduous in harsh winters, very invasive, and easy to prune.

SOIL: Any soil at all, other than one that is soggy or wet. Very drought tolerant.

PROPAGATION: Very easy to root cuttings in the summer or dig and transplant seedlings. Widely available in garden centers, though they are often mislabeled with generic names instead of true cultivars.

TIP: EVER TRY TO KILL A SHRUB by cutting it down, just to have it spring right back as vigorous as ever? This is known horticulturally as "rejuvenation" and, with the exception of junipers, is an excellent way to reclaim old, gnarly, half-dead, or overgrown ligustrum and other broadleaf evergreen shrubs— even azaleas. Do it early in the summer, and tip prune new shoots before fall.

Mock Orange
Philadelphus coronarius
Shade to part or full sun

Who needs dogwoods, when this Southern heirloom has even better flowers, and never fails to bloom? Whether you call it mock orange, English dogwood, or by its Latin name, this fairly large shrub brings a glorious fountain of pure white to both sun and shade gardens in mid-spring—and has fragrance to boot!

FLOWER: Dogwoods on a shrub is what they appear to be; four-petaled white flowers nearly two inches across, some single, some semi- or fully double, completely cover the arching branches in mid-spring, usually after azaleas. This old-garden shrub will bloom dependably in all parts of the South regardless of how mild or cold the winter. Many are fragrant (see Tip below), though if you want to be sure of what you get, root a division from an existing plant.

PLANT: Upright, arching, large deciduous shrub to ten or more feet high with many stems coming from suckers at the base to form a fountain of medium green; older canes have reddish brown or orange exfoliating (peeling) bark. Leaves are oval with pointed ends, three or four inches long and in pairs, some with variegation or golden tinges. Prune out older canes close to the ground to keep the big plants tidy and fresh, either in the winter when you can see what you are doing or right after flowering in late spring or early summer; new growth will quickly shoot back up and have time to set flower buds by fall.

INTERESTING KINDS: Tall, old-fashioned "English dogwood" (*Philadelphus coronarius*) is the most common, a bold species best suited for screens, 'Aureus' being a cultivar with bright golden-yellow leaves turning to light green in the summer; *P. × lemoinei* is a smaller species to around six feet with well-known single-flowering 'Avalanche' and double-flowering 'Enchantment' (which has somewhat confused parentage); *P. × virginalis* has several excellent cultivars, including the dwarf, double-flowering 'Glacier' (four to five feet tall) and 'Dwarf Minnesota Snowflake' (a mere three or four feet tall). 'Natchez', reportedly the showiest of them all, has flowers up to two inches across.

SOIL: Any well-drained soil of moderate fertility.

PROPAGATION: Hard to find in garden centers because they look so scraggly in pots in the spring, so either order from reputable mail-order or Internet plant centers or divide pieces of stems from around older plants in the winter. Mulch until established. Softwood cuttings can be taken in the summer.

TIP: ONE MAN'S FRAGRANCE is another man's stink, at least according to Gerard, the famous herbalist who wrote over three hundred years ago that the flowers of mock orange "have a pleasant and sweet smell, but in my judgement troubling . . . I once gathered the flowers and laid them on my chamber window, which smelled more strongly after they had lain a few hours, but with such an unacquainted savour that they awaked me from my sleep, so that I could not rest until I had cast them out."

Nandina
Nandina domestica
Full sun to dense shade

This is the plant I'd want on my grave, because it would never die. Fine foliage all year with gaudy red winter color, spring flowers, showy fall and winter berries that attract wild birds; lawn mowers can't kill it, nobody would steal it—what more could I want? And it's a perfect "textury" contrast with nearly every other plant!

FLOWER: Billowy, football-sized clusters of small white flowers with yellow stamens stand above the foliage in mid- to late spring; pea-sized berries follow, usually orange- to deep-red or sometimes golden yellow, sometimes so heavily that they bend the stalks completely down to the ground in the fall and winter before birds swoop them away.

PLANT: Leafy and bamboo-like (hence its common name, heavenly bamboo), each shrub produces many, sometimes dozens, of stiff stalks three up to eight or more feet tall, topped with brushy whorls of finely divided triangular fans of many small pointed oval leaflets; some entire leaves can be two feet wide and long. New growth is red or bronze before fading to green, then firing up again with brilliant bright-red or purplish winter color if planted in the full sun. Great for foundation plantings, hedges, groups or masses, understory shrubs, container specimens, or cemeteries. Prune by thinning older canes nearly to the ground.

INTERESTING KINDS: 'Compacta' is a fully shrubby cultivar that is best suited for many gardens, as it gets only three or four feet high or a little taller but still spreads and berries up well; 'Firepower' is a gnarly, twisted, red-and-burnt-orange compact form well suited for hot dry spots or mass planting; 'Harbour Dwarf' looks like "regular" nandina, but gets only two to three feet tall and spreads well; 'Gulf Stream' makes a dense, dark-green mound with no berries but has good red foliage in the winter. A yellow-berried form, 'Flora', has pale-green foliage, great for light shade.

SOIL: Any soil at all, no matter how miserable or hot or dry, or of low fertility. Mulches help keep roots cool the first year before they "take off" on their own and also keep lawn mowers and string trimmers off tender young trunks.

PROPAGATION: Seeds are slow and must be "scarified" out of fleshy fruits, but the easiest, fastest, and most economical way to increase nandinas is by digging entire plants, splitting them into smaller clumps, and replanting, done nearly any time of the year.

TIP: DO YOU HATE NANDINAS because they get too tall? Two solutions: Move them to a better location, or simply thin out some of the canes every year, cutting some close to the ground and some about halfway for a full effect and leaving some for spring flowers and winter berries.

Poncirus or Hardy Orange
Poncirus trifoliata
Full sun to fairly dense shade

Nearly everyone who sees a photo of this thorny hardy "wild lemon tree" recognizes it from an older garden they knew from childhood; the plants were used as rootstock for grapefruit and orange trees, and when folks bought souvenir plants from a visit to Florida, the only thing that survived the first winter was the rootstock. It has also been sold for many years as a "burglar" plant—buy a small bundle of seedlings for a hedge or under a window, and a thief would likely be begging for mercy before the police could get him out of the bush's prickly grip!

FLOWER: Spring flowers are two inches across, pure white, and smell like sweet citrus. Golf ball-sized, seed-filled fruits produced in the summer remain on the tree well into winter, sometimes all winter, and turn dusty orange-yellow. They are fragrant and so citrus-sour they are hard to use except for their high pectin content (for jelly-making).

PLANT: Large shrub to small tree has many limbs and branches which remain deep green year-round, all studded with an amazing number of large thorns, often three inches long, which are super sharp and can inflict painful, deep, slow-healing punctures. Leaves are tri-foliate (three leaflets) and leathery, and persist until first frost.

INTERESTING KINDS: 'Flying Dragon' is a more compact form, often used as a "dwarfing" rootstock on which other citrus trees are grafted because it causes the grafted tops to grow more slowly and compactly. 'Flying Dragon' has fantastically gnarly, twisted stems, and even the large thorns are curved around and back—if a gardener ever fell into one, there would be no way to get out intact! I use mine as a striking winter specimen in a small flower bed that needs a little boost when perennials are dormant.

SOIL: Any well-drained soil, acidic or alkaline will do. The plant grows under incredibly poor conditions, including low fertility and extreme drought.

PROPAGATION: Like other citrus, seed taken from fruits in late summer sprout quickly. Cuttings also root very well in midsummer. Leave small trees outside in pots, exposed to normal winter conditions to toughen them up (they can take the cold quite well). Small trees are easy to transplant; moving large hardy orange plants isn't a good idea since a taproot, once cut, will never redevelop, and it's not great for your back either (not to mention the possibility of getting scratched in the process!).

TIP: SPINY PLANTS CAN BE FUN, if you're careful. Stems of hardy orange are excellent for sticking sugar gumballs to for holiday tabletop decorations. A different sort of Easter decoration is colored eggs stuck to yucca leaves; curious neighbors will be intrigued by the strange "flowers!"

Prickly Pear Cactus

Opuntia compressa

Full sun to moderate shade

You don't have to be a sadist to enjoy this native cactus, which is hardy into Canada. It's an unusual texture plant for all seasons, especially in the winter when many perennials are "down" and shrubs are ordinary looking. The plant is so common we often overlook how exotic it is! Its flowers are a pure bonus, and if you're into exotic food, the cooked "pads" are loaded with vitamin C—just what the garden doctor ordered.

FLOWER: Very showy, many-petaled tulip-like tufts to four inches across, usually yellow but occasionally orange or red, appear on upper edges of the pads in late spring and summer, followed by large, purplish red, plum-like fruits that are covered with nearly invisible nettles and filled with seedy, but delicious, sweet pulp. Harvest the fruits (called *tunas* in Mexico) by rolling in newspaper to remove nettles, then peel and eat, being careful of the juice, which stains.

PLANT: Each pad is a thick, flattened stem, usually round but sometimes elongated, growing on the tops and edges of previous ones in an ever-increasing mound. The thorns, by the way, are really the modified leaves, believe it or not! Some varieties are smooth as a baby's bottom, often seen sold in upscale vegetable markets and restaurants as *nopales* (they taste like green beans or asparagus, with an okra-like slickness). Others are so thorny they cannot be handled because they are hard to grip—they "walk" off even thick gloves!

INTERESTING KINDS: Texas prickly pear (*Opuntia lindheimeri*) is a large, clumping cactus with long pads; *O. drummondii* has very small pads, under three inches across and very thorny; tree cholla (*O. imbricata*) is the very cold-hardy walkingstick cactus with tall (six- to eight-foot) cylindrical stems completely covered with thorns and magenta flowers. Also, a "prickle-less" form of prickly pear is showing up in nurseries.

SOIL: Prickly pear's main enemy is standing water, so any well-drained soil is best, including raised mounds, raised beds, containers, and rock gardens (of course). No need to mulch or protect from the cold, and only extremely small amounts of fertilizer are needed every year or two, max.

PROPAGATION: Twist off a pad and set it halfway in a sandy potting soil; roots will grow from the bottom (where it was originally attached), and new growth will appear around upper edges.

TIP: FOOL THE NEIGHBORS into thinking you know what you are doing when using unusual plants. Mix and match strong contrasting shapes, always including at least one that is familiar to help make things look "normal." For example, use prickly pear cactus beside drought-hardy nandina and dwarf golden arborvitae, then throw in two or three soft-tip yuccas. Together they work!

Pyracantha

Pyracantha coccinea

Full sun or light shade

Anyone who has ever had to mow a lawn with a pyracantha nearby knows where it gets the common name "firethorn"—the short but sharp thorns on each arching branch cause an immediate and long-lasting burning dermatitis. But the spring flowers and luscious winter berries make it worth having around, though perhaps in a neighbor's yard.

FLOWER: Tight two-inch clusters of small, white, musky "apple" blossoms appear in mid-spring on very short spurs of the previous year's growth (which is why hard pruning of pyracantha is a "no-no"). Extremely showy, pea-sized apple fruits, which are mealy tasting but perfectly edible, begin to "red up" in the fall and persist through the winter until a hard freeze browns them out or hordes of cedar waxwings or other hungry birds scarf them up.

PLANT: A wild jumble of upright long stems with many short twigs eventually gets to ten or twelve feet or more high and wide, making tight pruning either difficult or time-consuming unless the nearly vine-like shrub is espaliered along wires strung against a wall (in which case only small wayward or cluttered twigs need be removed).

INTERESTING KINDS: Old-fashioned firethorn varieties (*Pyracantha coccinea*) such as 'Lalandei', 'Kasan', and 'Wyattii', while beautiful, are susceptible to fire blight (see Tip below); even the popular Formosa firethorn (*P. koidzumii*, which has a variegated dwarf variety) can get blight, plus it is not cold hardy in the upper or mountain regions of the South. Newer hybrids and cultivars, which are both cold tolerant and fire blight resistant, include 'Fiery Cascade', 'Apache', 'Mohave', 'Teton', and the orange-berried *P. angustifolia* 'Yukon Belle'.

SOIL: Any well-drained soil will do for this vigorous shrub, as long as it does not stand in water more than a couple of hours after a rain. Too much fertilizer, including from the lawn, can cause succulent growth that hides berries and is more susceptible to fire blight and winter injury.

PROPAGATION: Summer cuttings of current season's growth.

TIP: FIRE BLIGHT IS BURNING THE SOUTH, and there isn't a lot to be done about it. The bacterium, which causes twigs and fruit clusters of pyracantha, ornamental pear, and fruiting apples and pears to turn brown like they've been burned, is spread by wild bees to flowers. Fire blight sprays are not cures, and they have to be applied while bees are working freshly opened flowers (the bacteriacide does not harm bees or people). Pruning infected plants usually has a mere cosmetic effect and often spreads the fungus on the pruning shears. Either spray while in bloom or not, then live with the results. Next time choose a blight-resistant variety.

Roses

Rosa species and hybrids

Full sun to very light shade

For too long, the "fancy rose" folks have been pushing us to become great rose **growers**, when all we want is to grow great **roses**. From Texas to the Carolinas, "rose rustlers" have been discovering and propagating (not stealing) the tried and true roses for the South, the "unkillable" ones you see in country gardens and cemeteries. Plant a few of these low-maintenance but high-reward beauties, and they will give you confidence to grow even more.

FLOWER: Colorful pointed buds clasped in tight green calyxes and borne either singly on long stems or in loose masses. Buds open into many petals of red, white, pink, yellow, orange, burgundy, near blue, and nearly every combination; there are singles and doubles, some open flowers remaining tight while others flop open shamelessly, and many are heady with fragrant perfume. Though some old varieties bloom only once in the spring, most continue to flower off and on through the summer and right up to the first frost of autumn. Pruning stems back by a third after flowering will stimulate increased new flowering shoot and bud formation, but many shrubs continue to flower repeatedly with no summer pruning at all.

PLANT: Small compact bushes to tall leggy shrubs and a few multiple-stemmed "vines" which require tying to keep them on trellises or arbors. Most plants have thorny stems and beautiful leaves up to six inches long with five to seven or more oval leaflets each an inch or more long. Foliage is a major concern for rose growers, because a large percentage of roses are highly susceptible to leaf diseases (black spot and powdery mildew) for which even regular fungicide sprays have only moderate success at best; many roses have been bred or selected for disease resistance. Another major chore with roses is annual pruning; while there is plenty of advice on the subject, there really are no rules across the board for pruning roses. Forget all that "fourth of an inch above an outward facing bud" stuff, the general idea is to simply cut all the stems of repeat-blooming shrubs back by halfway or more in the winter to get rid of old or weak growth and to stimulate strong new flowering stems to form in the spring; "once blooming" roses should be pruned after they finish flowering; with climbers, it's a simple matter of thinning older or weak canes and allowing new ones to develop.

INTERESTING KINDS: There are way too many great roses—old and modern, shrub and vine and bush—to be fair about what grows best for you (see Felder's Picks). But in general, there are five main kinds of roses most popular in the South: hybrid tea roses (upright with long stems and pointed buds, most susceptible to diseases); polyantha roses (small to medium bushes with solid masses of small flowers); floribunda roses (larger bushes with masses of larger flower clusters); old garden roses (shrubby and climbing roses that have been around since before the 1860s); and species roses (not hybrids, and have been around forever). There are others, of course, and there are now finally several great Southern rose books out there for your reference.

SOIL: Roses require well-drained soils of moderate fertility. Filling the bed or a wide hole with all the native soil that came out of it, amended with up to about a third that much potting soil, finely chipped bark, compost, or the like, really helps get them off to a good start; just don't overdo it. Organic mulches keep roots cool and moist in the summer (pine straw looks good but doesn't add much to the soil as it decomposes—better to use leaves, maybe top-dressed with pine straw or another more attractive mulch). Occasional deep watering and very light fertilizing at least every two or three years (no more than twice a year) will improve plant vigor and flowering.

PROPAGATION: Stem cuttings taken from mature new growth in the fall and winter, stuck most of the way into garden soil amended with sand or a half-and-half mixture of potting soil and sand. Rooting powders and covering cuttings with bottomless plastic bottles will increase the numbers that root.

TIP: HYBRID TEA ROSES DON'T NEED SPRAYING if you plan on yanking them out of the ground when they start looking bad. If you really like hybrid tea roses but don't want to spray, simply buy two or three new ones every year, then pull up two or three old ones that don't look so hot, rework the soil, and plant the new ones in the old holes. It takes discipline and tough decisions, but works without much fuss. Having companion plants in with roses helps, including liriope, daffodils, mint, daylilies, iris, salvia, and artemisia.

Felder's Picks: Roses Proven to Grow for Decades

My way of thinking is this: Most sane gardeners would be proud to have just a dozen good roses that bloom all the time without any care to speak of. So here are more than a dozen, just a few of the ones I have seen surviving and thriving across the South for many years in very poor rose-growing conditions—in real gardens, sometimes in the poorest parts of town, around neglected old country gardens, and even in cemeteries, all without sprays and a lot of watering, sometimes pruned poorly or not at all. Yet I also see them in upscale landscapes and botanical garden rose displays all over the country. They are a great starting point for building up confidence that anyone can grow America's Floral Emblem. Good climbing roses are listed in the chapter on vines.

'**Bonica**' (pink shrub)
'**Caldwell Pink**' (pink polyantha)
'**Carefree Delight**' (sturdy pink shrub, pictured at left)
'**Cecile Brünner**' (old sweetheart rose)
'**Duchesse de Brabant**' (fragrant shrub)
'**Europeana**' (red floribunda)
'**Heritage**' (the best David Austen rose)
'**La Marne**' (pink compact polyantha, pictured at right)
'**Louis Philippe**' (mauve shrub)
'**Martha Gonzales**' (red old-garden shrub)
'**Mister Lincoln**' (red hybrid tea)
'**Old Blush**' (pink old garden shrub)
Rosa chinensis mutabilis (mixed-color shrub)
'**The Fairy**' (light-pink small polyantha)

177

Spirea
Spiraea species
Sun to moderate shade

With their small, narrow leaves, clusters of tiny blossoms, and arching mounds of wiry stems, spireas are a fine-textured element in the garden, to contrast with more bold textured plants. Some forms have bright chartreuse or yellowish foliage that provides color even when the plant is out of bloom, is a foil for dark green or blue foliaged plants, and can be a shining backdrop for perennial and annual flowers.

FLOWER: Classic "bridal wreath" types have many clusters of small single or double white flowers produced along arching stems from the previous season's growth; the more shrubby pink spireas have broad clusters of pink, white, or red held above the current season's foliage from late spring through summer. Most have a dusty fragrance, not sweet or very noticeable. All spireas perform best when exposed to chilly winters and do better in the middle and upper South than along coastal areas.

PLANT: Durable, long-lived deciduous or semievergreen shrubs from two to six feet tall, tolerant of extreme weather conditions with no fertilizer or supplemental irrigation for decades. Prune spring-flowering bridal wreath spireas after they flower in late spring, and summer-flowering pink spireas in the late winter before new growth gets too far along.

INTERESTING KINDS: Bridal wreaths, in order of blooming: baby's breath (*Spiraea thunbergii*), earliest bloomer with many thin canes of single white flowers, with narrow leaves that turn reddish gold in the fall; true bridal wreath (*S. prunifolia*) flowers soon after baby's breath with clusters of small, tight, button-like, double, white flowers and small oval leaves; Reeves spirea (*S. cantoniensis*), clusters of white flowers surround thin, arching stems as serrated long leaves appear, the double form is 'Lanceolata' or 'Flore Pleno'; and Van Houtte spirea (*S.* × *vanhouttei*), the latest and perhaps most popular, with fairly large (two-inch) flat clusters of small white flowers held above new angular foliage (shaped like a ragged fingernail) at every leaf joint along the stems. Shrubby pink spireas, generally summer-blooming compact bushes, include hybrids and cultivars involving *S. japonica*, such as popular 'Anthony Waterer', 'Gold Mound' (chartreuse foliage), 'Limemound' (lime-green turning gold in the fall), and 'Bumalda'.

SOIL: Any well-drained soil, even tolerates close competition from mature tree roots. A light feeding in the spring helps foliage color. Adding organic matter to the soil at planting time, loosening potting soils, spreading roots, and mulching will get these long-lived shrubs off to a great start.

PROPAGATION: Division of mature plants, or short cuttings made in the fall or winter.

TIP: AZALEAS AREN'T THE ONLY SHOW IN TOWN when you consider how the even tougher spirea, forsythia, camellia, quince, mock orange, snowball, and loropetalum are all flowering around the same time—not to mention vines such as wisteria, trumpet honeysuckle, Carolina jessamine, cross vine, and small redbud and dogwood trees; why put all your eggs in one azalea basket?

Sumac
Rhus species
Full sun, at least half a day

My garden would not be complete without its tall central mound of sumac, planted on the pile of clay that came out of my water garden hole. I dug mine from a rural fencerow, the same kind of sumac cherished in European gardens and increasingly planted as outstanding specimens in modern American landscapes, from naturalistic hillsides to formal containers. And it isn't poisonous (see Tip below)!

FLOWER: Large, almost football-sized, pointed clusters of pale yellow or greenish small flowers held above foliage in late spring, an outstanding pollen or nectar source for bees, butterflies, and hummingbirds. Plants are either male or female; only the female flowers go on to form the fuzzy burgundy-red berries held in tight, triangular clusters above branches like fat fuzzy red candles, which are very showy well into winter.

PLANT: Fast growing, sparsely branched shrubs and small trees that grow in colonies from many suckers, creating a large flat- or rounded-top mound sometimes twenty or more feet high and several yards across in unrestricted areas. Because shoots come up nearly everywhere around, it can be a real chore pulling small plants—attached to roots headed back to the main clump—in the summer. Unbelievably gorgeous fall colors in leaves that are up to two feet long with twenty-one or more narrow, pointed leaflets.

INTERESTING KINDS: Shining sumac (*Rhus copallina*) has shiny leaves with "wings" lengthwise along twigs, good flower and fuzzy fruit clusters; smooth sumac (*R. glabra*) produces superb fruit clusters covered with velvety hairs; twigs of staghorn sumac (*R. typhina*) are covered in fuzzy hairs and include the small cutleaf sumac (*R. typhina* 'Laciniata') that is used by designers in shrub borders and large containers. Fragrant sumac (*R. aromatica*) is a spreading, upright ground cover type with three leaflets—very similar to poison ivy, to which sumac is related.

SOIL: The poorest, driest to be found. Sumac in moist, fertile soil will have poor fall color and get leggy and weak. Plant on top of a pile of hard-packed clay, and walk away from it.

PROPAGATION: Find a colony with good fruit clusters along a roadside near you, and dig (with permission) small trees from the edges, cutting them back to knee-high so they'll branch better.

TIP: POISON SUMAC has stubby foliage and clusters of white berries; it is nearly always found in low, wet, boggy soils, not on dry hillsides like "good" sumacs. If you aren't sure about a plant, clip a branch (carefully, into a trash bag) and take it to a county Extension Service office to send to the university for identification. Or buy the "sure thing" from a nursery.

Sweet Shrub
Calycanthus floridus
Shade or part sun

Before deodorants, ladies would find fragrant flowers and fruits to tuck into their blouses, beginning in mid-spring with the native sweet shrub. The almost generic-looking old-garden favorite, used very easily as an understory shrub or in mixed-shrub borders, adds a lush, upright shape under which ground covers and winter bulbs can really shine after the shrub's leaves turn yellow and fall off. This very popular old "pass-along" was once shared widely, which is a good thing because some of the newer mass-produced clones have less fragrance, meaning the very best kinds are to be had from older gardeners who are always very willing to share.

FLOWER: Loose water-lily-like clutch of narrow maroon petals, up to two inches across, known by older gardeners for their strawberry or over-ripe apple fragrance, produced in mid-spring just as leaves begin to come out (which quickly hide the flowers). Two-inch seedpods are not showy but are fragrant when crushed, revealing reddish brown seeds.

PLANT: Many-stemmed, upright shrub to ten or more feet tall, spreading into wide, multiple-stemmed shrubs or even small colonies with many suckers coming up from the roots. Somewhat sparse leaves are oval and pointed, to five inches long, shiny green with prominent veins, grayish green and slightly fuzzy beneath, and also fragrant when bruised. Fall colors of often golden yellow.

INTERESTING KINDS: 'Athens' is a yellow-flowering variety; California allspice (*Calycanthus occidentalis*) is a close relative that flowers in the late spring and well into summer.

SOIL: Native woodland plant that prefers well-drained woodsy soil, high in organic matter, but tolerates a wide range. Leaf mulch is very beneficial to help keep roots fed with organic matter.

PROPAGATION: Suckers are very easily dug, divided, and replanted in other areas. Seeds sown before the seed coats are rock hard and left outside to stratify, germinate the following spring.

TIP: UNDERSTORY TREES AND SHRUBS ARE OFTEN LACKING in contemporary gardens, in which gardeners try to hang on to their unnatural lawns even in the dense shade of mature trees (which in the long run usually fails, to the dismay of the unprepared). In the natural world, tall trees shade smaller ones, which in turn provide shelter for shrubs and support for vines, in an ever-descending hierarchy of layers. Though many popular understory plants are set out in full sun all by themselves, they typically do best in light shade and rich, woodsy, heavily mulched soils, providing the "walls" of a garden in which trees provide the roof. Great native understory plants for the South include sweet shrub, redbud, buckeye, dogwood, silverbell, yaupon holly, cherry laurel, wax myrtle; imported understory plants include privet, azaleas, and Japanese maples.

Weigela

Weigela florida

Sun or light shade

Some old-fashioned shrubs just won't fade away, including weigela, of which new cultivars are currently being developed in both North America and Europe for their "bridge" effect of flowering after azaleas and before crape myrtles. Easy to root and easy to prune once a year and then forget—until late spring flowers knock your socks off.

FLOWER: Narrow trumpet flowers an inch and a half or more long in loose clusters of deep-red, rose, lavender, pink, or white in mid- to late spring, with a few flower clusters appearing through the summer. The clusters appear at leaf joints all along the branches about the same time as the foliage, often weighing branches to the ground as if to show off the flowers. Outstanding hummingbird shrub.

PLANT: Arching branches arising from a central clump give this deciduous shrub a fountain-like effect up to six or eight feet tall or more (there are dwarf varieties also) and wider than tall. Narrow, oval leaves up to four inches long appear in pairs, dark green or even variegated with pale yellow or creamy white. Prune after flowering to preserve its fountain effect by cutting the entire shrub back to a foot or two from the ground so new shoots can arch back out undisturbed until the next spring's floral display, or selectively thin older canes and leave others to fill out as they will. Main thing is, don't shear weigela.

INTERESTING KINDS: 'Bristol Ruby' (ruby red), 'Bristol Snowflake' (white), 'Java Red', 'Variegata' (variegated leaves, rosy red flowers), 'Candida' (white tinged with green), 'Pink Delight' (compact shrub with deep-pink flowers), and 'Minuet' (dwarf variety to around three feet high with purplish foliage and flowers of red, purple, and yellow).

SOIL: Any well-drained soil, but prefers a good loamy soil for best foliage and flower color, and moderate fertility.

PROPAGATION: Roots very easily from dormant twigs taken in the late fall or winter or from softwood cuttings in the summer stuck in well-drained flower bed soil or a half-and-half mix of potting soil and sand. Layer by bending and looping a section of a long cane into the soil with the tip coming back out, held in place over the summer with a rock.

TIP: UNDERPLANT DECIDUOUS SHRUBS WITH BULBS, which get the sunlight they need in the winter and are dormant in the summer when shrubs are leafed out. Good bulbs for winter foliage and spring flowers include grape hyacinth, early-flowering daffodils, snowflake, painted arum, and even summer-flowering *Lycoris* (spider lily and naked ladies).

Yucca
Yucca species
Full sun to light shade

Yuccas have a bad rep—just because someone lost a beach ball to one. Truth is, soft-tipped varieties are neither dangerous nor invasive. Their bold forms and striking flowers are useful accents for architectural or tropical effects, plus they simply grow in tight, dry, sloped spots where not much else will, while contrasting well with other traditional Southern plants.

FLOWER: Tall tree-like panicles of two- to three-inch-wide white bells from spring to late summer depending on the species. Flower stalks arise from the center of each plant; there can be as many flower stalks as there are crowns in each clump. Very showy, slightly fragrant, and edible.

PLANT: Spreading rosettes of slender, sword-like leaves up to two and a half or more feet long with extremely sharp tips, often growing on tall trunks but some with thick mounding clumps of many rosettes. Slow-growing at first, they usually become quite solid and hard to get rid of—digging them completely out, or even burying them, often only slows them down. Tolerant of prolonged dry spells, they also tolerate normal rainfall, most hardy kinds being native to the Southeast.

INTERESTING KINDS: Mound-lily, often called Spanish dagger or soft-tip yucca (*Yucca gloriosa*), is one of the easiest to work with in landscapes, being nearly stemless and clump-forming, with somewhat flexible, soft foliage less likely to stab; 'Garland's Gold' has a yellow stripe down the center of each leaf and 'Variegata' has yellow markings. The smaller *Y. filifera* (*Y. flaccida*) also has soft foliage, with distinct thread-like fibers trailing from leaf edges, widely planted for its hardiness, tidy growth, and late-spring to early-summer flowers. The stiff-leaved Adam's needle (*Y. filamentosa*) has several cultivars, including 'Bright Edge' with yellow edges and 'Variegata' with cream-edged leaves that turn pinkish in winter. Spanish bayonet (*Y. aloifolia*) is an upright or sprawling multirosette plant with trunks ten feet or more tall with extremely stiff, sharp foliage that poses a real danger to pedestrians and beach balls. There are several other species similar to these, and several coastal and subtropical species for container culture.

SOIL: Any well-drained, dry soil with moderate to low fertility.

PROPAGATION: Division of clumps, or bury root sections of stems in sandy soil.

TIP: XERISCAPE IS NOT A DRY WORD when it comes to low-maintenance gardening. Far from being all rocks and yucca, it simply means designing and planting with rainfall in mind. Smaller lawn areas, more mulches and ground covers, groups of hardy trees underplanted with tough shrubs and old-time perennials. It's common sense gardening, without the pop-up sprinklers; choosing and using plants that have proven themselves to be hardy on rainfall alone for many decades and still look good—that's xeriscaping.

Other Great Shrubs:

I wish I could highlight them all, because they are all-time favorites to me and literally millions of other gardeners. But the following woody plants all share one problem: They are not universally tough, for one reason or another. If you can find them, give them a try anyway, and some may outlive your great-grandchildren.

Aucuba (*Aucuba japonica*) is an outstanding evergreen for deep shade; large oval pointed leaves often spotted with gold. It will burn in even winter sun and can freeze in the upper South.

Blueberry (*Vaccinium* species) includes medium to large deciduous shrubs with many suckers, delicate pinkish white spring flowers, showy summer fruit, and outstanding red fall colors. Sun or light shade; needs azalea-like soil preparation and occasional deep summer soakings.

Butterfly Bush (*Buddleja davidii*) features thick panicles of attractive flowers all summer; needs annual pruning like roses and regular deadheading for new flower production.

Chinese Photinia (*Photinia serratifolia*), a large roundish evergreen shrub, has bronze new foliage and huge round plate-like clusters of white flowers in the spring, red berries in fall.

Chinese Winter Hazel (*Loropetalum chinense*) (pictured) is a many-branched shrub with green or burgundy foliage and lots of white, pink, or burgundy flowers mostly in the spring; some cultivars are very showy and long flowering. Needs well-drained soil.

Cotoneaster (*Cotoneaster* species) is a spreading, small, branchy shrub or sprawling ground cover with long-lasting berries in fall and winter; too dense to weed, too thin not to. Good for rockeries or raised beds.

Elderberry (*Sambucus canadensis*) is a large, spreading, semiwoody herbaceous shrub with dinner-plate sized masses of white flowers in early summer and large heads of purple fall berries that birds love.

Fatsia (*Fatsia japonica*) has large, several-pointed evergreen leaves and is an outstanding texture plant. Must have year-round, even dense, shade and often gets frozen to the ground (but survives).

Fig (*Ficus carica*) is a huge, many-trunked deciduous shrub or small tree with large, sandpapery, coarse leaves and summer fruits for birds and sometimes people. Often gets winter damage.

Flowering Almond (*Prunus glandulosa*) is a small multistemmed deciduous shrub not notable except when covered with small, single or double, pink or white flowers in late winter. Very tough and showy!

Florida Anise (*Illicium floridanum*) is a native evergreen with thick, glossy leaves, a spicy anise fragrance, and interesting golf ball-sized red or white spring flowers. Best for damp shade but tolerates sun.

Florida Jasmine (*Jasminum floridum*) is an evergreen arching ground cover with showy late-winter yellow flowers. Not always cold hardy in upper South.

Gardenia (*Gardenia augusta*) is a popular old deciduous shrub with many varieties. Very glossy leaves and super-intensely fragrant white summer flowers. Not reliably hardy, suffers from white flies and mealybugs.

Indian Hawthorn (*Rhaphiolepis* species) is an evergreen shrub with showy mid- to late-spring flowers in full sun. Often suffers from diseased foliage or root rot, and winterkill in the middle South.

Japanese Snowball (*Viburnum macrocephalum*) is a very hardy, large deciduous shrub with huge round heads of white flowers blooming in mid-spring at the same time as azaleas.

Leucothoe (*Leucothoe* species) is a native evergreen with arching, drooping branches of glossy narrow leaves (often with a bronzy winter tinge) and clusters of urn-shaped white flowers in spring. Best as masses or screens in woodland gardens.

Mountain Laurel (*Kalmia latifolia*) is an interesting native small tree with showy clusters of colorful open trumpets in early summer. Requires azalea conditions and light shade.

Palmetto (*Sabal* species) features giant "palm" leaves on long stalks from short trunks, very wide and coarse. Tolerates shade or sun, moisture or drought, and any soil. Super hardy but hard to find.

Photinia (*Photinia* species) is a large shrub; some types have reddish new foliage (*P. fraseri*, *P. glabra*) and good flower clusters; often used as hedges but highly susceptible to leaf diseases and winter cold damage.

Pomegranate (*Punica granatum*) is a medium-sized deciduous shrub with many stems, showy ruffled orange-red summer flowers, and baseball-sized fall fruit. May suffer winter damage.

Sago (*Cycas revoluta*) is an ancient palm-like specimen with dark-green feather-like leaves to three feet long and a foot wide. Very showy specimen, best kept in a container (so it can be moved indoors) in areas where low temperatures in the teens are expected.

Strawberry Bush (*Euonymus americanus*) is a woodland native with sparse solid green branches and showy winter fruits of orange and red. Outstanding for shade.

Summersweet (*Clethra alnifolia*) is a native shrub with racemes of fragrant flowers; for moist, woodsy conditions.

Sweet Olive (*Osmanthus fragrans*) is an old-garden evergreen with small clusters of extremely fragrant white flowers in leaf axils in fall and winter. Often gets winter damage in upper South.

Tree Huckleberry or **Farkleberry** (*Vaccinium arboreum*), a loose, upright woodland native, has small black edible berries in the fall and winter. Outstanding fall red colors and interesting winter form.

Birds Love Shrubs

Not only do shrubs provide texture, flowers, and fragrance for our gardens, they also make terrific perching, feeding, and nesting sites for native birds. Anything evergreen or with berries is a plus, but the real key to providing

good wildlife habitat is **diversity**—special attention needs to be given to planting something for all seasons, because, after all, our native wildlife is out there all year, not just in the seasons convenient to humans.

Shrubs with good bird fruits include mahonia, nandina, pyracantha, holly, beautyberry (pictured), elaeagnus, ligustrum, prickly pear cactus, and sumac. Shrubs which make good cover include abelia, arborvitae, camellia, cleyera, elaeagnus, hollies, ligustrum, and cedar.

CORKSCREW PLANTS with gnarly, twisted trunks are often used as novelty accents, most effectively when placed against a backdrop of solid green evergreens such as magnolia or cedar, or against a building or fence. They can easily be highlighted with under-plantings of dwarf spring-

flowering bulbs such as grape hyacinth and 'Tête-à-Tête' daffodils. Very long-lived, small to medium sized flower bed shrubs with contorted trunks and stems include corkscrew hazel (*Corylus avellana* 'Contorta', pictured, sometimes called Harry Lauder's walking stick after an old Vaudeville entertainer), corkscrew flowering quince (*Chaenomeles* 'Contorta', with white or pink late winter flowers), and 'Flying Dragon' hardy orange (*Poncirus trifoliata* 'Flying Dragon', with extremely thorny, twisted stems).

Landscaping for Winter Interest

During what Southern garden writer Elizabeth Lawrence called our "two months of winter" we often find our landscapes and gardens bare of color and texture. Here are a few ways to spice up this otherwise dreary season.

■ Make sure weeds and frost-damaged perennials (ferns, lantana, cannas, etc.) are cut and composted, the lawn edged, and the garden raked free of leaf clutter. Clean up the garden, remove stakes, generally neaten stuff up.

■ Replace summer annuals with winter annuals such as pansies and violas, sweet Williams, ornamental cabbage and kale, and even colorful winter salad greens. The winter foliage texture of ornamental grasses, and perennials such as yarrow, iris, dianthus, and spring bulbs, looks great, too.

■ Add interesting shrubs and small trees for winter color, texture, and berries, including nandina, soft-tip yucca, pyracantha, crape myrtle (especially 'Natchez' for its mottled bark), palmetto, aucuba, mahonia, and many more. Break up lines of shrubs with plants having contrasting leaf shapes and foliage color.

■ Add winter-flowering shrubs such as *Camellia sasanqua* (blooms in fall and early winter), *Camellia japonica* (winter and early spring flowers), winter honeysuckle, flowering quince, mahonia, forsythia, spirea, and flowering almond.

■ Place a "hard feature" in the landscape, such as a large rock, birdbath, sculpture, urn, or even a trellis, gate, or small section of fence (split rail, picket, whatever suits your style).

■ Enlarge small plantings by working up the soil in a wide curve or other shape, and cover with mulch (pine straw or shredded bark), which gives instant good looks until you get around to planting more. Add a few sections of liriope or mondo grass as edging to give extra definition of the bed.

■ Plant bulbs and other perennials (store-bought or divided from your own garden) by mid-October to give them time to get settled in before winter rains and cold weather set in.

■ Overstuff a large pot on a sunny porch with several cold-hardy plants, including winter annuals, bulbs, cascading ground covers, small "textury" shrubs, etc. Group several indoor potted plants together near a window for a tropical touch (putting plants close to each other creates a humid zone and helps them cope with the low humidity of a typical house in winter).

■ Install and position low-voltage night lighting to illuminate steps without blinding visitors.

■ Set up a simple platform-type bird feeding station, stocked with black-oil sunflower seed. And cut the squirrels some slack—they're wildlife, too.

STOUTHEARTED
Trees

Walk away from your garden and, within a few short years, the entire place will become a shaded woodland. Because of our soils and climate, trees, vines, and large shrubs are the "climax species" in the Southern landscape, started from seeds spread by wind, birds, and other animals, and quickly growing large enough to shade out the "meadow" plants we call flowers.

Because they are so dramatic in size and effect, trees provide the most important landscape framework for your garden, apart from your home and other structures; they are the "walls" and "ceiling" where shrubs are the furniture, and flowers the knick-knacks. Trees enclose and cool, and they provide nesting places and food for wildlife. They capture the sound and motion of the wind and deliver color, texture, line, mass, and lots of other design goodies.

The selection of those which are super easy to grow and enjoy is astounding. Whether you choose tall or short, evergreen or bare in the winter, flowers or foliage, spring blooms or fall colors, there are kinds—and varieties within each kind—to suit every need and season.

This chapter deals with only a few of the very toughest that are planted in flower-garden-type landscapes. Most make fine specimen or stand-out trees because of their flowers or foliage. Some are easy to work into existing beds; others make good shade for more tender plants, and several are excellent "understory" or "in between" plants—taller than flowers, shorter than other trees.

It's an oddball fact, but a small tree will outgrow a larger tree of the same species if planted concurrently, nearly every time. I've watched this happen for many, many years now. This is because a smaller tree has a higher proportion of roots to top, so it doesn't waste time trying to play catch-up, as does the larger tree, which spends months just sitting there trying to stay alive as it builds its root system to accommodate its branches and foliage. Choosing a tree that is smaller can be important both for your wallet and your back, and it will help determine how quickly the tree will get established and begin growing.

Even if you plant small specimens, keep in mind that trees need elbow room to grow. Small ones can fill a void beneath other larger trees with their spreading branches and roots. It is best to include only very small tree species in new flower beds, and to wait until larger kinds are established before planting shade perennials and ground covers underneath. Meanwhile, nothing beats a clean layer of natural mulch to make trees "look right" while protecting the new roots from hot summer sun, cold winter nights, and attacks from lawn mowers and string trimmers. Plus, as leaves and bark decompose, they feed the soil around tree roots in a most natural way (it's how things have worked in the forest for a long, long time).

Protect Your Trees

A tree's worst fear is being hit by a lawn mower or string trimmer. Even one good cut on tender bark can interfere with food movement from leaves to

roots, which starves the roots and causes the tree to suffer for years to come. Meanwhile, it also introduces dirt and contaminants that can cause long-term heart rot. You get the picture.

Prevent this number-one cause of tree death by mulching around the base (in a ring around the area, not a mound up on the trunk) and edging the planting hole with bricks, rocks, or other ornate shield. Or plant a ground cover such as liriope. Keep in mind that two or more trees can be "connected" at their bases by a large mulched area, in which small shade-loving shrubs or perennials such as ferns, hosta, monkey grass, or ajuga can be planted. The whole area will take on a more "finished" look.

Getting Trees in the Ground

Soil preparation for trees is not nearly as complicated as some horticulturists make it seem. To encourage their roots to roam far and wide to access water and food, trees need to get adjusted to their new home quickly; in fact, when planting new trees around Habitat for Humanity homes, I rarely add anything at all to the native soil—no matter how hard the clay. Here are a few quick planting tips for trees:

- Dig a **wide** hole, not a deep one, chopping grooves into the sides and bottom of the hole.
- Loosen tree roots from potting soil, and mix the potting soil with the native soil.
- For balled-and-burlapped trees, remove any wire and as much burlap as possible.
- Set the tree so its original soil line is even with or barely higher than the soil around it.
- Fill in around roots with original soil (with the potting soil mixed in).
- Water thoroughly.
- Cover the planting area with leaves, bark, or other natural mulch.
- Water subsequently only when very, very dry—keeping a tree too wet will cause root rot.

After-planting care for trees is about as easy as it gets. Five or six good soakings the first summer, one or two the next year, and the trees should make it on their own for decades after that. In general, little or no fertilizer is needed the first year a tree is planted, because it really needs to get its roots established before putting on a lot of top growth. A little "root stimulator" can help, but don't push a new tree too much—let it get rooted, and it will really "jump" the next year. Any fertilizer given to nearby flowers or lawn will generally take care of the tree's needs, as well.

To Prune, or Not to Prune?

When should a tree be cut? Forget what you've been told, and think like a tree. If there are dead or broken limbs or branches, or one or more are getting in your way or shading a plant too much, then by all means remove them—any time of the year—leaving no stubs. That is, cut nearly flush right where the limb or branch is attached, just to the outside of the growth "collar" at the base of the branch; otherwise, rot may get into the stub before it heals. If you cut off the collar, the tree will have a much harder time healing over the cut.

If you want to "limb up" a tree to allow more sunlight or a better view, do a few branches a year, leaving some here and there for a natural shape instead of zipping straight up the trunk leaving a "top knot" effect.

If you just want to "thin out" some cluttered or competing branches, it makes little difference to the plant which ones go and which stay.

If you want to "bob it back" like a shrub, most experts—and I—recommend that you get a poodle dog instead and leave the tree alone.

And by the way, "pruning paints" are purely cosmetic and have no effect on how fast a cut heals or whether or not insects and fungi get into the cut area. Use them only for approval from a spouse or neighbor.

AN INSTANT TREE IS EASIER THAN YOU'D THINK—if you think about how easy a large deck umbrella can be. One large-diameter post—at least ten feet high—set into the ground, then planted with a vine, can create the same effect as a "real" tree. Setting up a two-post arbor—again, at least ten feet high, using six by six posts instead of cheap four by four's—is only a little more expensive, with nearly twice the appeal. See the vines chapter for more ideas.

 Best for Beginners:

- Crape Myrtle
- Bradford Pear (specimen)
- Lilac Chaste Tree
- 'Little Gem' Magnolia
- Redbud

- Cedar
- Tree Hollies
- Bald Cypress
- River Birch

Kinda Tricky:

- Oriental Magnolias
- Bradford Pears (in long rows)
- Dogwood
- Fruit Trees (peaches, plums, pecans)

- Leyland Cypress
- Wax Myrtle
- any tree that gets its trunk hit with a lawn mower

Go Native

Many great trees are native to the Southeast.
Below are a few suitable for general landscape use:

LARGE:

- American Holly
- Bald Cypress
- Eastern Red Cedar
- Ginkgo
- Persimmon
- Red Maple

- River Birch
- Southern, Big-Leaf, and Cucumber Magnolias
- Tulip Poplar
- Willow, Water, and Live Oaks

SMALL:

- Dogwood (tricky to get established)
- Grancy Greybeard
- Magnolia 'Little Gem'
- Parsley Hawthorn
- Pawpaw (pictured above)
- Possum Haw
- Red and Bottlebrush Buckeyes
- Redbud

- Serviceberry
- Silverbell
- Smoke Tree
- Spicebush
- Sweet Bay Magnolia
- Wax Myrtle
- Wild Plum
- Witch-Hazel
- Yellow-Wood

Crape Myrtle

Lagerstroemia indica

Full sun to light shade

Who needs Northern lilacs when we have the most incredible flowering shrub in the country in every cemetery in the South? Crape myrtles are glorious in bloom or even in mid-winter, especially if planted near a magnolia or surrounded with nandina or silvery gray artemisia for contrast.

FLOWER: Large, loose, football-sized panicles of crinkled white, red, pink, lavender, or striped flowers are showy from early summer to frost; flowering is always best in the full sun. Clusters of round seedpods appear after flowering, and remain through the winter; some gardeners love them, others snip them off. Birds do eat the seeds.

PLANT: Upright to round shrubs or small trees, usually with multiple trunks and many branches, with oval leaves up to two inches or more long; leaves often have outstanding red, orange, or yellow fall colors until frost. Trunks are very showy and "architectural" even in the winter; most are light brown or taupe, and some have attractive cinnamon blotches. Pruning is usually not necessary except to thin out clutter or dead limbs.

INTERESTING KINDS: The best "old garden" crape myrtles would have to be 'William Toovey' (deep watermelon red) and 'Near East' (light pink, poor cold tolerance in the upper South). Other good ones with good cold tolerance include 'Regal Red', 'Catawba' (dark purple), 'Centennial' (dwarf, dark purple), 'Centennial Spirit' (dark wine red), and 'Potomac' (clear pink).

Traditional crape myrtles have been crossed with the tall, strongly upright, mottled-bark Japanese crape myrtle (*L. fauriei*) for some very showy hybrids which are generally mildew resistant and cold hardy. Most have Native American tribe names, including 'Acoma' (white), 'Biloxi' (light pink), 'Cherokee' (red), 'Hopi' (medium pink), 'Muskogee' (light lavender), 'Natchez' (white), 'Osage' (clear light pink), 'Tuskegee' (dark pink), 'Yuma', and 'Zuni' (both medium lavender). There are a lot of others in the commercial trade, including some dwarf varieties with "Southern" names ('Lafayette', 'Mardi Gras', 'Baton Rouge', 'New Orleans', and 'Delta Blush'); feel lucky if you can find them properly named! Other good small varieties are 'Chickasaw', 'Pocomoke', 'Sacramento', 'Houston', and 'World's Fair'.

SOIL: Any well-drained soil, moist or dry, sand or clay, with or without fertility.

PROPAGATION: Foot-long stem cuttings taken in the late fall through mid-winter, inserted in sandy soil and left to root over the first summer. Seedlings can be dug from flower beds.

TIP: "CRAPE MURDER" IS NOT NECESSARY to have attractive flowers. In late winter, simply thin out unwanted trunks near the ground or cluttered limbs at their point of origin, then lightly snip back last year's twigs about halfway. No need to butcher any more than that! Light pruning (to pencil-thick growth) in midsummer can promote a more luscious fall spectacle.

Cut-Leaf Lilac
Syringa × *laciniata*
Full sun or part shade

Hate to not even mention a lilac, even if it is one of the four most difficult plants for mid- to lower-South gardeners (the others being most of the popular peonies, English lavender, and Texas bluebonnets). But lilac is so popular, and so hardy in the North, that I must share some information about a particular one that does fairly well for us. Cut-leaf lilac is not the same as the huge standard lilac (*Syringa vulgaris*, "vulgaris" meaning "common"), but at least it flowers—and has fragrance. It can be worked into the back of a bed where it doesn't detract from other plants. And it does smell good—when rains don't ruin its flowers. How is **that** for faint praise?

FLOWER: Many clusters of lilac-colored flowers are not very large, but they are produced, and are even fragrant, throughout all parts of our region—even in the lower and coastal South.

PLANT: The small, open tree is of no particular interest most of the year, except for deep-green, parsley-like foliage.

INTERESTING KINDS: There are a few lilacs that are smaller and more shrubby that can work in the South as well. *Syringa meyeri* gets four or more feet tall with violet flowers; its cultivar 'Palibin' is a more compact form. The similar *S. patula* is nine feet high or more, with fragrant lavender flowers; it, too, has a smaller cultivar, called 'Miss Kim', which is three feet tall and wide, with purple buds opening to pale blue flowers.

SOIL: Lilacs require well-drained soils that are neutral or slightly alkaline. If your soil is acidic, work limestone into a wide planting hole and scatter more around the outer edges of the plant's root system every three or four years.

PROPAGATION: Lilacs generally root fairly easily from stem cuttings taken in the fall or winter, stuck directly into well-prepared garden soil as with rose cuttings.

TIP: LILACS DON'T DO "SOUTH" VERY WELL— at least most don't. Whenever someone disputes this general observation, the plant nearly always turns out to be small, scraggly, sparsely flowering, and only faintly fragrant. I can understand Americans wanting to "make" something work (whether or not it makes sense), and the horticulturist in me says, "Here's how we can give it a try, by modifying all sorts of conditions." But the **gardener** in me wonders why we insist on trying borderline plants from another region when we have stuff that other folks in other parts of our huge country would all but kill for in their own gardens?

Anyway, lilacs generally do best where there are colder winters than we have and prefer to stay cold all winter as opposed to our fickle ups and downs. And they suffer severely from long, hot, humid summer nights in the South. Best to give them a try in well-drained soil on the north side of a building for protection from winter sun, and then hope it cools down at night in August.

Or just grow gardenias.

Ginkgo
Ginkgo biloba
Full sun

The maidenhair tree is a bona fide antique—perfect leaf fossils date it back to dinosaur days. The ones I remember from my childhood hometown were stately old trees with deep, chocolate-brown bark that contrasted starkly with the breathtakingly brilliant yellow-gold fall leaves. The ones I studied during my college horticulture days were ill smelling because of fetid decaying fruit.

FLOWER: Small flowers are borne in spring on short catkins or stalks. Trees are either male or female; if you have a choice, you definitely want a male. Female trees produce round, messy, smelly "fruits" (actually not true fruits but naked seeds).

PLANT: The tall, single-trunked tree is so slow growing (a foot or two a year is about all you can expect) it can be a good addition to even a small garden for many, many years. Its bark is fissured and dark brown. Its leaves, each of which is fan-shaped like an oversized leaflet from a maidenhair fern, often with one deep slit, are medium-green and leathery. Fall color comes with a whoosh, as the tree turns solid yellow all at once. The leaves persist for a week or two or more, but then fall suddenly into a yellow carpet beneath the tree.

INTERESTING KINDS: Ginkgo trees are separate male and female, with only the female producing foul-smelling fruits; most named varieties are male selections, with predictable shapes and growth habits. 'Autumn Gold' is a tall, upright "tree" shape; 'Saratoga' is rounded, with deeply slit leaves that droop; 'Princeton Sentry' has a taller, more narrow shape; there are many others.

SOIL: Any deep, loose, well-drained soil, alkaline or acidic, will grow great ginkgos; excess fertilizer or irrigation can reduce the fall color impact by making plants too succulent.

PROPAGATION: Seedling variation is too much of a gamble—you won't know if you're getting a male or female plant; best to graft or even take root cuttings from mature trees in early to midsummer (semihardwood cuttings).

TIP: WHAT MAKES FALL COLORS SO BRILLIANT on some trees and not on others? It depends largely on the health and vigor of a plant, soil type, moisture conditions, and fertility. A plant grown on the "lean" side generally has better fall color because its nutrients—the ones used in its leaves—get used up as leaves begin to shut down for the fall and winter. A plant grown in rich soil and lots of moisture will be more "succulent," will not readily prepare for winter, and will not "harden off" as well as one grown in tougher conditions.

By the way, all those colors—the reds, purples, scarlets, golds, and yellows—are there all year, only "covered up" by the hard-working green chlorophyll. As photosynthesis shuts down and the green gets used up, the other colors begin to show. Anything that slows this process promotes good fall colors; a sudden frost or prolonged wet or dry spell ruins the show.

Grancy Graybeard
Chionanthus virginicus
Full sun or shade

What would compel a grown man from Memphis, Tennessee, to scatter seed of a native tree across the countryside from the window of his private airplane, as he travels around the South on business? Nothing else seems to be in bloom when "old man's beard" or fringe tree turns itself on as a pure white spotlight in the landscape. This small tree gets more comments from gardeners than nearly any other plant because it is so lacy and stunning at a time when most spring trees have faded from bloom and summer plants have yet to kick in. On top of all this, graybeards are extremely tolerant of urban air pollution, making them tidy street trees when not overlooked in favor of more trendy plants. Yet they are difficult to locate in "garden variety" garden centers—hence the man who sows seed from the air.

FLOWER: When in late-spring bloom, each tree becomes a spectacular, solid mass of slightly fragrant, white, fringe-like flowers, each with four slender petals, held in showy, lacy clusters of four inches or longer. Plants are either male or female, but both are showy; if both are present, the female will produce small, dark fruits that are very attractive to birds.

PLANT: Upright, somewhat generic, shrubby-looking tree, not very distinctive, with glossy green, pointed oval leaves that have deep or bright-yellow fall colors. Highly variable in shape due to genetics.

INTERESTING KINDS: The native Southern fringe tree, sometimes called "old man's beard," is good enough to have just on its own. But the Chinese fringe tree (*Chionanthus retusus*) is more shrub-like, with smaller flower clusters, which bloom earlier and look like white lilacs. Its furrowed bark is gray-brown, almost golden on new stems, and provides winter interest.

SOIL: Grancy graybeard tolerates any well-drained soil, including rocky outcroppings and other poor, dry conditions. Tolerates competition from other trees nearby but also holds its own out in the middle of a lawn.

PROPAGATION: Very slow from seed, usually a minimum of two years from when they are sown (the man in the airplane grows them by the dozens in pots, left outdoors for two winters and two summers). Can be layered, but usually they are just bought as seedlings from progressive garden centers.

TIP: BY ITSELF, A GRANCY GRAYBEARD is a handsome specimen tree; when surrounded with contrasting foliage plants, especially those tolerating dry conditions such as artemisia, iris, or dwarf nandina, the plant becomes a "mother hen," providing midday shade. A "wrap-around" seat can be just the elegant touch this sometimes-stark tree needs during the winter or summer.

Lilac Chaste Tree

Vitex agnus-castus

Full sun or very light shade

Vitex is an old-garden plant that is making a huge comeback as a large border shrub or even a specimen plant when limbed up near a patio or along a sidewalk. It's my mom's favorite non-rose summer flowering tree, but raises eyebrows in my little cottage garden (see Tip below).

FLOWER: Dense, upright panicles to nearly a foot long crusted with small blue, lavender, pink, or white flowers, produced from late spring into midsummer or later, which are slightly fragrant and covered with butterflies, bees, and hummingbirds. A striking show in midsummer, especially when cool blue is such a hard color to come by. Light tip pruning after the main flower flush may yield new flowering growth, but most gardeners simply let the large shrubs go to seed; the narrow spikes of dark, round seedheads are somewhat weedy looking to some, but give the plant a fine texture.

PLANT: Small rounded, umbrella-like tree or large shrub, multi-trunked with grayish brown bark and many branches of dense twigs, which can become a litter problem as they fall. Aromatic leaves (used in ancient times as an herbal treatment) have five to seven narrow leaflets arranged in a hand shape—almost exactly like marijuana, for those who notice such things—and are dark green above, silvery gray underneath, which makes an interesting shimmer when the wind blows. Pruning is mostly limited to removing lower limbs and thinning cluttered and downward-facing branches and twigs to promote an upright growth habit (the easier to walk or sit under). The medium density of the tree's shade makes it possible to grow ground covers and a few perennials such as purple coneflower, artemisia, or even daylilies beneath to accentuate the multiple stems of the vitex.

INTERESTING KINDS: *Vitex agnus-castus* forma *latifolia* is large and cold hardy, but not as flowery as 'Abbeville Blue' or 'Rosea', which are to me much more attractive than either of the two common white varieties *V. agnus-castus* forma *alba* and 'Silver Spire'. Others are available from mail order and Internet nurseries, but watch out for *V. trifolia*, which is hardy only in the lower South. *Vitex negundo* has more delicate, toothed foliage and is hardy to the upper South.

SOIL: Any well-drained soil, although flowering seems to be best in fairly dry or poor soils similar to the tree's Mediterranean origins.

PROPAGATION: Easy from seed sown outdoors in the fall or from foot-long cuttings taken in late fall or winter.

TIP: JUST SAY NO TO PLANTS that look "druggie" in the garden—chaste tree, cleome, and Texas star hibiscus all have leaves that look somewhat like marijuana, which may not cause visits from the local constabulary, but can certainly gets second looks from casual visitors. If that makes you nervous, don't attract unwanted attention by using these plants, although you might find it provides occasions to "talk gardening" with curious neighbors.

Magnolia
Magnolia grandiflora 'Little Gem'
Full sun or moderate shade

Anyone who hates magnolias has a real problem with living in the South. The biggest two complaints are the size of the trees and the quantity of leaf litter—both solved by the compact, nearly dwarf 'Little Gem', which is the longest-flowering magnolia ever.

FLOWER: Tulip-shaped white buds open into fragrant bowls of pure white with yellow stamens in late spring and summer, even into fall. Seeds are showy red berry-like fruits emerging from bristly pods.

PLANT: Upright, narrow, evergreen shrub to fifteen feet or more with foliage that is deep glossy green above and fuzzy brown underneath. New growth from spring to fall covers the older foliage, which may turn bright yellow before shedding; leaf litter may be a problem around walks or patios, but is easily cleaned up, or better yet, hidden when the tree is underplanted with liriope. 'Little Gem' makes a superb container specimen, choice "textury" companion to other shrubs, and even a nice flowering hedge when planted six or eight feet apart.

INTERESTING KINDS: Other great small magnolias for flower garden use include other compact cultivars of the "regular" Southern magnolia, such as 'Saint Mary', 'Victoria', and the very cold-hardy 'Edith Bogue' and 'Bracken's Brown Beauty'. A small magnolia that fits into ordinary-sized landscapes is sweet bay magnolia (*Magnolia virginiana*), a tall but narrow, smaller-leaved, semi-evergreen tree with aromatic foliage and mid-spring flowers, good for large tubs or as an understory tree. Larger, deciduous relatives (all native to the U.S.) with large leaves, less obvious but still fragrant flowers, and wide spreading branches include big-leaf magnolia (M. *macrophylla*), cucumber tree (M. *acuminata*), and umbrella tree (M. *tripetala*). Cultivars of cucumber tree, such as 'Miss Honeybee', have smaller, creamy yellow flowers.

SOIL: Any well-drained soil, even heavy clay if amended slightly with organic matter to help new side roots spread quickly. Mulch to keep roots cool. An occasional deep soaking—no more than every three or four weeks—will keep in-ground magnolias going strong without harming roots.

PROPAGATION: Best to buy new grafted plants (which flower the first year you set them out) as needed. Hard to root, very slow from seed, and grafting is a lost art with most gardeners.

TIP: DON'T BE STINGY WITH SPACE when adding some native magnolia species to your landscape. Unless you're planting a smaller type such as sweet bay or 'Little Gem', give them plenty of elbowroom. A big-leaf magnolia can grow up to forty feet tall and half that wide, with leaves almost three feet long. But don't let their size scare you off—they make spectacular, structural statements in a large lawn area. And when it's sporting its full complement of giant leaves, everyone will want to know what that tree is!

Oriental Magnolia

Magnolia species
Sun or light shade

It seems like the blooming of "tulip" magnolias, which include several different species of deciduous trees of Oriental origin, actually **causes** a freeze; warm spells in mid-winter make the summer-generic trees erupt into huge splashes of pink, purple, or white blossoms, most larger than your hand. Then, even though the trees are winter-hardy up to the Great Lakes, a frost invariably knocks off the flowers or browns them out. Happens nearly every year. Still, their Mardi Gras exuberance usually brings spring into the heart and mind; their spectacle makes them worth the risk.

FLOWER: Each stem tip has several large, fuzzy, showy, pointed buds that open into bowl-shaped saucers or pompoms of white petals, each up to six or more inches across. Depending on the cultivar, flowers can be pink, rose, purplish, or white, with creamy-white to pale pink centers. They are often highly fragrant, which is much more pronounced on warm, humid days.

PLANT: Single- or multi-trunk trees with upright branching can eventually get fairly large, up to thirty feet tall and half that wide. In the summer they are not all that noteworthy, but provide excellent summer shade for ferns, hostas, and other plants that need protection from hot sun. Trunks are smooth and grayish. Oval leaves, which get up to seven inches long, tend to look ratty after a hot, dry summer before dropping with at best a little yellow fall color.

INTERESTING KINDS: When it comes to deciduous magnolias—Oriental, saucer, Yulan, Japanese, whatever—everyone with a horticultural background will argue about which is which, but to the general gardening public they all look and grow sorta alike. And for the most part, they all perform about the same, from a garden-variety gardener's perspective. However, there are quite a few named cultivars that flower later than the generic ones available, making them less likely to freeze. One of the best, though slow-growing, small flowering trees for the mid-winter garden is star magnolia (*Magnolia stellata*), up to fifteen feet across, which makes a cloud of white, floppy, water lily blooms. Saucer magnolia (M. × *soulangiana*) has tulip-shaped flowers of cream or white with a pink or lavender blush.

SOIL: Magnolias grow in a wide range of soils, but look best when their roots go deeply into well-drained sites, or have a wide area in which to roam; heavy soils can stunt the overall growth of the trees, or cause their foliage to be even rattier (still they survive and flower for decades). To get one started well, dig a wide hole, and add a moderate amount of organic matter.

PROPAGATION: Not practical, but can be done from seed, cuttings, or grafting. Best to get one from a reputable garden center.

TIP: WHY WON'T MY MAGNOLIA BLOOM is a common question when seedling trees have been set out, which have huge variations in genetics and performance; buy named or grafted cultivars. Also, excess water or fertilizer from nearby lawns encourages foliage growth over flowers. Root prune by cutting a few outer roots in the late summer, which can stress plants into flower bud formation.

Red Buckeye
Aesculus pavia
Shade to part sun

A buckeye seed carried in your pocket is supposed to bring good luck. I'd rather plant mine! I'm surprised the somewhat gawky, small woodland native isn't called "red salvia tree" for its spikes of reddish orange flowers in the late winter to early spring, or "hummingbird tree" for its intense attraction for hungry little hummers as they return to the South from wintering grounds. No matter, when red buckeyes begin to flower, woodland glades and shaded home landscapes light up. Their big, shiny seeds look good enough to eat, but are inedible (and even considered poisonous, though squirrels eat them).

FLOWER: Buckeyes have late winter to early spring, nearly foot-long spikes of reddish orange flowers, followed by clusters of golf ball-sized leathery seed capsules that split open by late summer to release up to four or five large, shiny, mahogany-colored seeds.

PLANT: Rounded, many-branched tree, rarely over twelve or fourteen feet tall, has almost tropical-looking leaves fanned out with finger-like, multiple leaflets. Buckeyes are one of the first to shed foliage in the late summer and early fall. Usually found growing in colonies, almost always on slopes in the woods.

INTERESTING KINDS: Ohio buckeye (*Aesculus glabra*) is much larger, with greenish yellow flowers and prickly seedpods; yellow or sweet buckeye (*A. flava*) is a huge native tree with dark-green foliage and yellow flowers. The bottlebrush buckeye (*A. parviflora*) is a spreading large shrub with long, showy panicles of white flowers and bright yellow fall foliage color, very good for massing as an understory edging. Texas buckeye (*A. glabra* var. *arguta*) is a small tree with pale yellow flowers in the spring and many pounds of seed per tree.

SOIL: Any moist, well-drained soil, well mulched.

PROPAGATION: Buckeye seeds, collected as soon as the leathery pouches split in late summer, will sprout within weeks of being planted outdoors in good soil or in potting soil (place flat side down, cover only lightly with soil, and protect from squirrel and chipmunk pilfering). Seedling buckeye trees grow nearly a foot tall before first frost, maturing over the next year to flower the second spring. Seeds are so easy to sprout that they often do so under the parent tree and quickly form a colony. Allowing seeds to dry and shrivel will lower their germination ability. It's best to plant before fall and leave small trees outside in pots, exposed to normal winter conditions to toughen them up (they can take the cold quite well). Small trees are also easy to transplant.

TIP: WE TAKE FOR GRANTED the common names of plants, and say them over and over again without giving them a second thought. But once you think about the words, your curiosity might be piqued. "Buckeye" comes from the resemblance of the seeds to the brown eyes of a deer; "haw" refers to the fruit of the hawthorn and similar trees, thus "possum haw" (though a holly) means "fruit for possums;" "crape myrtle" comes from the foliage similarity to myrtle trees, and the crape-like blooms ("crape" and "crepe" are both acceptable spellings for the crinkled cloth).

Redbud
Cercis canadensis
Light shade or sun

If it weren't for dogwoods and ornamental pears—the "party girls" of spring—native redbuds would be the hottest plants in the late-winter, early-spring landscape, with their dependable show of color and no-fuss temperaments. They have a reputation for being short-lived (twenty to thirty years), but generally fill in as understory trees with no care at all, replacing themselves with new seedlings. And by the way, a naturalistic group of three or four redbuds can be as breathtakingly beautiful as a dogwood.

FLOWER: Showy clusters of small, pea-like, reddish pink or white flowers, rarely with any fragrance at all, form along trunks, branches, and twigs, sometimes in nearly solid masses, especially after a good winter chill. Flat, bean-like seedpods persist well into the following winter, long after fall colors have faded and leaves have fallen.

PLANT: Redbuds are vase-shaped trees with rounded crowns, often with multiple trunks; because their wood is not very strong, older trees often form sturdy, fresh sprouts from the base to replace dead or damaged older trunks. Foliage is generally heart-shaped, the size of a man's hand, and glossy green, turning yellow in the fall.

INTERESTING KINDS: There is much variation among wild seedlings, so for a particular effect it is best to buy a named variety. Many are now available, including some with burgundy, chartreuse, or variegated foliage or thicker, waxier blue-green leaves that can tolerate harsher sun and heat. 'Alba' has white flowers, and 'Flame' has double flowers. Chinese redbud (*Cercis chinensis*), especially the heavy-flowering 'Avondale', has dense flower clusters and bright, glossy-green leaves. Western redbuds (*C. occidentalis* and *C. reniformis*, including 'Oklahoma') are much more drought tolerant, perfectly at home in all parts of the South.

SOIL: Any well-drained soil, acidic or alkaline, preferably moist but not wet. Redbuds are understory woodland trees; when planted in broiling hot sun, a mulch of natural leaf litter will help protect roots from hot soils and extreme drought.

PROPAGATION: Seeds sown in the fall will sprout readily the following spring, especially if placed in very hot (but not boiling) water and allowed to soak as the water cools overnight before sowing. If you don't sow them outdoors in the fall, then after soaking, put them in a plastic bag in the refrigerator for two or three months before planting in the spring. Special varieties are grafted onto wild redbud rootstock.

TIP: REDBUDS ARE EDIBLE! The pink spring flowers are perfectly delicious, tasting exactly like raw peanuts (after all, they're both in the pea family). Not that they're in high demand, but just try one or two sometime when no one is looking. And imagine them on a crisp, homegrown salad.

Silverbell
Halesia species
Shade or sun

Silverbell tree is as close to a dogwood substitute as anyone will ever find—and ten times tougher. Scattered throughout the South as native understory trees, silverbells bring the woodlands to life right after dogwoods have faded from memory. The challenge is to find a garden center that values long-time customer "silverbell satisfaction" over quick dogwood sales.

FLOWER: The lovely, bell-shaped flowers, each half an inch or longer, are produced in clusters along long, slender stems just as new foliage appears, which takes away some of their impact (but they are delightful when viewed from underneath the trees, especially on spring walks in a woodland garden). Interesting but inedible fruits are brown and winged, and persist into the following winter.

PLANT: Rounded, usually multi-trunked trees (often pruned into single trunks by landscape gardeners) have finely toothed, oval leaves up to six inches long with a little yellow fall color.

INTERESTING KINDS: Carolina silverbell or snowdrop tree (*Halesia tetraptera*) blooms just as foliage appears and has four-winged fruit. Two-winged silverbell (*H. diptera*), the most common in commercial trade, has deeply lobed flowers that appear well after foliage, making it less showy from a distance; but 'Magniflora' is a profuse bloomer with larger, showier flowers. Mountain silverbell (*H. monticola*) is a very large silverbell tree and includes 'Rosea' with light-pink flowers.

SOIL: Silverbell is an upland species tree, usually found growing naturally in woodsy soils on bluffs or high on riverbanks where logging has not destroyed their habitat. They will not tolerate heavy or wet soils, but are fuss-free once established.

PROPAGATION: Seeds take up to two years to sprout, making them difficult for most gardeners; stems root fairly readily in a greenhouse, especially if rooting hormones are used. It's best to buy from a garden center that specializes in good native plants.

TIP: WHEN IN DOUBT, PLANT IN GROUPS. Woodland trees love company, to the point that if you don't give them neighbors, they will ignore your best efforts at "making" them grow. Just as you never see a dogwood growing along a sunny fencerow—they grow best on shaded slopes—you won't find silverbells or other woodland natives surviving for long standing alone in hot, sunny landscapes. Best to put them under existing trees or to plant a shade tree and then plant silverbells on the east side for protection from hot afternoon sun. Leaves used as mulch also help a great deal by shading the soil and roots, and "feeding" woodland trees as they decompose, creating a nice woodsy soil.

Bottle Tree

Silica transparencii 'Gaudi'

Full sun to dense shade

Originating in ancient Arabia, this specimen migrated to the South to create a dazzling focal point that is close to zero-maintenance perfection, while being whimsical, daring, artistic—and nowhere nearly as unusual or painful as hanging ornaments from holes punched in ears.

FLOWER: Small to medium, hollow glass cylinders of clear, amber, green, blue, and occasionally a rare red, found on the ends of stems, remain every single day of the year (particularly colorful when back-lit by sunshine). Though occasionally damaged by hailstorms, bottle tree can be quickly and easily repaired.

PLANT: Generally upright to eight or ten feet, with few to many branches. Sometimes a strictly upright specimen similar to a large fence post with stout nails, often more like an old Christmas tree with limbs bobbed back to finger-sized branches, occasionally a rambling collection of several lesser trees wired together; rarely one is seen that looks as if it were heavy welded rebar. Collectors save glass flowers to line kitchen or bathroom windows, with a stained glass effect. Some bottles have been seen as neck-down edging around nice flower beds (particularly in Europe, where gardeners have used them this way for centuries).

INTERESTING KINDS: Solid-green or solid-amber bottle trees are edged out by unique cultivars, including 'Milk of Magnesia' (pure cobalt blue); 'Beer Bottle Delight' (delicate blend of greens, browns, and transparent); 'Kaleidoscope Stroke' (popular multicolor display, often no particular pattern); 'Texas Bluebonnet' (a rare form with green lower "leaves" and blue upper "flowers" seen only in one garden in east Texas).

SOIL: Any firm soil will support a heavy bottle tree, though ready-mix concrete can be used for strength. Occasional watering cleans the foliage and flowers; selecting vines such as cypress, moonflower, or a tidy climbing rose such as 'Red Cascades' can enhance the bottle tree if not overdone. Mardi Gras beads and old necklaces have been seen in the nicer neighborhoods.

PROPAGATION: The tree itself is easily made any time of the year, sometimes taking just a few minutes. Most bottles are very easy to locate, either at home or behind local pubs. Upscale restaurants often share choice longneck amber or even blue bottles at no charge. Annual bottle collector meetings can yield some very fine colors at a reasonable cost, as can Internet auction sites and garage sales.

TIP: GARDEN ACCESSORIES CAN BE SERIOUS, classical, contemporary, whimsical, or downright humorous, but add a special accent or personal touch. Birdbaths, urns, statuary, driftwood, boulders, bottle trees, whatever—in your own personal space, "anything goes." After all, no matter what you do, your neighbors will talk about you anyway!

Other Good Trees:

Bald Cypress (*Taxodium distichum*) is a tall, narrow, many-twigged deciduous tree for many soil types (including dry), with ferny green foliage and rusty red fall colors. Very little leaf litter.

Black Cherry (*Prunus serotina*) is one of the showiest red fall color trees in the South.

Cedar (*Juniperus virginiana*), one of the best evergreen screening plants for sun or light shade, has a narrow teardrop shape. May have dusty light-blue berries to complement good green foliage.

Chinaberry (*Melia azedarach*) is an old-timey favorite for its rounded form, glossy fern-like leaves, fragrant lavender spring flowers, and orange fruit balls in winter (which can be messy).

Chinese or **Lacebark Elm** (*Ulmus parvifolia*), one of the blight-resistant elms, has long, spreading, drooping branches of leathery green leaves, and outstanding mottled bark for winter interest.

Chinese Parasol Tree (*Firmiana simplex*) is a tall, upright, sparsely branched tree with large leaves and showy summer flowers and papery fall seedpods. Trunk and stems stay bright green.

Chinese Tallow-Tree (*Sapium sebiferum*), a roundish tree considered invasive by hard-core experts, has the most brilliant fall colors. Females have popcorn-like seed clusters.

Flowering Cherry (pictured), **Crabapple, Pear, Plum,** etc. (*Prunus* species and *Pyrus* species) are extremely showy small trees for early spring flowers; they often lose flowers to late frosts, suffer root problems in heavy or irrigated soils, and generally are best used as short-lived "party girls." Foliage alone makes some worth growing, and some have great structural interest and winter bark.

Glory Bower (*Clerodendrum trichotomum*) has extremely showy and fragrant summer flowers and attractive fruit clusters, for sun or shade. Not hardy in the upper South.

Golden Rain Tree (*Koelreuteria paniculata*) is a rounded tree with ferny foliage and large showy clusters of yellow flowers in early summer, followed by showy papery seedpods.

Japanese Flowering Apricot (*Prunus mume*) is one of the toughest winter-flowering trees around, blooming way before anything else. Tolerates a wide range of soils.

Japanese Maple (*Acer palmatum*), a small to medium specimen tree, has many cultivars with delicate leaf forms (including burgundy foliage cultivars). Suffers in full sun and dry weather.

Japanese Pagoda Tree (*Sophora japonica*), a small rounded tree with ferny leaves, has foot-long sprays of yellowish white summer flowers, as well as showy seedpods.

Japanese Persimmon (*Diospyros kaki*) is a small deciduous tree with leathery leaves and large, extremely showy orange fruits held after frost. Not entirely winter hardy in the upper South.

Jujube (*Ziziphus jujuba*) is an upright tree with glossy summer foliage, thumb-sized edible summer fruit, and an interesting bark effect.

Ornamental Pear (*Pyrus calleryana*), upright and usually teardrop-shaped, provides an excellent focal point with showy spring flowers and brilliant red fall colors. Often breaks up in ice storms.

Pawpaw (*Asimina triloba*), an upright, rounded native to moist soils, has maroon winter flowers and egg-sized or larger "custard apple" fruits in summer. Great orange fall colors.

Quince (*Pseudocydonia sinensis*), similar to crape myrtle in growth habit, flowers in the spring and has beautiful large, golden, edible pear-like fruits in the fall. Attractive bark.

Sassafras (*Sassafras albidum*), a colony-forming tree, has orange fall colors and root bark from which root beer was once made. Great host for larvae of showy butterflies.

Serviceberry (*Amelanchier* species), a graceful small tree for the middle and upper South, has white or pinkish spring flowers, edible summer fruits, good fall color. Easy to plant beneath.

Smoke Tree (*Cotinus coggygria*), a small shrubby tree, has many cultivars with burgundy foliage; hairy seed plumes clothing the entire tree in a smoke-like effect. Grows in tough conditions. Native species (*C. obovatus*) has outstanding fall color, but is harder to locate in the nursery trade.

Snowbell (*Styrax* species), including native and Japanese species of small trees, is good for light shade, with spring clusters of fragrant white flowers that droop like bells from twigs. Easy to plant beneath.

Sourwood (*Oxydendrum arboreum*) (pictured), with sprays of finger-like summer flowers and brilliant fall colors, is a popular native tree for slopes and banks, especially in the mid- and upper South.

Wax Myrtle (*Myrica cerifera*), a large evergreen native, has olive-drab leaves and dusty-blue, waxy fruit clustered along twigs. Very fast-growing, sun or shade, but often gets too big and begins to fall apart, especially under ice loads in the middle and upper South.

Windmill Palm (*Trachycarpus fortunei*), the cold-hardiest palm, has a tall, hairy, single trunk topped with palm foliage. Risks winterkill from severe freezes even in the middle South.

Witch-Hazel (*Hamamelis virginiana*), winter-flowering in sun or especially shade gardens, has crepe-paper-like flowers of yellow or gold.

Help! I'm a Garden Nerd!

Ever find a sprig of rosemary soaking in a water glass beside the sink, left over from a nice meal out on the town the evening before? Anyone who brings food home to root has a problem, possibly an addiction. I can just hear it now, at a twelve-step meeting:

"Hi, my name is Felder, and I am a gardener..." ("Welcome, Felder, we're glad you are here. Come back often.")

"I gardened just this morning." ("Amen.") "Pulled a few weeds on the way down to pick up the morning paper, and before I knew it, started dividing daylilies and repainting a fencepost. During carpool, I found a mail-order catalog under my car seat, and people behind me at the stoplight had to honk to get my attention back on the road.

"I need help, can't stop gardening on my own. Even though I don't play golf or own a bass boat, I am sorry for my family because I spent my last pay-check on a new greenhouse door, a big bucket of Miracle Grow, and some shrubs I don't even need, 'cause they were on sale..."

Sound close to home? Here's a simple test to see if you, too, need help:

Do you grow ten or more different kinds of the same plant (rose, daylily, daffodil, iris, African violet, camellia, tomato, whatever), and know their names? Extra points if they're labeled. Do you subscribe to three or more garden magazines? Do you think Roger Swain is funny?

Do you keep a small shovel in your car trunk? Turn your compost weekly? Blow leaves on Sunday morning? Buy birdseed by the fifty pound sack? Own a $40 pair of pruning shears (bonus points for a leather scabbard)? Are entire flats of flowers still sitting in the driveway because there's simply no more space to plant?

Have you ever willingly taken a tour of a garden by flashlight? Do we need to search your purse or camera case for purloined seeds after a visit to a botanical garden?

Extra points if your cuticles are dirty right now. And last, but not least, triple points of you would appreciate a special someone sending you a load of manure for an anniversary...

I'm not suggesting we gardeners should quit—though we all claim we can, any time. Maybe our motto should be **One Flower at A Time**. And remember, denial is a symptom!

Vines
WITH VIGOR

Nearly every landscaper agrees that vines are the most overlooked group of plants available to gardeners. Yet they are everywhere, clambering up trees in the native woods, sprawling along roadsides, cascading down hillsides and creek banks, and softening the edges of fences and arbors in every small town and country garden. There are dozens of great vines that need little or no care at all, other than occasional pruning to keep them out of our faces and off of other plants.

Technically, vines are just flexible stems that don't stop growing; they constantly get longer, reach higher, and spread into new areas. Some are multiple-branched and make good screens or ground covers. There are annuals to be replanted every year or tender tropical plants that must be brought in every winter. Others are herbaceous perennials that leap from the ground every spring or long-lived woody landscape features that provide a year-round framework of texture for many years. Some grow so fast they can take over a porch in a few weeks or months; others seem to take forever to get established and depend on their supports to give the desired vertical effect until they catch on.

Vines and their supports lend crucial "vertical appeal" to landscapes. They provide framing, creating focal points and lifting our view from the lawn and flower beds to eye level and above. They mask bare walls to provide fast shade on the hot side of a house or hide ugly scenery. Several provide erosion control or grow in areas that are too difficult to mow or too shady for grass. They provide colorful flowers in the spring, summer, and fall; gorgeous autumn colors; and evergreen texture or accents through our sometimes-dreary winter. On the following pages are great vines for the South.

YOU CAN EASILY MAKE A TROPICAL CONNECTION with vines that normally you see only while on vacation in frost-free parts of the country. Many dozens of exotic vines can be enjoyed either as temporary summer beauties or, by bringing them indoors over the winter, as long-lived companions. Without a doubt, the most popular "big three" are mandevilla, with large, clear pink trumpets; allamanda and its clusters of rich yellow flowers; and bougainvillea, a large tropical vine that has masses of papery bracts of red, white, or shocking pink. These sun-loving tropical vines are popular in large containers or around mailboxes, but must all be brought indoors to a sunny window in the winter. Drastic pruning promotes tidy new flowering growth and helps them get over the shock of being brought indoors or being put back outside. All require regular watering and occasional light feedings (half strength). For instance, keeping bougainvillea too wet or overfed can cause poor flowering.

 Best for Beginners:

- *Climbing Roses*
- *Cypress Vine*
- *English Ivy*
- *Gourds*
- *Hyacinth Bean*
- *Moonflower*
- *Wisteria* (easy to grow)
- *Carolina Jessamine*
- *Morning Glory*

Kinda Tricky:

(Either because they need special care, or vigilance to keep them from becoming invasive.)

- *Clematis*
- *Japanese Honeysuckle*
- *Muscadine Grape*
- *Wisteria* (sometimes won't bloom)
- *Tomato*
- *Trumpet Creeper*
- *Poison Ivy*

Carolina Jessamine or "Yellow Jasmine"

Gelsemium sempervirens

Sun or part shade

One of the first vines to bloom in late winter, the Southern native jessamine—which most gardeners, not knowing or ignoring the correct name, simply call "yellow jasmine"—twists and climbs to the tops of woodland edge trees and shrubs. Often seen only when in full bloom along miles of woodland roads and highways, Carolina jessamine is a good source of nectar for bees early in the season, but its pollen has been known to kill young bees when it is the main source of food during early brood production (don't worry, the bees quickly recover with new broods). Carolina jessamine is a favorite vine for small arbors where evergreen screening is needed, but even it can tear up lattice-work. When using this vine around the mailbox, be sure to prune it after flowering to keep it in bounds.

FLOWER: Cheerful, medium-yellow trumpets up to two inches long are produced in great clusters in the late winter with an occasional flush of flowers in the summer and fall.

PLANT: Moderate grower to twenty feet long, with many stems wrapping and twisting around supports (including shrubs and nearby trees). Jessamine can be used as a loose ground cover, especially on banks. The small, pointed leaves remain green all winter, making it one of the few dependable ever-green vines for "toning down" arbors, entryways, fences, and even mailboxes (though it has to be cut back from time to time on small supports).

INTERESTING KINDS: 'Pride of Augusta' (or 'Plena') is a double-flowering form sometimes seen in garden centers and mail-order sources.

SOIL: Any soil, moist or dry, but it does best in deep, well-drained, woods-edge soils, and it can tolerate both seasonal wet spells and drought. Light feeding in the spring will produce lush growth, but too much can cause leggy vines with few flowers. Mulch roots to keep them cool in the summer.

PROPAGATION: Layer long vines, or simply buy what you need. Carolina jessamine is widely available and usually inexpensive in gallon pots already growing on a redwood or cedar support. Can also be grown from seed.

TIP: PRUNING IS EASY if your spring-flowering Carolina jessamine gets way too big. Either cut it low to the ground after it finishes its heaviest bloom and let it get started all over again for the next spring or, when it is used as a screen and gets "leggy," simply thin out unwanted growth through the summer, leaving some tall vines but cutting some fairly low to the ground to promote new growth lower down. Do not prune heavily in late summer or winter, or you risk losing all of next spring's flowers.

Clematis

Clematis species and hybrids

Sun or light shade

Normally I would not include clematis in a list of unkillable plants because so many of the fancy hybrids die from being planted poorly or from severe weather damage. But some very fine old tough varieties are available for planting on mailboxes, trellises, and particularly on the canes of climbing roses. Clematis flowers make stunning cut flowers, especially when floated in a bowl (seal cut stems by burning with a match).

FLOWER: Generally large, flat, multipetaled showstoppers, from two to nearly ten inches across, in white, purple, blue, red, pink, yellow, and bicolors, produced on either new growth or old stems, depending on the species (hence the pruning dilemma). Most also have decorative plumed seedpods after flowering.

PLANT: Vines climb from a few feet to several yards, with dark green leaves usually divided into leaflets. Because the foliage is sometimes sparse, clematis is usually not planted alone as screening; it's better to use it in combination with other plants or as a detail against wooden fences or lattice. Clematis grows by wrapping around stakes, arbors, or other plants (sweet autumn clematis is often considered a rank weed that can take over nearby shrubs and small trees). Some hybrids have weak stems that are easily broken and need protection from strong winds.

INTERESTING KINDS: Jackmanii group (large purple or white flowers, blooms on new growth), *Clematis henryii* (huge creamy white blossoms with dark stamens), *C. armandii* (medium-sized white flowers on super-vigorous stems that require constant pinching and pruning), *C. crispa* (North American native with sparse, bell-shaped, lavender flowers, not a very vigorous vine), *C. paniculata* (sweet autumn clematis, fairly invasive evergreen with super showy small white flowers in the fall), and many hybrids.

SOIL: Clematis requires a loose, fast-draining soil that is at least initially high in organic matter—soil preparation is generally the same as for roses. A deep leaf mulch is important for keeping roots cool in the summer, but some gardeners instead use a flat stone or ground covers such as mondo grass or liriope around the base of clematis.

PROPAGATION: Buy new vines as needed.

TIP: THE MOST COMMON QUESTION concerning clematis is about pruning. Some bloom on new growth and should be pruned in the winter. Others flower on old wood and may be cut after flowering in the spring. How do you tell, if you aren't sure which type you have? Either look it up in a clematis book or Web site (which usually has more detail than most people need to know) or simply do only minor corrective pruning as needed, then wait a year to see how yours flowers.

Climbing Roses
Rosa species and hybrids
Full sun

Nothing in the horticultural world says romance better than an arch covered with fragrant roses—but nothing in the gardening world says "high maintenance" more than roses either. I grow over fifty different kinds, including climbers that bloom all the time, and I don't even own a sprayer! Choosing good roses comes from decades of watching others fail, then growing those that survive with flair and fragrance. Climbers cover arches, walls, and fences with beauty and scent—and without a lot of trouble.

FLOWER: Loose clusters of often-fragrant pink, white, red, or yellow flowers, usually on the ends of arching canes, produced in mid-spring with some cultivars repeating in flushes throughout the summer and fall. Some types occasionally have red fruits, called "hips."

PLANT: Vining shrubs that need to be tied to supports, with usually thorny canes reaching several yards long. Older vines often reach twenty feet or more and require sturdy supports at least ten feet off the ground to allow for thorny branches to cascade without catching people passing underneath. Prune any time to remove older or wayward canes.

INTERESTING KINDS: These are a good start: Lady Banks or banksia rose (*Rosa banksiae*, pictured), perhaps the most famous climber, with flowers of dusty yellow or white in the spring only (and thornless), not cold hardy in the upper South; Cherokee rose (*R. laevigata*), another spring bloomer with huge white flowers and glossy leaves (state flower of Georgia); 'Climbing Old Blush', medium pink in masses from spring to fall; 'New Dawn', a prolific bloomer with huge pinkish-white fragrant flowers all season; 'Don Juan', hearty red flowering climber; 'Zéphirine Dröuhin', thornless and dark pink, blooms all the time; 'Red Cascades', a small "sprangly" nonstop red rose that can be trained up to eight feet.

SOIL: Fertile, well-drained soil is a must. At planting time, work in generous amounts of organic matter to the native soil in a wide hole, then mulch. For the best flowers, fertilize lightly every year or two and at least every couple of months in dry seasons.

PROPAGATION: Stem cuttings taken fall through mid-winter should be stuck in a fifty-fifty mix of sand and soil (or sand and potting soil, if rooting in pots). Dipping cut ends in rooting powders is not necessary, but it helps. Cover cuttings with individual "greenhouses" made by cutting the bottoms off of two-liter plastic cola bottles. Rooting take a couple of months.

TIP: **FORCE FLOWERS THE ENTIRE LENGTH** of running rose stems by bending the stems over nearly to the point of breaking and then tying them down for a week or more. This "pegging" stresses the plants just enough to cause emergency flower "breaks" at nearly every leaf joint on the stressed areas, stimulating flower bud formation.

Coral or Trumpet Honeysuckle
Lonicera sempervirens
Sun or shade

Don't be scared away from this terrific vine just because it's a honeysuckle! Completely unlike the invasive Japanese honeysuckle, this vigorous woodland native stays put and is never a nuisance. It's one of the first plants of the year to flower (sometimes in mid-February for me), just in time for early hummingbirds coming north from the coastal areas, and its red berries are attractive to seed-eating birds as well. Often called "coral" honeysuckle because of its reddish flower, this informal vine is perfect for short trellises, mailboxes, and lattice and is especially good in naturalistic settings.

FLOWER: Orange-scarlet tubular trumpets with yellow throats, up to two inches long; flowers most heavily in the late winter and spring, but often throughout the summer and fall as well. Clusters of flowers appear in the center of two fused leaves at the ends of branches. Berries are bright orange and showy in the summer.

PLANT: Noninvasive and loose, to about eight feet long, the vine does not attach itself as readily to structures and needs tying at first. It can actually be pruned into an almost shrub-like mass. Mostly evergreen except during severe winters, it can develop bare lower stems; remedy this with selective pruning to promote new growth down low. Sometimes aphids get on flowers and distort them, but these pests are easily washed off or killed with a natural insecticidal soap applied twice, a few days apart.

INTERESTING KINDS: 'Sulphurea' has yellowish flowers; 'Superba' is bright scarlet; 'Magnifica' has large flowers, bright red on the outside and yellow on the inside; *Lonicera* × *brownii* 'Dropmore Scarlet' is a hybrid between *L. sempervirens* and another native honeysuckle and has blue-green leaves and scarlet flowers; another hybrid between native species is goldflame honeysuckle (*L.* × *heckrottii*), which has blue-green leaves and pink buds that open into flowers that are bright coral outside and rich golden inside.

SOIL: Rich, woodsy conditions until roots get established. Mulching helps keep roots cool in the summer. Tolerates wet or dry conditions.

PROPAGATION: Slow to grow from seeds, this honeysuckle is easily grown from cuttings or layering, or simply buy what you need from garden centers, where fairly inexpensive plants are often sold in pots already growing on redwood or cedar stakes.

TIP: VINES CLIMB IN WEIRD WAYS, such as twining their stems around supports (cypress vine, smilax, honeysuckle, wisteria), using special extensions called tendrils that reach out to wrap around supports (grapes, gourds, cross vine, sweet pea, passion flower), clinging with tendrils that have hooks or claws or with small stem roots with adhesive disks (trumpet creeper, creeping fig, Virginia creeper, wintercreeper euonymus), or being tied up with soft twine (climbing roses, thorny roses, tomatoes, coral honeysuckle). Clematis actually twists the stalks of its leaves around supports.

Cross Vine

Bignonia capreolata

Sun to part shade

Late winter into early spring brings an unusual smoky blaze to treetops along country roads when cross vine comes into bloom. The high-climbing native vine, which gets its name from the "X" seen when looking down the cut ends of vines (like looking down a drinking straw), is also infamous with kids who have tried smoking pieces of the vine (somewhat harmlessly) like a cigarette. Hummingbirds and bumblebees literally crawl onto its thumb-sized flowers, which appear only in sunny places, and sometimes so high in the trees that you are unaware of them until they begin to fall to the ground. Its rapid growth makes the vine ideal for covering walls, although its foliage is not so thick that it obscures its support.

FLOWER: Fat orange buds open into two-inch trumpets with two lips, reddish orange on the outside and yellowish on the inside, produced in loose clusters in leaf joints, very showy in the early spring, with a few flower clusters appearing through the summer and fall. Produced mostly on new shoots growing off older vines, flowers retain their color after they fall, leaving an attractive, bright ground clutter.

PLANT: Fast-growing vine to fifty feet or more, usually flowering only in the tops of trees where sunlight is available to the plant. Oblong leaves are four inches long, produced in "pairs of pairs"—a pair of leaflets on both sides of leaf joints like four large butterfly wings (very interesting pattern when the vine grows up tree trunks). The vine, sometimes confused with poison ivy (which has only three leaflets per leaf joint), grows by twining and clasping with strong tendrils that wrap or stick tightly to whatever surface they touch.

INTERESTING KINDS: Free-blooming 'Tangerine Beauty' has exceptionally bright, apricot-orange tubes, which continue to flower prolifically through the summer and fall.

SOIL: Any soil, including heavy or wet. Tolerates extreme drought.

PROPAGATION: Root or layer stem sections in the summer. It is available commercially from mail order or garden centers; even though it is not a "mainstream" plant, it is in commercial production—ask a local garden center manager to order it from wholesale growers.

TIP: DIGGING PLANTS FROM THE WILD is usually seen as unethical, and, with endangered plants, it is illegal. If you feel absolutely compelled, make sure the plant is not endangered and always get permission from the landowner. The rule of thumb for when to dig plants is "in the season opposite of when it blooms the heaviest." Always cut large plants back to balance the top to the reduced roots, and replant as soon as possible or pot up until the appropriate season for planting.

Cypress Vine

Ipomoea quamoclit

Full sun or very light shade

Feeling unlucky with plants? This delicate, ferny vine is so easy you might actually regret getting it started; the incredibly fast-growing annual vine can wrap up everything within reach. It's so tough that I've seen it growing on the guardrails of interstate highways! Good news, though: it is easy to control by simply pulling down excess vines once a year and letting the rest keep flowering. Best of all, it's loaded with flowers, butterflies, and hummingbirds from spring until frost; my mother has one vine that flowers under a small shade tree, where hummingbirds roost until they get enough energy to go back to work on all the flowers. On top of all that, the vine comes back from seed for many years, sprouting all around the original plants.

FLOWER: Bright red, flaring tubular darlings scattered profusely over the entire vine, right up until frost. One of the best butterfly and hummingbird flowers around, yet too small to be as attractive to heavy bees.

PLANT: Super-fast-growing vine, twining up to fifteen or more feet, often growing thickly enough to make a light ground cover. Its foliage is airy and ferny, individual compound leaves looking exactly like those of a cypress tree. Medium-green vine can overpower nearby small shrubs, but makes an outstanding addition to arbors and even as a companion to other vines or small, multitrunked trees.

INTERESTING KINDS: A white-flowering form can be found and shared between gardeners. Cardinal climber (*Ipomoea* × *multifida*) has identical flowers, but the two-inch wide leaves, instead of being fernlike, are roundish and hand-shaped with points.

SOIL: Prefers soil moist and well drained, but grows anywhere at all, including very poor soils. Flowers best with moisture but not much fertilizer (which promotes lush vines, but not flowers).

PROPAGATION: Small black seeds are easy to collect. Cypress vine reseeds very well, especially around outer edges of a garden where the mulch may be thinner. If mulch is thick, expose a little "real dirt" and sow a few seeds, then water lightly. They'll sprout when the soil warms in the spring.

TIP: EXTEND THE BEAUTY ALL DAY by growing cypress vine with other annual vines, including morning glory and moonflower, so you can enjoy them morning, noon, and night. Their foliage complements one another, and at the end of the season, they can all be cleaned up at the same time. Be sure to collect seeds from each vine to mix together in decorative envelopes to share with friends or give as "can't fail" gifts to children. Save a few for yourself, in case the unthinkable happens and they don't come back in your garden.

English Ivy
Hedera helix
Shade or part sun

No shade garden is complete without ivy. The evergreen vine is used most commonly as a rugged, foot-thick ground cover in even the dense shade of live oak trees, and its vines will climb up to forty feet in trees, out onto limbs, and cascade back towards the ground. It will root right into wooden arbors, house siding, and even brick mortar.

FLOWER: Not showy enough to speak of, although mature vines (really old ones, hanging from trees) may have clusters of small, greenish flowers followed by black berries. Best bet for contrast is the use of variegated forms to interplant with bulbs, hostas, ferns, or other shade-loving flowers.

PLANT: Tough vine that roots as it grows, either in the ground or on supports. Dull, dark-green leathery leaves, usually with pointed lobes, are not produced so thickly they will shade other perennials, but masses of the vine can fill in well, creating solid ground covers that prevent erosion on steep shady slopes. Variegated forms are available, as are kinds with ruffled leaves. Foliage of mature English ivy, found growing in trees, is more oval, and cuttings taken from this part of the plant will make small shrubs, instead of vines.

INTERESTING KINDS: There are dozens of ivy cultivars, many of which are best suited for growing in pots (some are not as winter hardy in northern areas). Variegated, curly-leaf, ruffled, and many shapes and sizes can be found in garden centers and through the American Ivy Society (www.ivy.org) whose members sell interesting cultivars. Algerian ivy (*Hedera canariensis*) has much larger, more luxurious foliage, but is not as cold hardy.

SOIL: Ivy grows best in loose, well-drained soils. Root rot is common where it is planted in heavy or wet soils, or when ivy is fertilized heavily. Plants kept moist often develop leaf spots as well, which can be controlled with pruning and less frequent irrigation. Ivy grown in the sun needs occasional watering, which should be done in the morning so foliage dries quickly.

PROPAGATION: Sections of vines six or eight inches long root quite readily, especially in the fall. Insert them into well-prepared soil and keep moist, not wet. Roots will form before spring.

TIP: "DOES IVY KILL TREES?" That's a common question, and everybody's mother says it will. But at the risk of starting an argument with Mama, it won't—unless it is so thick it completely shades the leaves of shrubs or small trees, or breaks them under the combined weight. If insects hiding in the thick vines are a concern, simply cut it all down every few years and let it start over again.

Gourds
Lagenaria, Luffa, and *Cucurbita* species
Full sun

A friend once called gourds "vegetal white-out" for their ability to cover up the most glaring holes in a landscape scene. Growing almost as rampantly as kudzu, some can top a mature crape myrtle in a single season, festooning it with large fruits that dry into huge ornaments. From the giant birdhouse and dipper gourds, to the tiny ornamental kinds with warty skins and interesting colors and shapes, to the back-scrubbing loofah variety, gourds are among the toughest annual vines around.

FLOWER: Loofah and small kinds of gourds have small, yellow flowers; large true gourds have big, flat, white flowers. Separate male and female flowers are produced on the same plants, and both have to be open and pollinated by bees or moths for gourds to grow. You can tell the difference easily by looking close: male flowers are on simple stems, females are on the ends of small immature gourds. If pollen makes it from the male to the female, the gourd will develop; otherwise, the immature fruit will shrivel and drop off. Hint: You can snip a pollen-laden "brush" from a male flower and dab the pollen in the female flower. Sounds weird, but it works.

PLANT: Fast-growing vines with large leaves can climb fifteen feet or more, using strong, long tendrils to wrap around everything they touch. Gourd farmers grow them in fields like pumpkins, but most gardeners put up a sturdy wire or wooden trellis. Large gourd vines require a lot of space, so plant them along chain link or another large fence. Some gardeners build special "gourd houses"—tall arbors over which gourds can clamber, with fruits hanging like ornaments. Take care when interplanting gourds with other vines or training them up small trees—the lush growth of the gourd vine can hinder the growth of the other plants.

INTERESTING KINDS: Loofah (can be skinned and the insides used as a dish washer or for scrubbing body or hands), dipper (long-handled), basket (huge and roundish), ornamental (many shapes and sizes and colors), and many others. Contact the American Gourd Society (www.americangourdsociety.org) for tips on growing, preserving, and ordering seeds of unusual varieties.

SOIL: Needs a well-drained soil, but not a lot of water or fertilizer. Mulches help keep roots moist and cool.

PROPAGATION: Wait until well into spring to plant seeds—planting can continue until the end of June for gourd production by fall, so no need to rush! Or start in containers kept in full direct sunlight to keep young plants from getting "stretchy," and then transplant when the soil warms.

TIP: GOURDS CAN DRY right on the vine, even until after a hard freeze. Preserve them by scrubbing off any mold (unless you like its mottled appearance), washing with chlorine bleach and water, and allowing to dry thoroughly. Coat with paste wax, lacquer, or shellac.

Hyacinth Bean
Lablab purpureus (or *Dolichos lablab*)
Full sun

The purple flowers and burgundy beans on this twining vine never fail to stop traffic! Among the tallest I have seen are on a long, rustic arbor made of tree limbs at Monticello, Thomas Jefferson's mountaintop home in Virginia. Up close, the vine resembles kudzu, perfect for quick screening on simple arbors or trellises, but it rarely survives any but the mildest frosts, so there is no danger of it "getting away" and becoming a weedy nuisance.

FLOWER: Late summer and fall spikes up to a foot long stand above the foliage and are topped with loose clusters of lavender-purple, sometimes white, sweetpea-like flowers. Very pretty, almost like upright wisteria flowers. Dark, maroon-burgundy beans nearly three inches or so long are flat except for the lumps made by seeds, similar to butterbeans (lima beans).

PLANT: Twining summer annual vine with large, divided green leaves that fan out like kudzu, up to twelve or more feet long. Requires a trellis, arbor, pergola, or other rough structure to twist around.

INTERESTING COMPANIONS: Plant by itself or with complementary cypress vine.

SOIL: Any well-drained garden soil, with moderate fertility and an occasional deep soaking when the plant is in bloom and no rain is in sight. Mulches help conserve moisture and keep roots cool. May be grown in a large container, placed near a post or arbor, or with a large "teepee" placed in the pot.

PROPAGATION: Easily grown from seed, planted after all danger of frost is past, preferably after the soil has warmed to prevent seed rot. Sometimes birds will be a problem pulling up seedlings.

TIP: YOUNG VINES FROM SEED MAY DIE for several reasons. Seeds planted too early in cool, wet soils often rot; wait until mid-April before sowing seeds of tender annuals. Crickets, cutworms, slugs, or rabbits may chew the stems at soil level; prevent this by surrounding the seedlings with a collar made from a plastic container with the bottom cut out. Then surround the plastic with sand. Birds may pull small seedlings; cover the seeded area with a small amount of bird netting, a small "hat" of wire fencing, or a medium-sized leafy branch cut from a shrub or tree stuck in the ground over the area (choose a branch that will hold its leaves until the seedlings get established). Finally, a string trimmer can wipe out a plant quicker than the blink of an eye, so protect vines with mulch, small stones, a bottomed-out plastic container, or another, more visible, plant.

Japanese Honeysuckle
Lonicera japonica
Sun or light shade

Few plants cause folks to get their knickers in a knot more than honeysuckle! Not just because it's an invasive "weed" that takes over hedgerows, woodlands, and azaleas, but also because it's actually a good-looking plant with fragrant flowers. One of my jobs at a nursery in Texas was rooting pieces to sell as ground-hugging erosion control plants; I have seen it sold in New York City for an astounding $75— for courtyard containers! This serious weed is a beautiful vine, perfect for fast privacy and erosion control, with outstanding fragrance and delightful nectar, beloved by hummingbirds and kids of all ages—and really not all that hard to keep in bounds.

FLOWER: Tubular white-to-cream flowers with flaring lips in clusters from spring to fall, which fade to a dull yellow upon maturity. Each extremely fragrant tube has a partial drop of pure nectar. Get to it by pinching off the tip end and pulling the long, slender pistil through the narrow tube; then put that drop on the tip of the tongue, where "sweet" taste buds are concentrated.

PLANT: Vigorous vine with deep-green leaves that remain evergreen most winters. The vine stem is "exfoliating" (has loosely hanging, shredded bark) and can reach twenty or more feet. Spreads from "runner" vines to overgrow and smother nearby shrubs. Prune close to the ground every year to keep it in bounds, or train along the top of a fence where flowers and foliage can be appreciated, while you can keep an eye on "runners" trying to get out of control.

INTERESTING KINDS: 'Halliana' has very white flowers changing to yellow; 'Purpurea' has purple-tinged leaves and flowers that are maroon outside and white inside; 'Aureoreticulata' has leaves veined in gold.

SOIL: Any soil that does not stand in water for more than a few days. Fertilizer causes rampant growth and reduces flowering.

PROPAGATION: Easy from rooted cuttings nearly any time of the year, best in the summer. Root divisions also sprout. Few people would mind an earnest gardener digging a few plants from along fencerows. Often spreads by birds eating berries and dropping seeds from perches.

TIP: CONTROL HONEYSUCKLE by planting in a bottomed-out large pot sunk in the ground, away from other desirable plants so you can keep an eye on its spread; simply pinch off unwanted runners. Where you need to eradicate it, prune close to the ground repeatedly and pull up roots; several herbicides are effective controls if applied to new growth after plants have been pruned.

Moonflower or Moonvine

Ipomoea alba

Full sun or very light shade

One of the most magical events in a new gardener's life is watching moonflowers open at dusk. The large white flowers spring suddenly from relatively small "twists" of buds, releasing a fragrance into the evening air that all but overwhelms anyone whose nose is too close. If you are lucky—or unlucky, as the case may be—you will experience the most magical of night creatures, a huge, brownish, hand-sized moth that lumbers up, almost silently, and sips nectar from each flower, hovering like an oversized night hummingbird. The unlucky part comes when you realize that the moth is the adult of the voracious, plant-chomping, giant tomato hornworm.

I grow moonflower on one of my seven tall iron posts set in the front yard, beside a deck where we spend many early evenings enjoying the flowers, the fragrance, and the moths (which also pollinate other night-blooming flowers, including cleome and ginger lily, *Hedychium*). It can also be planted under small, airy trees such as crape myrtle for a companion effect.

FLOWER: Flat white summer and fall trumpets up to six inches across, sometimes tinged with purple, often streaked with green, open from pointed buds shaped like swirls of soft ice cream. They remain open, almost glowing, all night, sometimes into the morning if the day is overcast. Very fragrant.

PLANT: Fast-growing, twisting vine up to twenty-five or thirty feet, wraps around arbor pots or teepees made of sturdy reinforcing rods (rebar) at least ten feet tall. Luxuriously large and heart-shaped, leaves are spaced closely on the vine. Grows best in warm seasons.

INTERESTING RELATIVES: Morning glory, sweet potato, cypress vine.

SOIL: Any moist, well-drained soil with moderate fertility. To help promote fast root growth, do not mulch until the soil warms up. Water only occasionally during extreme dry spells.

PROPAGATION: Grow from seeds, which have a hard coat and should be soaked for a day or two and even nicked slightly with toenail clippers or a knife to help them take up moisture and begin sprouting. Plant in pots indoors in a sunny, warm spot before setting out well after the soil has begun to heat up.

TIP: PLACES WHERE ANNUAL VINES GROW all summer are usually bare in the winter and slow to fill in during the spring. Add interest with a wind chime or other hanging accessory to give your eye something to enjoy in the bare months. Plant liriope, artemisia, or another non-invasive, drought-tolerant perennial, ground cover, or small shrub around the base of arbors or teepees to visually anchor the structures while summer vines are beginning to grow.

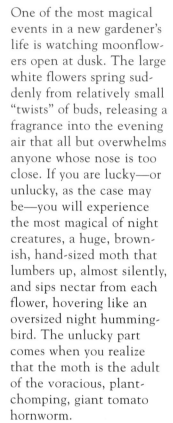

Muscadine Grape
Vitis rotundifolia
Sun

Our winters are too mild, our summers too humid, our pests too overwhelming to grow most of the popular eating and wine grapes of the world. But the native muscadine grape is tough enough to grow in the woods and along riverbanks and produce several dozen pounds of aromatic berries, perfect for eating fresh or making pies, jellies, and fresh juice—or turning into wine.

Modern hybrid varieties produce more heavily, ripen more evenly, and have less pungency than the wild and older varieties, which are pulpy and strong-flavored. They have practically no needs other than an annual fall or winter pruning, essential for berry production and vine control.

FLOWER: Tiny clusters of off-white blooms hidden in the leaves. The small to large grapes—golden yellow, red, or deep purple—are the reason for growing muscadines; a single vine can easily produce sixty or more pounds of grapes every fall.

PLANT: Woody vine that climbs with tendrils. Five-inch roundish leaves with small points around the edges, golden-yellow in the fall. Vigorous vines will grow to the tops of large trees in search of sunlight or cover an arbor several feet thick with layers of growth. It's best to train vines to drape over a single-wire arbor (see Tip below) and prune it hard every winter, leaving short (three- or four-inch) stubs of the previous year's growth.

INTERESTING KINDS: Many old muscadines were female and required a male vine nearby for pollination. Newer kinds are self-pollinating, so only one vine is needed for production. Popular varieties include 'Carlos' (bronze-colored fruit, self-pollinating), 'Noble' (purple-black fruit, self-pollinating), and 'Scuppernong' (an old female variety, requiring a male or self-pollinating vine nearby).

SOIL: Any good, well-drained soil, not rich or highly prepared or growth will be rank. Feed lightly every spring, and water only during the most severe droughts.

PROPAGATION: Layer vines over the summer; cuttings are difficult to root except in the summer in high-humidity greenhouse conditions. Buy named varieties locally or by mail order.

TIP: KEEP A TRELLIS SIMPLE, or you will have trouble keeping the vines pruned and picked. Each vine should be kept to no more than twenty or twenty-five feet. Plant along a sunny chain-link fence, or set sturdy posts ten or twelve feet apart; use three posts for one vine, and add two posts for each additional vine. Tightly stretch a heavy-gauge wire about chin-high between the posts, and train each vine to grow up to the wire, then tip-prune it to cause two "arms" to grow towards the next posts, in a "T" or "Y." For more details on planting, training, and pruning grapes, call your county agricultural extension agent.

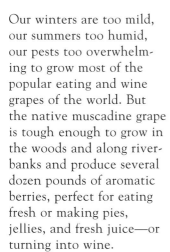

Poison Ivy

Toxicodendron radicans (or *Rhus radicans*)

Sun or shade

Not many garden experts would write about poison ivy as a landscape plant, but since it's here, let's see what we can glean from it—or at least learn to recognize it. Captain John Smith first called the plant "poison ivy" in 1609 after being warned about it by Native Americans (who believed it was put in the woods to make people more careful). Its fall colors, best viewed from afar, are among the most spectacular show around, looking like "flames" licking up tree trunks. Tolerant of shade or sun, poison ivy may be best used as a screen along the back property, perhaps as a "burglar" plant or to keep kids from cutting through the yard.

FLOWER: Pale yellowish, not showy at all in the summer. Pale yellow or white berries—a distinct way to recognize poison ivy, oak, and sumac—cluster loosely in late summer.

PLANT: "Running" vine that forms large ground cover colonies with upright stems like small shrubs. Rope-like stems growing thirty feet or more up trees are often covered in dense, hairy aerial roots and sometimes have outstretched branches up to ten feet long. Leaves are distinct—three large leaflets with edges either smooth or toothed. Incredibly beautiful fall colors of bright red, yellow, or deep orange. All parts are poisonous.

INTERESTING RELATIVES: Poison oak, an "erect vine" that grows more like a shrub, sometimes climbing, with three lobed, oak-like leaflets. Poison sumac is a small, multi-branched tree, each leaf having many leaflets (usually seven to thirteen); it usually grows only in low, wet areas and has pale yellow or whitish berries. Not to be confused with ornamental sumacs (see sumac entry in the shrubs chapter).

SOIL: Well-drained, especially in good woodland soils. Very drought tolerant and needs no fertilizer.

PROPAGATION: Seed, or transplant small plants with pieces of root. Wear gloves.

TIP: KILLING POISON IVY is not hard. Be aware that its oil (urushiol) can remain active for years, even on dead plants, tools, and gloves, and can cause a rash long after you are done working around the plants. Wash clothes thoroughly after working around poison ivy!

Find a way—or someone who "so far" isn't allergic—to cut the old plants close to the ground. New shoots will sprout back out within a few weeks or in the spring. When the new growth is up and actively growing (after a good rain), spray its foliage with Roundup® used exactly according to directions. Repeat treatment as needed until control is complete. Note: Roundup® is not absorbed through tree trunks or roots and does not persist in the soil. It kills only plants whose leaves have been sprayed.

Smilax or Greenbriar
Smilax species
Sun or even dense shade

Many gardeners have cut their hands trying to pry smilax out of the ground, only to have it sprout right back up. This Southeastern native vine is one of the most common evergreens in the woods and has been used for floral garlands and wreaths for many generations. Perhaps the most typical way it is used in landscapes is over doorways, porches, and breezeways, where its loose, rambling stems can be trained and tied into clean, tidy, arching frames. The large fleshy or woody tubers of some species are used to make sarsaparilla, and its new shoots are edible—smilax is in the same family as asparagus.

FLOWER: Very inconspicuous green clusters. Dull reddish brown berries can be somewhat attractive.

PLANT: The vine has moderate growth, using tendrils for support. New shoots arising from a hardy underground tuber are often thorny. Old vines are smooth and olive-green. Glossy deep-green and sometimes variegated leaves are pointed, oblong, or round, up to four inches long or across, and persistently evergreen in the worst winter.

INTERESTING KINDS: Jackson vine (*Smilax smallii*), not as vigorous as the common species, is favored by florists for its six-inch leaves with prominent veins that retain their color long after cutting. But "florist smilax" is really a true asparagus (*Asparagus asparagoides*). The "common" smilax is *Smilax lanceolata*.

SOIL: Any, even heavy clay, wet or dry, woodland or roadside. Very tough tubers need little if any care—ever.

PROPAGATION: Usually done by digging and moving the big, tough tubers from under shrubs and trees where birds have dropped seeds in years past. Cultivars are available through specialty mail-order nurseries.

TIP: SOME VINES MAKE EXCELLENT GROUND COVERS because they spread quickly and their leaves and matted roots are dense enough to hold soils even on slopes too steep to mow. Evergreen vines that spread rapidly include English ivy (*Hedera helix*), Algerian ivy (*Hedera canariensis*), wintercreeper euonymus (*Euonymus fortunei*), and Asiatic jasmine or Japanese star jasmine (*Trachelospermum asiaticum*). Non-vine choices are dwarf bamboo (*Sasa* spp.) and pachysandra (*Pachysandra terminalis*, for the upper and mountainous South only, or in shade in the middle South).

Newly planted ground covers on slopes will need help at first. Either plant them through holes cut in landscape fabric laid over the area or cover them with pine straw mulch "strapped down" with string mesh. While it is important to allow a few fallen tree leaves to "feed" the soil under trees, one way to keep the excess from being a nuisance is to lay lightweight bird netting over the ground cover in the fall to catch the leaves, then lift it away after the bulk of the leaves has fallen.

Trumpet Vine
Campsis radicans
Sun or light shade

I was once astounded to find trumpet vine (sometimes called trumpet creeper) being sold for ten bucks under the name "hummingbird vine"—when it grows along every fencerow and up every abandoned railroad telegraph pole in the South! It's a good buy (for someone who doesn't know how to just look around), because even though the vine is rampant and invasive, it actually does attract hummingbirds, plus it shades decks in summer and lets in the warm sun in the winter.

FLOWER: Clusters of thumb-sized buds on the ends of arching stems open into bright orange or reddish tubular flowers large enough for hummingbirds and bumblebees to crawl in and out for nectar, produced from late spring and early summer right up until frost. Large, canoe-like seed pods five or six inches long split open to release flat seeds that float away on downy parachutes.

PLANT: Extremely vigorous vine climbs forty or more feet long by twisting and attaching with aerial roots that spread out like short spider legs—even onto metal poles. It's best to plant this vine where you can walk or mow around it, to keep it from spreading. Foot-long leaves hold nine or more pointed leaflets, like those on a pecan tree. When the leaves fall in autumn, the current season's stems remain tan; I prune mine lightly every winter to keep its canopy-like growth habit. Some people report a mild allergic reaction to contact with leaves, but I'm allergic to everything and have never had a problem.

INTERESTING KINDS: Hybrid 'Crimson Trumpet' is deep red; 'Flava' is yellow or pale orange; *Campsis* × *tagliabuana* 'Madame Galen', a hybrid between C. *radicans* and C. *grandiflora*, is bright orange to red; Chinese trumpet creeper (C. *grandiflora* or C. *chinensis*) is not as large a vine as the native, but has slightly larger, red flowers.

SOIL: Dry, miserable, low-fertility soils produce fine growth and prolific flowers.

PROPAGATION: Very easy from seeds sown in the late summer (when they first start blowing around) in pots left outside to be exposed to cold temperatures. Very easy to dig small vines growing as root suckers near established plants. Cultivars are available through specialty mail-order nurseries.

TIP: DON'T BE WEAK when it comes to making an arbor, pergola, or other vine support. Vines often outgrow "store-bought" arbors, and it isn't unusual for climbing roses and wisteria to tear up wooden lattice. Use sturdy four-by-six- or six-by-six-foot posts at least ten feet high to allow for vines to grow over and hang down a bit. One of the best "fabrics" for use between heavy posts is heavy-gauge concrete reinforcing mesh, with large openings to allow vines to grow through readily.

Wisteria or Chinese Wisteria

Wisteria sinensis

Sun or light shade

First thing in the spring, around azalea time, some still-naked roadside trees look as if they are solid purple with clusters of wisteria flowers dripping down. Wisteria, one of the most invasive imports to this country, has taken over almost as much as its cousin kudzu! Yet few vines say "spring in the South" like wisteria, trained on sturdy arbors, draped across porches and breezeways, or even pruned like oversized bonsai trees into leggy cascading shrubs.

FLOWER: Large, hanging clusters of bluish purple or white, very fragrant, before leaves appear in late winter. Seeds (which are poisonous) form in long fuzzy pods. Late-summer flowers are common, usually because of weather stress.

PLANT: This incredibly vigorous vine can get up to a hundred feet long, sending "runners" in every direction to climb everything in their path by twining, often strangling or crushing shrubs and small trees to death. Requires regular pruning to keep it in bounds. Leaves are long and compound with up to thirteen leaflets.

INTERESTING KINDS: 'Alba' is white, 'Caroline' is deep blue-purple, 'Jako' has extra-large fragrant flower clusters. Japanese wisteria (*Wisteria floribunda*) has pink, white, or purple flowers in eighteen-inch clusters after leaves appear ('Longissima' flower clusters can get three feet long!); native American wisterias (*W. frutescens* and *W. macrostachys*) have pale lilac flowers in six- to twelve-inch clusters after leaves appear and are not as invasive or destructive.

SOIL: Grows anywhere at all except waterlogged soils, but blooms best in poor, dry, low-fertility soils. Often seen flowering best in trees along the back slopes of highways and around abandoned homes.

PROPAGATION: Seedlings take many years to mature and flower, so it's best to buy mature plants grown from cuttings or grafted, preferably already flowering. Or, root your own stem cuttings from mature, blooming-age stems in the winter.

TIP: "WHY WON'T MY WISTERIA BLOOM?" is a very common question—and there's no easy answer. Often it's because wisteria gets too much fertilizer through far-ranging roots growing under lawns (in the same family as kudzu, wisteria converts its own nitrogen from the air and doesn't need additional nitrogen from fertilizer). Too rich a soil, too much water, and too much shade all contribute to rank vine growth over flower production. Also, many seed-grown plants are just not very floriferous for several years. Try to buy this plant with at least one flower stem on it—to ensure that it is able and old enough to flower, or root a piece from a vigorously blooming branch from someone's garden. Or try "root pruning," which means just that—making a few vertical cuts a few feet out from the vine, in the summer, which stresses the vine and causes flower bud formation. Really.

HONEYSUCKLE AND POISON IVY are normally not the first—or even last—choices for use in landscapes, but they have their places. Some gardeners and naturalists get upset over the use of "invasive exotic" plants in landscapes, such as Japanese honeysuckle and wintercreeper, because they have escaped from gardens and begun to take over natural areas, sometimes displacing native plants. But just as the similarly invasive wisteria is often carefully placed and tended, other "botanical pythons" can be controlled or converted into mannerly garden favorites. And many native plants can be "invasive" as well—a single oak tree can shade out a beautiful flower or vegetable garden.

But it is good to consider the impact of "weedy" vines on neighbors and nearby natural areas. Think twice before planting them, make sure they are in a good spot for control, and take care to keep them in bounds.

Other Great Southern Vines

There are many good vines for Southern gardens, but some either require water, spraying, or some other kind of maintenance, aren't as tough in all parts of the South, or are nearly impossible to find at garden centers. You may have to shop around to find these or keep them in pots, but they are worth a little extra effort.

Akebia (*Akebia quinata*) is often called five-leaf akebia for its interesting foliage. Great tracery effect as it twines up supports to fifteen feet. Interesting fruit looks like a small sausage.

Bittersweet (*Celastrus scandens*) is sometimes viewed as a "Northern kudzu" because it is so rampant and can crush or strangle small plants that get in its way. Attractive orange fruit coverings and red seeds are good for dried arrangements. Needs both male and female plants to fruit.

Black-Eyed Susan Vine (*Thunbergia alata*) is an old-fashioned summer annual, grown quickly every year from seed as a small climber or hanging basket plant. Lots of orange, yellow, or white flowers with dark throats. Related to twenty-foot sky vine (*T. grandiflora*), an annual with blue flowers.

Boston Ivy (*Parthenocissus tricuspidata*), the famous "Ivy League" ivy that clambers all over buildings with exotic smooth waves of big bright-green leaves, usually three-leafed, that turn orange, red, or burgundy before dropping in autumn. Tolerates cold better than heat.

Confederate Jasmine (*Trachelospermum jasminoides*), one of the most popular old fragrant vines of the Deep South, is not hardy in the upper South but makes a superb potted specimen. Climbs to ten feet or more with glossy evergreen leaves and intensely fragrant white blossoms. Tolerates light shade.

Creeping Fig (*Ficus pumila*), an evergreen vine often grown on walls and even the risers of steps, is covered with small, heart-shaped leaves. May get killed to the ground some winters, but usually recovers quickly.

Firecracker Vine (*Manettia cordifolia*), a thickly twisting mass of thin vines with small pointed leaves, climbs to ten feet and is covered with small tubular scarlet flowers that can be "popped" before they open. Perennial in most of the South, but needs digging and saving indoors, or container growing in upper South areas.

Japanese Climbing Fern (*Lygodium japonicum*) is a twining, lacy fern vine that has escaped cultivation and become weedy in some areas of the lower South. Fine-textured leaves form a narrow triangle several inches across on wiry stems. Great container plant and hardy outdoors in all but northernmost areas.

Love in a Puff (*Cardiospermum halicacabum*), treated as an annual, is a twining summer vine that can reach ten feet or more. Small white flowers are followed by hollow, three-compartment fruits that contain hard, black, pea-sized seeds with a perfect white heart marking on each.

Scarlet Runner Bean (*Phaseolus coccineus*), an antique summer bean, climbs readily and has reddish orange flowers all summer. Very attractive on wooden teepees in a garden setting.

Climbing Hydrangea (*Hydrangea anomala* or *H. petiolaris*), a hardy, deciduous vine, has small roundish leaves, flattened lace-cap clusters of white flowers, and peeling cinnamon-colored bark in the winter. Attaches to walls with aerial rootlets.

Evergreen Wisteria (*Millettia reticulata*) is evergreen only in the lower South, but produces fragrant, rich purple wisteria-like flowers above the foliage all summer.

Passion Vine or **Maypop** (*Passiflora incarnata*), one of the Gulf fritillary butterfly's main host plants, grows well in extremely poor soils, climbing and wrapping over everything it gets close to. One of the most exotic, spicy-scented flowers in the garden. Exotic, tropical species are not hardy.

Potato Vine (*Solanum jasminoides*), twining to nearly thirty feet, is a great arbor plant that is not cold hardy but blooms seriously all season with big clusters of inch-wide white flowers tinged with blue.

Silver Lace Vine (*Polygonum aubertii*) is a fast-growing vine that can cover a hundred square feet in a season. Covered with heart-shaped leaves and frothy masses of small white flowers from summer to fall. May need pruning to keep it in bounds, but it recovers quickly. Very drought tolerant.

Sweet Pea (*Lathyrus latifolius*), perennial in most of the South, is a strong vine with blue-green foliage and reddish purple, pink, or white flowers that bloom into summer if not allowed to go to seed. Tolerates drought much better than the traditional annual sweet pea (*L. odoratus*), which has to be planted in the fall or late winter to have time to bloom before heat kills it.

Tater Vine (*Dioscorea bulbifera*) is a favorite old "pass-along" plant with huge, heart-shaped leaves on twining vines. Grows from small tubers that form high on the vine in leaf axils in the late summer. Not winter hardy in the middle or upper South, but can be stored as dry tubers indoors.

Virginia Creeper (*Parthenocissus quinquefolia*) is a very common and fast-growing vine for sun or shade, with five leaflets. Often confused with three-leaflet poison ivy. Perfect for growing on tree trunks, fences, and walls; can take wooden shingles off a roof or wall and may need pruning to keep it out of rain gutters along roof lines. When grown in sun, it has attractive purplish berries on red stems and strong fall colors.

The Southern Cottage Garden: Out of the Parlor, into the Den

Cottage gardening is a style with the freedom of growing what you like, where you like, and how you like. Anyone can have a slice of one, a place to plant stuff "every which way" and enjoy using all the senses.

No two cottage gardeners—or their gardens—are alike, though most share certain characteristics, including a love of being outdoors, keen observation, attention to detail, appreciation of variety, and a sharing spirit. Their gardens, filled with plants having proven hardiness and often shared between a diverse lot of gardeners, typically provide a strong sense of place.

Common elements of cottage gardens around the world, including in the South:

■ There is no apparent design to outsiders, but it has a definite "personal" layout—usually best viewed inside-out (from inside the house, not from the street).

■ A fence, hedge, gates, and divided "rooms" connected with meandering paths create a sense of enclosure, as if you are in a special place (which you are).

■ The lawn is minimal, or non-existent; grass is used in a "throw-rug" effect well defined by edged beds.

■ Outdoor living is evident, from lots of seating, and signs of gardening activities (tools, gloves, pots, water cans, etc.) in full view, where they can be reached easily.

■ A strong vertical effect is created with flowering trees, arbors, and posts supporting vines.

■ Plant diversity is incredible, almost to the point of being overdone: shrubs (evergreens often pruned creatively), roses, vines, bulbs, perennials, annuals, vegetables, and herbs provide a year-round display of texture, color, and fragrance.

■ Potted plants and hanging baskets are everywhere, using a wide variety of containers.

■ Few, if any, pesticides are used, partly because they are troublesome and partly because cottage gardeners rarely tolerate plants that have serious pests or diseases.

■ There is abundant wildlife, often deliberately attracted, fed, and housed, especially birds and butterflies, but also tolerated are rabbits, lizards, big yellow-and-black garden spiders, and the occasional non-poisonous snake left hiding under the rock pile to eat rodents.

■ Expect to find many "hard features" such as birdbaths, urns, small statuary, signs, whimsical "yard art," and found objects (rocks, driftwood, etc.).

Not all of these are requirements. The main thing is to have fun growing plants for the love of it, to indulge in a few creative fantasies. Don't worry—**it doesn't have to be an all-consuming obsession!**

Garden Lingo

Love that *lingua franca!* Comfortable gardeners often speak plain, and plainly, to one another, slipping into a relaxed dance with country sayings and clichés that cause outsiders—and high school English teachers—to shudder.

It's not that we don't know better; though cognizant of the often confusing rules of our language, sometimes we prefer down-home lingo over more polished, high falutin' discourse. I've been criticized by more technical-minded fellow scientists for using vernacular, homespun phrases, as if "talking Southrun" is just plain lazy. But some of our quirky descriptors are more meaningful to me than being precise.

For example, I recognize intellectually that it's not possible to put something both "up" and "under" at the same time, but how else can you get something "out from up under" the porch? And you need to "ask me something quick" 'cause I "just happen" to be busy.

I've picked up a few fun aphorisms from my English gardening buddy Rita Hall, who "bloody falls on her bum" every time she hears someone say they're "fixin' to do" something— which we always seem to be doing: Fixin' to set out some 'maters. Fixin' to blow the leaves. Fixin' to jerk a knot in the boy's neck. Fixin' to git on a plane, or on a train.

Rita, who "bungs" (crams) plants into the ground, got her "nappies in a twist" (shorts in a knot) when she heard me tell someone that their green tomatoes would "red up" after being picked. "Red up? What's that mean?" she laughed.

Yet she says anyone who doesn't speak in a local jargon is just putting on airs—and real people can tell; after just a few minutes of hearing someone from England talk, Rita can spot their dialect, and pinpoint what part of England they are from. And on two trips to England, I've heard her revert to a normal English accent within an hour of getting through customs.

Jargon rules! A fellow called my radio program the other day to share how his rose bush— which he had pulled out of a pasture using a tractor so he could get the main root—had "growed up so good" that when it flowered "it was just a bo-kay." We all could tell how proud he was.

If you don't understand our patter—from the French *patois*—you ain't from around here, are you?

Still, there are some terms you outta know from this book, so here is my glossary (those that are not listed here, can be found in ANY garden book, anywhere, any time):

Glossary: A place in a book to look up words you might not know.

Agriculture Extension Service: Local county or parish branch of an agricultural university, with publications and advice on various aspects of gardening.

Annual: Seed- or cutting-grown plant that dies within a few months of when it is planted, usually from either hot or cold weather; some perennials in other parts of the world are annuals here.

Biennial: Green leaves one year, flowers the next. Then it's gone.

Bones: Evergreen plants and hard features which give a year-round structure to a garden or landscape, especially in winter.

Comes Back: Opposite of "goes down."

Cultivar: Variety that usually can't be grown true from seed, but has to be "cloned" (divided or rooted).

Cut Back: To prune stems moderately, leaving some of previous season's growth, to clean it up or to encourage new growth.

Deadhead: To remove spent flowers and seedheads, in order to frustrate plants into reblooming.

Dilettante: A gardener who dabbles in a little of everything, and knows more about some things that most folks don't really care about.

Divide: Pull or cut apart soil-level sections of a multiple-branched perennial or woody plant to make more plants, best done in the season opposite of when a plant flowers.

Dormancy: Often mistaken for death. The resting period for a plant, usually during either cold weather or really hot, dry weather, depending on the species.

Double Dig: British and Californian masochistic practice in which holes are dug twice too deep, causing root rot when they fill up with water in our wet winter and spring.

Force: To make a plant grow unnaturally, as in a vase on the TV; often done with bulbs, and cut stems of spring flowering shrubs.

Garden Club Lady: A member of an organized social club whose garden-related meetings often include plant swaps and flower shows; often performs valuable community beautification and educational services.

Goes Down: When either summer or winter perennials go dormant and their aboveground foliage disappears.

Herbaceous: Perennial that goes down part of the year, or is not woody.

Layer: To bury a part of a vine or shrub stem and let it root while still attached to the "mother" plant.

Master Gardener: Trained gardening volunteer with the Extension Service.

Melt: To collapse from heat and drought and overwatering and frustration with our climate; can happen to plants or gardeners.

Peg: To bend a vine or shrub, such as a rose, severely, attaching it to the ground with stakes, which forces flower buds to form all along the stem instead of just at the tip.

Perennial: A plant that lives for several to many years. Can be woody or herbaceous.

Pinching: To deadhead with your fingers, or to nip the tip off a plant so that it will branch down below.

Reseeding: Drops seeds everywhere that sprout the next season (think wildflowers and weeds).

Rogue Out: To remove a few unwanted plants somewhat brutally, by hand or with implements of destruction.

Root: Used as a verb—cut branches from plants, stick in soil or water, and grow new plants. Used as a noun—the part of the plant that goes in the ground when planting.

Run: To spread rapidly by way of vigorous underground stems; sometimes a good thing for ground covers, sometimes a weedy way of something "getting away from you" in flower beds.

Southern: Capitalized word representing a culture of people, plants, and environmental conditions peculiar to the southeastern portions of the United States.

Variety: Distinct kind of a certain type of plant that can be grown from seed.

Woody Plant: Perennial vine, shrub, or tree that has permanent stems and branches that get bigger every year.

Bibliography

Bender, Steve. *The Southern Living Garden Book.* Birmingham, AL: Oxmoor House, 1998.

Bender, Steve and Felder Rushing. *Passalong Plants.* Chapel Hill, NC: UNC Press, 1993.

Chaplin, Lois Trigg. *The Southern Gardener's Book of Lists: The Best Plants For All Your Needs, Wants, & Whims.* Dallas, TX: Taylor Publishing, 1994.

Dutton, Joan Parry. *Plants of Colonial Williamsburg.* Colonial Williamsburg Foundation, 1990.

Feltwell, John and Neil Odenwald. *Live Oak Splendor: Gardens Along The Mississippi from Natchez to New Orleans.* Dallas, TX: Taylor Publishing, 1992.i

Grant, Greg and Dr. William Welch. *The Southern Heirloom Garden.* Dallas, TX: Taylor Publishing, 1995.

Hill, Madalene and Gwen Barclay, with Jean Hardy. *Southern Herb Growing,* Fredericksburg, TX: Shearer Publishing, 1987.

Lawrence, Elizabeth. *A Southern Garden.* Chapel Hill, NC: UNC Press, 1942. Reprinted 2001.

Lawrence, Elizabeth. *Gardening for Love: The Market Bulletins.* Durham, NC: Duke University Press, 1988.

Odenwald, Neil and Dr. William Welch. *The Bountiful Flower Garden: Growing and Sharing Cut Flowers in the South.* Dallas, TX: Taylor Publishing, 2000.

Odenwald, Neil and James Turner. *Identification, Selection and Use of Southern Plants for Landscape Design,* 3d ed. Baton Rouge, LA: Claitor's Publishing Division, 1996.

Ogden, Scott. *Garden Bulbs for the South.* Dallas, TX: Taylor Publishing, 1994.

Phillips, Harry. *Growing and Propagating Wildflowers.* Chapel Hill, NC: UNC Press, 1985.

Seidenberg, Charlotte. *The New Orleans Garden.* Jackson, MS: University Press of Mississippi, 1993.

Shoup, G. Michael. *Roses in the Southern Garden.* Brenham, TX: Antique Rose Emporium, 2000.

Wasowski, Sally with Andy Wasowski. *Gardening with Native Plants of the South.* Dallas, TX: Taylor Publishing, 1994.

Welch, Dr. William. *Perennial Garden Color: Perennials, Cottage Gardens, Old Roses, and Companion Plants.* Dallas, TX: Taylor Publishing, 1989.

Wilson, Jim. *Bulletproof Plants for the South.* Dallas, TX: Taylor Publishing, 1999.

Photo Credits

Thomas Eltzroth: 23, 26 (first), 27 (first), 28 (second), 29 (second), 30, 32, 33 (first), 34, 35 (first), 36 (second), 38 (second), 39, 40, 43, 50, 52, 53, 59, 60, 62, 63, 64, 66, 68, 69, 71, 73, 75 (second, third, fourth), 76 (first), 77 (third), 79, 81, 83, 85, 87, 96, 99, 101, 103, 107, 109, 112, 115, 116, 119, 122, 123, 126, 131, 136 (first), 137 (second), 140 (first), 141 (first), 143, 144, 150, 152, 156, 157, 158, 160, 167, 168, 170, 171, 172, 175, 176, 179, 182, 192, 193, 204, 209, 210, 212, 215, 217, 224

Felder Rushing: 4 (photo courtesy of the author), 7, 9, 12, 14, 19, 24, 25, 27 (second), 31 (second), 37 (first), 47, 51, 56, 57, 75 (first), 76 (third), 77 (first), 88, 91, 94, 100, 104, 133, 134, 135, 137 (first), 138 (first), 139, 140 (second), 141 (second), 142, 148, 149, 173, 183, 191, 198, 200, 203, 208, 223, 230, 233 (photo courtesy of the author)

Jerry Pavia: 26 (second), 28 (first), 29 (first), 31 (first), 35 (second), 36 (first), 37 (second), 54, 61, 76 (fourth), 77 (second, fourth), 97, 105, 106, 110, 111, 120, 127, 128, 147, 155, 161, 162, 164, 165, 166, 169, 174, 177, 185 (first), 189, 197, 201, 205, 207, 213, 216, 218

Liz Ball and Rick Ray: 21, 33 (second), 38 (first), 45, 48, 58, 67, 74, 102, 113, 114, 117, 118, 121, 124, 125, 151, 153, 159, 178, 181, 185 (second), 187, 194, 195, 199, 211, 222, 225

Pamela Harper: 98, 145, 154, 180, 202, 214, 220

William Adams: 76 (second), 108, 136 (second)

Charles Mann: 49, 77 (fifth), 219

André Viette: 55, 196

Michael Dirr: 65

Lorenzo Gunn: 138 (second)

Gerard Krewer: 221

Ralph Snodsmith: 163

Meet the Author

Felder Rushing is a 10th-generation Southern gardener whose ancestors moved from Virginia to South Carolina in the 1600s, then to Mississippi in the late 1700s. His quirky, overstuffed, low-maintenance cottage garden with its "yard art" has been featured in several books, many magazines, and newspapers, including *Southern Living*, *Better Homes and Gardens*, *Garden Design*, *Landscape Architecture*, *House and Garden*, *The New York Times*, and others. He has studied in gardens all across North America, Europe, South America, and Africa.

Felder's twice-weekly garden columns and live, call-in radio program are syndicated, and he has had hundreds of articles and photographs published in over twenty-five magazines, including *Fine Gardening*, *National Geographic*, *Organic Gardening*, and the *Brooklyn Botanic Garden Record*. He has written or co-authored ten garden books, appears regularly on HGTV and the Discovery Channel, and lectures every year from coast to coast. He serves as contributing editor for *Horticulture Magazine* and *Garden Design*.

Felder is a national director of the Garden Writers Association, serves on the board of directors of the American Horticulture Society, and recently retired after nearly twenty-five years as Mississippi's "consumer horticulturist" with the MSU Extension Service.

One of his proudest moments was in 1990 when he was presented with an honorary membership in the Garden Clubs of Mississippi—of which his horticulturist great-grandmother was a charter member in 1936.

Rushing, who believes that too many of his fellow horticulture experts complicate things unnecessarily, says, "We are daunted, not dumb." His lifework has been trying to make gardening as easy as it is fun.

Index

Featured plant selections are indicated in **boldface**.